COMPLIMENTS OF

 Northern Trust

northerntrust.com

Early Praise for **FutureThink**

"*FutureThink* stretches the boundaries of our perception and opens new avenues for development. Incisive and useful!"

—**General Wesley Clark**, U.S. Army (ret.), former NATO commander

"We have exposed many of our people to the thinking technologies contained in this book, and they have proven extremely useful. I recommend this book to anyone who needs to get a grip on what the future may hold."

—**Beth Comstock**, chief marketing officer, General Electric

"This primer on critical thinking is a vitamin-B shot to the brain. I loved it."

—**Barry I. Herstein**, senior vice president, International Marketing and Communications, American Express

"Weiner and Brown have taken the innovative and far-reaching vision that earned them respect and admiration in the foresight community and translated it into practical advice for daily business decision-making. Their insights into social dynamics and corporate governance strategies are extraordinarily useful."

—**Tim Mack**, president, World Future Society

"Weiner and Brown see connections and causalities that no one else sees. *FutureThink* rattles convention and clichés and does nothing short of challenge the way we look at the world."

—**Ed Nardoza**, editor-in-chief, *Women's Wear Daily*

FutureThink

How to Think Clearly in a Time of Change

Edie Weiner and Arnold Brown

Pearson Prentice Hall
An Imprint of Pearson Education
Upper Saddle River, NJ • New York • London • San Francisco
Toronto • Sydney • Tokyo • Singapor • Hong Kong
Cape Town • Madrid • Paris • Milan • Munich • Amsterdam

Library of Congress Catalog Number: 2005925103

Publisher: Tim Moore
Acquisitions Editor: Paula Sinnott
Editorial Assistant: Susie Abraham
Development Editor: Russ Hall
Marketing Manager: John Pierce
International Marketing Manager: Tim Galligan
Cover Designer: Sandra Schroeder
Managing Editor: Gina Kanouse
Project Editor: Christy Hackerd
Copy Editor: Gayle Johnson
Indexer: Angie Bess
Compositor: Tolman Creek Design
Manufacturing Buyer: Dan Uhrig

**Prentice Hall offers excellent discounts on this book when ordered in quantity for bulk purchases or special sales.
For more information, please contact U.S. Corporate and Government Sales, 1-800-382-3419, corpsales@pearsontechgroup.com. For sales outside the U.S., please contact International Sales at international@pearsoned.com.**

Printed in the United States of America

First Printing, September 2005

ISBN 0-13-185674-X

Pearson Education LTD.
Pearson Education Australia PTY, Limited.
Pearson Education Singapore, Pte. Ltd.
Pearson Education North Asia, Ltd.
Pearson Education Canada, Ltd.
Pearson Educatión de Mexico, S.A. de C.V.
Pearson Education—Japan
Pearson Education Malaysia, Pte. Ltd.

Dedicated to all those who have strengthened our ability to understand and interpret the world: our clients over 35 years, our friends, and our loved ones. Many of them are still with us; many, like Pam and Kathy, are still alive in our thoughts and gratitude. We love you all.

CONTENTS

Acknowledgments   xiii

Introduction   xv

Part I Personal Traps: Individual Biases and Blocks to Seeing and Understanding Change   1

Chapter 1: Looking Through Alien Eyes   7

Figure-Ground   8

Example #1: Male/Female   9

Example #2: Youth/Aging   11

Example #3: Able/Challenged   13

Example #4: Stability/Transition   15

Children Can Be Aliens   18

The Lesson of Alien Eyes   18

Chapter 2: Trend/Countertrend   23

Example #1: No Responsibility Self-Reliance   25

Example #2: The Sociology of Apology   28

Example #3: The Emerging Diseases of Affluence   31

Example #4: Technology, Thy Name Is Poetry   34

Example #5: Consuming Versus Saving Safety 36

Example #6: The Decline of Community and the Rise of a New Consumer Durable 38

So Newton Was a Futurist 41

Chapter 3: Substituting the Spiral for the Pendulum   43

Example #1: The Social Fabric 45

Example #2: Cycles in Business Oversight 48

Example #3: The Markets 51

Chapter 4: The Extremes Inform the Middle   53

Example #1: Corporate Social Responsibility Versus Free-Market Capitalism 56

Example #2: The Techies Versus the Luddites 58

Example #3: Free Speech Versus Censorship 61

Example #4: Traditional Versus Nontraditional Gender Roles 64

How to Study and Use the Extremes 68

Part II Organizational Traps: Institutional Biases and Blocks to Responding to Change   69

Chapter 5: Efficiency Breeds Vulnerability   71

Example #1: Acceleration Through Electronics 73

Example #2: Efficiency in Government 74

Example #3: Warped Speed 75

The Continuing Importance of Redundancy 78

Chapter 6: The Multiplier Effect of New Distribution Channels 81

Example #1: Media 82

Example #2: Print Versus the Internet 83

Example #3: The Campus Versus Online Learning 85

Example #4: Retailing 86

Example #5: Health Care 87

Choices and Options 88

How Multiplication Can Help You See the Future 88

Attention Is the Monetary Unit 91

Chapter 7: Entropy 93

Example #1: Taxation 94

Example #2: The Internet 98

Example #3: Addiction to Adrenaline 99

Complexity and Entropy 101

Chapter 8: Integrity Begets Quality 105

Example #1: Getting and Keeping a Customer 107

Example #2: Apple Juice Should Be Made from Apples 110

Example #3: Do Unto Others... 111

Surface Social Responsibility Is Not Integrity 112

Stewardship and Integrity 115

Part III Springing the Trap: Seeing the Big Picture 117

Chapter 9: The Law of Large Numbers 119

Example #1: Critical Mass 120

Example #2: Peer Pressure 122

Example #3: Bell-Shaped Curves 123

What Lies Ahead 126

Chapter 10: Demography 129

Example #1: Demography and Islam 130

Example #2: Why the Number of Youths Matters 133

Example #3: Asian Demographics 134

Example #4: Immigration 135

Example #5: Aging 137

Age and Relevance 139

Example #6: "Ymigration" 142

Example #7: The U.S. Becomes the Southern Hemisphere 143

Example #8: The Burgeoning Global Middle Class 143

Example # 9: Women 145

Example #10: Marketing to Children 146

Example #11: Where People Go 147

Caveat on Demography 147

Beware of Extrapolation 148

Chapter 11: Compromise Versus Lowest Common Denominators 151

Example #1: Employee Diversity 154

Example #2: Majority Rules 157

Example #3: International Conflict 158

Example #4: When the Denominators Are 4 and 8 160

Example #5: What's in a Definition? 162

Example #6: John and Mary Public 165

The Bottom Line 166

Part IV Imagining the Way: Using Metaphors to Free Your Mind 169

Chapter 12: The Three-Legged Stools of the Political Agenda 171

Example #1: The Foundation of the Republic 171

Example #2: The Political Parties 174

Example #3: The Male/Female Perspective 176

Chapter 13: Right-of-Way 179

Example #1: Customer-Centered Versus Sale-Centered 181

Example #2: Tunnel Vision 183

Example #3: The Infrastructure Dilemma 185

Example #4: The Amazon River 187

What Are Your Potential Rights-of-Way? 188

Chapter 14: Football Meets Shopping 191

We Always Shopped 192

First Down 194

Second Down 197

Third Down 198

Fourth Down 199

Chapter 15: Managing by Harnessing Evolution 203

The New Natural 205

Example #1: Cross-Breeding to Manage the Biosphere 205

Example #2: Evolution and the Management of Health and Social Services 207

Example #3: Managing Telecom 207

Example #4: Managing Biotech 209

Example #5: The Business of Managing Human Evolution 212

Survival of the Fittest 216

The Next Big Management Tool 218

Chapter 16: Self-Defeating and Self-Fulfilling Prophecies 221

Example #1: Orwell and Gates 221

Example #2: Government and Nongovernmental Organizations 223

Example #3: Your Mind and Body 225

Example #4: How to Make It Happen 226

Conclusion 229

Anticipation Is Key 231

What Type of Business Will Succeed? 233

Question Consensus 234

References 235

Index 267

ACKNOWLEDGMENTS

We owe a lot to our clients, who over the years have believed in us so strongly and who have so enthusiastically supported our efforts to help people think better. Many other people who have heard us speak on this subject have urged us, sometimes with great fervor, to write a book—this book. We thank them for prodding us enough to help overcome our reluctance (we don't like writing books).

In particular, our thanks go to Suzanne Rotondo, then a senior editor at Harvard Business School Press, who, having heard us speak on this subject, practically demanded that we do the book for her. Unfortunately, when she left Harvard (not because she contracted with us, we hope), we were unable to reconcile their editorial viewpoint with ours. It was then that Jerry Parisella introduced us to Paula Sinnott, a senior editor at Wharton School Press. Paula immediately understood what we were trying to do, and she brought a welcome new level of enthusiasm to the project. She, together with fellow editors Russ Hall, Christy Hackerd, and Gayle Johnson, then helped us enormously in making this the compellingly useful book we believe it now is.

We cannot thank enough our own people who worked so hard and so uncomplainingly, not only with research, typing, writing, and editing, but also with good advice and suggestions—Cindy Mooney, Jared Weiner, Michael Rhoads, Jim Perry, and Erica Orange.

In conclusion, we repeat the vow we took after each of our previous books: Never again. No más. Fuggedaboutit.

P.S.: Whatever errors this book may have are entirely the fault of somebody else.

INTRODUCTION

The future, obviously, is about change. Our look at change begins with Cassandra. That beautiful daughter of King Priam of Troy caught the eye of Apollo, who wooed her by giving her the power to see the future. (Apparently he never heard of jewelry.) But when she spurned him, Apollo made sure the other Trojans wouldn't believe Cassandra's prophecies.

The Cassandra metaphor tells us that having good information about the future—being right—is not enough. You must see what the prophet sees, believe it, and, most importantly, know how to respond to it.

The prevalence in business literature today of knee-jerk clichés and management fads has caused many people to overlook the basics of good thinking. After more than 35 years of studying constant and confusing change, we have learned that the future can be grasped only when you combine objective information about change with clear-eyed thinking. We do this using thinking techniques that we have crafted over the years. These are aids you can use to prepare (and train) your mind to accept the signals of change, much as a farmer must prepare the ground to accept seeds for crops. They are ways to liberate your mind from the assumptions, prejudices, pre-judgments, and yearnings that hold it prisoner.

Some extraordinary experiments have revealed what psychologists call inattentional blindness. Subjects in one experiment, as reported in *Scientific American* in March 2004, were told to focus on how many passes a basketball team made in a one-minute video. About halfway through the video, a gorilla emerged and walked across the basketball court. Half the participants in the experiment did not see the gorilla. The more you focus on something, the less able you become to see unexpected or unanticipated happenings. Just as when you drive you have to frequently use the rear- and side-view mirrors while focusing on the road ahead, so do you have to make yourself aware, even if only peripherally, of what may be coming up alongside or behind you.

The techniques we describe in this book are timeless because they are rooted in physical principles, diversity of thinking, long-wave observations, and good old-fashioned common sense. This book, therefore, defines the ABCs of clearly seeing patterns, weighing choices, understanding trends, getting the future right, making good and innovative decisions about the future, and, indeed, influencing what that future will be.

Many people believe that if they win the lottery, they will be set for life. Statistics show, however, that a large percentage of those who hit it big are bankrupt a few years later. Why? Because it's not about the money. It's about having your head screwed on right.

After more than three decades of working with Fortune 500 companies, trade and professional associations, start-up ventures, government agencies, academic institutions, and everyday people, we have learned (often the hard way) that there are good and bad ways of understanding what may come.

Seeming contradictions make seeing the future difficult. But in the physical world, every action has an equal and opposite reaction. The same holds true in the world of social, economic, and political affairs. For those who cannot understand trend/countertrend (Chapter 2), the world moves in one direction only, and they are constantly surprised by events and forces they did not see coming. This is one example of the thinking techniques we have articulated during our many years of analysis, consulting, and speaking.

Techniques for Effective Thinking

The Cassandra myth is a compelling metaphor. Such metaphors help create perception and understanding, as you will see in this book, because they can help you grasp contexts. For example, a football game can clarify priorities in competitive retailing and customer attraction and retention (Chapter 14). Or understanding the history of the railroads can put the Internet into perspective, and, more importantly, make powerfully clear the too-often neglected and extremely valuable asset that is the right-of-way (Chapter 13).

We turn to the principles of mathematics, such as the Law of Large Numbers, to help you see the inevitability (and the drivers) of such powerful forces as deviancy and terrorism (Chapter 9). And in physics, the Second Law of Thermodynamics—Entropy—explains why benchmarking often fails and why you should thoroughly analyze any formula in terms of whether it is factual or merely a cliché (Chapter 7).

These ways of observing are simple, illuminating, and, now more than ever, essential.

There are plenty of sources of information about what's going on in the external environment. Organizations pay a lot of money for such information. But the money spent, and the time and resources spent, can be wasted if organizations neglect to focus on how best to think about the new information.

New York Times columnist Thomas Friedman, in commenting about the criticism of the U.S. intelligence apparatus after 9/11, wrote that what occurred was a failure not of intelligence but of imagination. The U.S. government had information—good information. It just couldn't see how to think about it in the most effective way. As novelist John le Carré wrote, "The greatest spies are worth nothing if their intelligence is not wisely used."

It's Not Just About Information

The first thing the two of us learned when we began tracking change in the 1960s was that how people respond to information is as important as—if not more important than—the information itself. We found, for example, that often people's fear of change led them to reject or deny information about change, even in the face of enormous competitive and technological forces. So we had to find ways to help them see the positive possibilities, to remove or diminish what they saw as threatening, without in any way changing the truth of the information. This meant encouraging them to look for positive implications.

Similarly, wherever we saw roadblocks to the effective use of information about change, we searched for and tested techniques that could help all of us become more open to the information—and better able to use it the way it should be used. "The real voyage of discovery," wrote Marcel Proust, "consists not in seeking new landscapes, but in having new eyes," or, as you will see in Chapter 1, seeing with "alien eyes."

A client once told us that meeting with us was like "a spa for the brain." Our thinking techniques wake up minds. Listeners are jolted out of the rut of stereotypical and lazy thinking, out of the knee-jerk responses that all of us fall into because they require so little effort. A cliché has it that most of us use only 10 percent of our brain's capacity. These thinking techniques can enable you to go beyond that low level—and to enjoy that exercise as well as profit from it.

These are time-tested thinking processes. We have used them to acclaim with all kinds of audiences, from the most senior business, association, and government leaders to groups of practicing professionals and middle managers, from entrepreneurs to teenagers. Without exception, the response has been overwhelmingly favorable. We find ourselves being quoted frequently in our clients' offices, in articles written by people who hear our speeches, or by experts ranging from anthropologists to business-school professors. And we are constantly asked if we can provide all our thinking techniques in written form. It is as if people have been waiting for a believable, useful guide to navigating a new and unfamiliar world.

When asked for a one-sentence definition of what we do, our answer is that we give hope. We can help you see that you do not have to be a passive victim of change, that you can instead control the consequences of change.

Hope is important. We live in a time of rapid and massive change, a time that can, as Thomas Paine said, "try men's souls." It is a fearful time because change is frightening. And, to again quote le Carré, "Frightened people never learn."

As you read this book, we ask that you discard the accumulation of things that prevent you from seeing clearly. Remind yourself that, in today's (and tomorrow's) rapidly changing world, what matters is not what you know, but what you are capable of learning. And what you are capable of putting to good use. For as Aristotle wrote, "In practical matters, the end is not mere speculative knowledge of what is to be done, but rather the doing of it." Our hope is that this book will help you in the doing of it.

Part I

Personal Traps: Individual Biases and Blocks to Seeing and Understanding Change

You learn from the time you are born, or perhaps even before. You learn the vocabulary that shapes your thinking, the customs of your culture, the beliefs of your caregivers, and the aesthetics that delight or repel you. Going through school, you learn history the way your teachers and texts present it, you learn about the physical world based on your society's acceptance or rejection of theories and discoveries, and you learn to express yourself in a prescribed manner to succeed in your classes and fit in with your peers.

The older you get, and the more knowledge you acquire, the more mental baggage that gets loaded into your consciousness. That consciousness becomes your thinking, your beliefs, and your problem-solving.

If you go on to acquire specialized knowledge to pursue a career or profession, even more baggage is loaded onto your already-weighty mental cart. Although all that freight is necessary to excel at everything from carpentry to doctoring to accounting to teaching to policing, carrying such a load has a negative side. It is stacked so high that it blocks your vision, limits the freedom of your understanding, and, unknown to you, pushes you into a walled and turreted world where you believe you are immune to conflicting worldviews or emerging new realities. When the walls are breached, as they will be, by events and changes, you are then faced with a choice: You can go down fighting against new knowledge, or you can learn and grow and conquer.

The Limits of Expertise

As trend analysts, we would never turn only to doctors to help us see the future of health care, or only to army generals to define the future of national security. People generally, both professionally and personally, know so much about what they know that they are the last to see that future differently. Whether bankers or bakers, we derive our psychic and financial rewards from all the time put in to master our work and attain whatever status we have. It is in our own self-interest to protect that and to make sure that everyone else who wants to be where we are has to pay the same price, learn the same things, and do things the same way. It is no wonder that we are constantly surprised by new competition from left field or by upstarts who question why things are done the way they are and who prove that what we do is ineffective or, even worse, irrelevant to the world of things to come.

When someone has too much information to see clearly, we call that *educated incapacity*. To thrive—indeed, to survive—on the fast-paced journey into the 21st century, you need to selectively (but accurately) shed all of this educated incapacity—the baggage of accumulated knowledge that makes you incapable of change. As you become more experienced, forgetting curves become much harder to navigate than learning curves.

The Japanese word *sunao* means "the untrapped mind." Konosuke Matsushita, the pioneering Japanese industrialist, said that a *sunao* spirit is essential. "Without it," he wrote, "one can enjoy neither genuine success in management, nor genuine happiness in life." But how do you free your mind when language and imagery are what you use to define all that you know, and these are products of your past?

Even the most brilliant thinkers of every age are stuck in their mental trenches. Thomas Edison believed that widespread use of alternating current (AC) would burn down a city. British scientists at the dawn of rocketry believed that there was no way for a vehicle to escape the earth's gravitational pull because the amount of payload required for fuel alone would make the journey impossible. Before railroads came along, the thinking of "astute" and "knowledgeable" experts was that humans could not travel faster than 15 miles per hour, because if they did, blood would spurt from their noses and ears.

The ancient astronomers, with all their supposed celestial knowledge, were blind to the fundamental movements of the solar system. It was Copernicus who protested their conventional wisdom. Steve Jobs and the other personal computer pioneers recognized the promise of home computers, at a time when computer experts saw them as mere toys. In fact, it was Ken Olsen, CEO of Digital Equipment Corporation (DEC), who stated famously that he could not see any reason why anyone would want a computer in their home. When an adhesive bandage manufacturer ran focus groups on its products, even its African-American interviewees did not mention the need for a darker bandage. A major pharmaceutical company was frustrated that its researchers peaked in their 40s and were expensive to continue to employ until retirement. Yet its human resources executives were paying top dollar for each

new chemistry graduate specializing in the expanding field of toxi-
cology. Even these experts couldn't see the possibility of retraining
existing researchers to become toxicologists.

Questioning Assumptions

Experts, and their constituents, constantly run in place on their educated incapacity wheel, rarely testing their assumptions or shifting
their frame of reference. When they do, startling things occur.

Think about this: If you already know where someone stands on
any given position, you are not likely to sit up and take notice when
he continues making the same point. You've heard it already, so you
engage your brain in only a limited capacity in listening. If the person tends to agree with you, you're even less likely to mentally
debate and consider his point; you relax instead, content to know
your understanding is confirmed. But if you think you know where
someone stands, and that person confuses you by taking a contrary
approach, what happens? You pay a great deal more attention
because *now* your mind is rattled. You see what seems to be a square
peg in a round hole. You need to compute, reflect, and reconsider
your own thoughts. This is why leaders can accomplish monumental
breakthroughs when they approach things counter to their track
record. This is why it took Richard Nixon, a son of the McCarthy era,
to open up Red China. And it's why Bill Clinton, a liberal, was able
to reform welfare.

In this increasingly complex world, people have more questions
about everything, from the future of terrorism to the future of education. They keep hoping experts will provide the answers. But what
difference would it make, armed with all the answers, if both you
and the experts were asking all the wrong questions? This is what
usually happens.

Shedding intellectual baggage can be difficult, and it's scary. But it can also be exhilarating, empowering, highly rewarding—and, indeed, necessary in today's changing world.

Four thinking techniques are most helpful in allowing you to overcome educated incapacity: *Looking Through Alien Eyes*, *Trend/Countertrend*, *Substituting the Spiral for the Pendulum*, and *The Extremes Inform the Middle*. Each of these can help you shed some baggage and become more flexible. Taken together, they can allow for a whole new interpretation not only of what is, but also of what is possible.

1

LOOKING THROUGH
ALIEN EYES

There may be only two kinds of intelligent life-forms who do not suffer from educated incapacity—aliens from another planet and children.

About 30 years ago, an animated film from Canada showed two aliens who had been sent to Earth to observe it and report back on it to their native planet. After two weeks, the aliens concluded that Earth was inhabited by four-wheeled vehicles called automobiles, each of which owned at least one two-legged slave called a human. Every morning a loud noise went off to wake the human so that he could take the automobile to a social club (parking lot), where the auto hung out all day with other cars while the human went into a building to work to support it. This cartoon was an eye-opener for us. It became clear that, seen from a completely unbiased perspective, another reality emerges.

Figure-Ground

Figure-ground experiments, which use illustrations that can be seen in at least two clear ways, teach us the same thing. Figure-ground is often illustrated with a picture of a vase (figure) that can also be perceived as the profile of two faces (ground). Depending which you focus on, you see one or the other.

As a psychology major in college, one of us (Weiner) created an experiment around figure-ground illustrations. The experiment used three such pictures that were created for the study. One picture was of a diamond, cut in quarters from corner to corner, with a squiggly line on the bottom. There were 20 subjects. Ten were told it was a picture of a kite in the sky with clouds, and ten were told it was a window with four panes, curtains, and flowers on the sill. After 10 minutes of diversion, each subject was asked to draw exactly what he or she had seen in the picture. Each person's drawing more closely resembled what he or she was told than what was actually shown. Those shown the "window" drew curved curtains and flowers; those shown the "kite" drew clouds and even included a kite string. What they were told about the picture when they first saw it determined their perception of the figure and the ground. This is educated incapacity.

The bottom line is that if you see a kite, you see a market for string. If you see a window, you see a market for glass. *Kite*: weather is important. *Window*: weather is irrelevant. *Clouds*: the stuff daydreams are made of. *Flower box*: buy dirt. Depending on your focus, your entire perspective changes, along with all the products, services, behaviors, and systems that come into play. Your perspective is a product of what you were taught. This is what we mean by educated incapacity. The following sections discuss four more examples.

Example #1: Male/Female

For centuries, throughout much of modern agricultural, industrial, and post-industrial life, men were seen as economically more important, with women far less so. Since most processes, products, and services were designed with the dominantly perceived figure in mind, everything from financial services to corporate structures reflected the male's needs.

As we move into the 21st century, however, and we adjust our lenses to see what the alien would see, women (the ground) clearly become the figure.

For one thing, they are the majority of the global adult population. For another, they are making extraordinary economic, political, and social advances (although they are still greatly underrepresented in science and technology), to the point where they run nations, advise leaders, have overwhelming say over use of discretionary income in some countries, are increasingly the major breadwinner in their households, and are often sole parents to their children. At the dawn of this new century, unmarried women give birth to 62% of the babies in Iceland, 49% in Norway, 41% in France, 38% in Britain, and 31% in Ireland and the U.S., as reported in the *New York Times* on March 24, 2002.

To some, this means businesses have to learn to market more effectively to women. But the alien seeing today's realities would naively believe that most products and services on Earth were *designed* for women and that the challenge would be marketing those more effectively to men.

Often when this point is made, the most vocal objections come from women. They believe that there should be no difference in the design of products and services for men and women, and that they (women) should have equal access to, and be accorded equal respect in, the purchase. This proves that you should not just survey women to understand what the future of the female market would look like. Like men, they too suffer from knowing too much about the past and therefore become unable to see how things can change.

A New Perspective

The alien, for example, looking at financial services would design other kinds of insurance and savings vehicles. Women face profoundly different sets of risks and needs over the course of their lifetimes. They are subject to complications of pregnancy and childbirth, to the physical and emotional effects of menopause, to spending more time alone in old age, to caregiving responsibility for children and parents, to age discrimination in their love lives, to financial discrimination in their work lives.

Take the case of disability insurance in the U.S. It was once sold almost exclusively to the male (breadwinner) market. Enlightened marketers (and group insurers, presented with more women in the workforce) now underwrite women, to the point where men and women are about equally covered. The obvious response to seeing the woman's increased economic role and earnings is to assume that she, as well as he, must be protected in the event of disability.

Now let's pose this question: In two-worker households with children, when the woman earns a great deal more than the man, on whose life is disability insurance more needed? Most enlightened people would probably say the woman. But the alien, looking with no mental baggage, would say the children. That is because, as women's economic status in the household changes, *everything* changes, including the value of healthy children. Healthy children allow the parents, especially the mother, to work and not stay home or pay for expensive professional caregiving. In a world of knowledge work, an adult's disability does not necessarily mean an end to earning money. But a child's disability requires expensive resources (time, energy, dollars) to be reallocated by society and the household unit. To repeat: When you switch the figure and the ground, *everything* changes. *Everything*.

Example #2: Youth/Aging

Another significant example of figure-ground educated incapacity relates to the age of the population. All through modern history, the average age of most of the world's population was under 40. In the past half-century, marketing data was based on the assumption that people over 60 were a niche. For the purposes of targeting various age segments, it was not unusual to see the population broken into age category groupings beginning at age 18. Researchers would gauge the attitudes and behaviors of persons 18 to 25, 26 to 35, 36 to 45, 46 to 55, 56 to 65, and 66 and over. Those over 65, then, faded into the ground, while the bulk of the figure was made up of younger people. The amazing thing about this is that these breakdowns are still the norm. Why is this amazing? Consider that the Census Bureau and the National Institute on Aging project that, by 2030, close to one-fourth of all Europeans will be over 65. In North America, the projection is for over 20 percent. All of Europe is aging, but it's not just Europe. China and Japan both have serious issues concerning aging. (See Chapter 10, "Demography.")

A New Perspective

An alien would see that in the industrialized world, *older* persons are becoming the figure, and the rest of the population will make up the ground. We cannot minimize the implications of this for the coming years. Remember, when the figure and the ground change places, *everything* changes. In this case, that means *the entire life cycle*.

The retirement age of 65 was set early in the past century. At that time, the average life expectancy of an adult working male was about 67, so workers who made it to their 65th birthday would have several months off before they died. Today, the average life expectancy of working adults (including all the women who have entered the workforce) has risen to the low 80s. Using the same logic, the official retirement age should now be *80*!

Fifty years ago, as a male college graduate, you could expect to work for about 40 years before officially retiring. The early part of your work years was dedicated to career climbing and family formation. The middle part of those years was dedicated to home purchasing and children's education. What remained was peak income and pre-retirement saving years. Then it was pretty much over—time to hang out the "gone fishing" sign and enjoy the grandchildren.

Look at the reality today. Baby boomers (born between 1946 and 1964) who will live to be over 80 are having to figure out what to do in a world where they are no longer mentally or physically spent at 65, but where the workplace has told them at 50 that they are getting too old for the new jobs. Men who retire at 62 have wives at the peak of their careers who don't want to quit their positions to keep their husbands company for the next 30 years. Young people just leaving college now look forward to a work life that could very well span 65 *years*.

Your child's wanting to take a few years off after graduation to join a jazz band or ski in Aspen might not be such a bad idea. It's better to do that at 22 than at 80, although nothing will stop the older crowd from joining them. No one in his or her right mind would want to settle on one job for over 60 years. Second and third careers are on the rise. So are second and third marriages—so much so that many children have stepbrothers and half-sisters old enough to be their aunts and uncles. Generation Xers—those born between 1965 and 1978—are beginning to have to care for their aging baby boomer parents. *USA Today*, in April 2002, reported on a study by Sage Products that said that 20 percent of Gen Xers spend 30 to 49 hours a week providing parental care.

People should now start saving for retirement in their 20s because it is too late to ponder financing 30 more years at the age of 57, especially when there are fewer employer-sponsored pension plans to count on.

Does the marketplace reflect all of this? Fashion manufacturers and retailers that bemoan the decline in their sales are still focusing on the younger population, while older women with money to spend can find only a few places selling stylish clothing suitable for the shifts in their bodies and lifestyles. This is one reason for the continuing success of Chico's. The glaring truth is that all sorts of new or revised products and services are called for at every stage of the life cycle because of the aging of the world. To an alien this is obvious. But most people are still stuck in the old model of youth being the figure and older persons just one of the subgroups that make up the ground.

Example #3: Able/Challenged

A third dramatic example of figure-ground educated incapacity relates to the physically challenged. Society assumed that the figure is comprised of physically able people and that those with one or more handicaps make up the ground. An alien would observe some-thing altogether different. Adding together all the people who are obese or have asthma (major epidemics in the world); women who have ever been pregnant; athletes with chronic pain of some sort; those who have broken an arm or leg at some point in their lives; suf-ferers of carpal tunnel syndrome and tennis elbow; victims of neuro-muscular diseases; the growing numbers of elderly; people with back pain, arthritis, stress, or depression; and those who have sight, hear-ing, or permanent mobility problems, you can conclude that living one's life to the normal expected age without ever being physically challenged is the exception to the rule.

There is an old saying in the design community: "When you design for the physically challenged, you design for everyone." Nobody enjoys blouses that button in the back. When cities were forced to lower sidewalk curbs to accommodate wheelchairs, the per-centage of wheelchair users who used those dipped curbs paled in comparison to the bikers, strollers, inline skaters, wheeled-luggage draggers, shoppers with grocery wagons, fast-food deliverers, and others who benefited.

Now that the baby boomers are moving up in years, their eyesight is diminishing. Magnification reading glasses are common now. Yet most restaurants still print menus in small type, even though they are often read in dim lighting. Is it any wonder that people order the chicken or the special that has been recited to them? Containers of home cleaning products, many drugstore items, and credit card bills are impossible to make out without holding a magnifying glass in front of the reading glasses. From TV control panels to automobile dashboards, the whole world is designed for the eyes of adolescents, at the peak of their physical form and prowess.

A New Perspective

Any alien can see that the perfectly fit are just a small segment of the population. If we were to switch figure and ground, moving the physically challenged into the dominant position, everything would change. For one thing, perhaps all toilet stalls in airports would accommodate people with luggage, not just the one we all rush to because it's designed for wheelchairs. Designing larger, easier-to-use, more convenient products for a physically challenged audience would also make life a lot easier for people who are not viewed as "physically challenged" in the traditional sense.

Case in point: OXO designs household, cooking, cleaning, and gardening products that are easy to use. OXO's signature product lines include the Good Grips collection and the Softworks product line, with handles that are large, softer, and more comfortable. These products offer attractive features for any consumer, but they were originally designed for the physically challenged consumer. The technology behind the Good Grips product line was made possible by a visionary named Sam Farber, who understood that millions of Americans (including his wife) were suffering from debilitating arthritis and had trouble with mundane tasks such as gripping kitchen utensils. Good Grips were designed to accommodate arthritic customers, but they are so comfortable and convenient that millions of nonarthritic Americans now have these products as well. Again, switch the figure and the ground to see that by serving the physically challenged, you can reap the benefits of providing a superior product to everyone.

Example #4: Stability/Transition

One last example of figure-ground is that of life stages. We tend to define people by what stage of life they are in: married, adolescent, student, retired, and so on. The emerging reality is that far more of us seem to be spending more time *between* stages in our lives. And for most people, more of these junctures exist than ever before. Perhaps it's appropriate to finally recognize that these between times are becoming the figure, while stability is becoming the ground.

At least 300,000 illegal immigrants enter the U.S. each year, and people around the globe are moving constantly to places where they bide their time until they can find work. The youth culture is synonymous with mobility, and young people increasingly move from place to place in search of ever-better financial opportunities and lifestyles, domestically and globally. Colombia and Venezuela are seeing tens of thousands of middle- and upper-class citizens emigrating (including the most talented professionals and entrepreneurs) because of seemingly intractable violence and poverty, leading to a new class of temporarily dislocated persons called "airline people" in places like Miami. The U.S., along with other countries, has many foreign students and dual-citizenship workers who will return to their homelands after brief stints on campus and in expatriate environments. Indeed, expatriate workers all over the globe are on temporary assignments for any number of reasons. For example, as reported in the *Wall Street Journal* in November 2000, India is sending women abroad to learn how life is lived elsewhere, and their husbands quit their jobs to follow them into this short-term situation. Japanese women are going to Long Island, New York, to get manicurist credentials that are highly valued back home.

Changes in what was the traditional life cycle are a major contributor to what you might call *betweenity*. Children are now entering physical puberty too soon, before they are emotionally ready, throwing them into a new stage between childhood and adolescence. Living longer is leading to more midlife crises and self-recriminations as people seek to transition from material success to spiritual and social significance. The lengthened life span is causing people to examine more than one way of life and consider more than one career. Add downsizings to the mix, and many more cocktail party conversations center around betweenity—where someone was, the fact that he or she is not working now, and where he or she would like to be next.

Widowhood, too, lasts a lot longer now. *U.S. News & World Report* wrote on September 11, 2000, that almost 700,000 U.S. women become widowed annually, and they stay widowed for an average of 14 years. This creates an important betweenity because some will see widowhood as a stage between two lives, and others will see it as a stage between marriage and death. While more widowers than widows remarry, more also commit suicide, perhaps because, for them, this experience of *betweenity* is unbearable.

Currently, more executive women are moving back into the role of housewife because their spouses earn a great deal of money. As they find themselves adopting retro roles with which they are uncomfortable, confusion results, and some see themselves biding their time until they return to positions of independence and economic responsibility.

The workplace, which used to frown on betweenity, is now encouraging or capitalizing on it. Increasing numbers of college students are doing internships, which employers use to attract and retain these betweeners. At the other end, increasing numbers of workers who leave their positions are seen as just being between accepting a new job and returning to the old. "Boomerangs" are former employees who left to go to Internet startups and then returned to their original jobs. In the year 2000, at e.Com, those who left were not forgotten, but rather put on an unpaid leave of absence. Another company didn't hold an exit interview for 45 days, hoping the resignee would change his or her mind and return.

As we live longer and move more and as transitions in people's lives become socially acceptable, the time spent *between* life stages is becoming as important as the time spent *in* them. These between times can be highly stressful. The UK's Association of Insurance and Risk Managers notes that stress is likely to be the number one emerging risk of the 21st century. Although the Association attributes much of this to pressures emanating from the workplace, it also comes from not being in a comfortably settled and projectable point in life. Betweenity is spurring a growing demand for a host of stress-reducing products and services, from religion and meditation to psychological counseling and daytime TV programming, career coaching and self-assessment books, and seminars and tapes.

Betweenity is becoming a new and potentially important tool for recruitment and for easing people into retirement. Betweeners are lucrative markets for relocation services that range from moving vans to quickie foreign-language courses. People who are between may be tapped for volunteerism or extended cruises or as markets for hobby-related goods and services.

A New Perspective

While much market research concentrates on how people identify themselves—professionally, maritally, geographically, and so on—we will face the growing challenge of redefining the figure and the ground and seeing the large and growing segment of the public who can only define themselves by what they currently are *not*. Whether it is the youngster who takes a few years off after school to explore the first of many futures, or the oldster who has left a lifelong career and/or marriage and ponders what's next, or the professional who is reinventing his or her life, the time we spend in betweenity is becoming time to be seriously reckoned with by marketers, public policy makers, financial institutions, and employers.

Children Can Be Aliens

Twenty years ago, when the son of one of us was four years old, he came into the room as a baseball game began on TV. The national anthem was playing, and he asked what was going on. When he was told that this was the beginning of a baseball game, he exclaimed, "I can see that! But why are they playing hockey music?"

On any given day, you can walk into a store like the Gap to shop for jeans, proceed to the bins on the wall, and select from the sizes that are arranged top to bottom, small to extra large. A child would immediately argue that the stack should be reversed, with the small sizes on the bottom, where little people can reach them, and the larger ones on top so that bigger people don't have to bend over.

The Lesson of Alien Eyes

For any business, seeing things from a fresh reality is one of the most powerful lessons. Suppose an alien lands on Earth and, to study earthlings better, he wants to dress like one. The alien would observe that in many developed countries, the majority of earthlings (male and female alike) wear pants. Having done his homework on how to buy pants on Earth, the alien knows this can be done through any number of distribution channels—catalog, TV, online, store, flea market—so he asks 10 people at random how they bought their slacks. The majority say in a store. When pressed as to why, most say they wanted to try them on. Having no preconceived mental baggage about the delivery channels, the alien conjures up an image, based on his research, that a clothing store on Earth—capitalizing on its advantage over other channels—would be a large fitting room, or many large, well-appointed, high-tech fitting rooms.

If the alien walked into a typical clothing store, there would be a major disconnect. He would find the fitting rooms to be little closets in the back, with no technology to serve the customer. That is because although the alien can quickly and clearly see the supposed advantage of the store, the store designers are stuck in the world they knew before the new distribution channels became popular. The stores' inability to understand their real competitive advantage in these changing times will give further impetus to those who design online technology that allows clothing to be customized for each individual body type.

Levi's has led the way in clothing customization. Levi's understands that jeans are a very personal item for millions of Americans and that having the exact right fit is paramount. The inherent problem is that most of us simply cannot find a pair of jeans that fits perfectly. Levi's began incorporating personal customization, but from its retail outlets. The notion that a store should be one large fitting room finally materialized. In essence, a customer goes into a Levi's retail outlet and is measured to the last detail. Once this process is done, the customer selects the style, cut, and fabric he or she wants, and voilà—the pants are manufactured to specification for the customer. This process of in-store customization, while seeming revolutionary, is something that should have been developed years earlier. By adopting an alien's outlook, the "fitting room" environment for clothing customization is a no-brainer. This process increased customer satisfaction, and it helped Levi's cut costs and reduce inventory surplus. While the beginning attempts at this kind of customization might not all prove profitable, the process is inevitable. As the costs of doing it decrease, and as customer demand increases, eventually marketing will have to provide it.

Now, Internet product customization is all the rage. Many companies have begun personalizing their services in all types of product areas. A few e-tailers have been particularly successful when it comes to streamlining their operations using customization. Amazon.com is perhaps the most striking example of an e-tailer that has improved its customer service by developing a profile and set of preferences for each of its users. Amazon keeps track of all its customers' purchases and can couple that electronic record with the customer's new order to offer product recommendations. This can make life a lot easier for someone who otherwise would have to search for a while to find something he or she wanted.

Another good example of an e-tailer effectively doing Internet profiling and customization is Reflect.com, an extension of Procter & Gamble. Reflect.com is a website that uses profiles of female customers to offer them customized packages of cosmetics and other personal care items. The profile is based on a questionnaire that elicits customer responses about things such as hair, skin type, and various lifestyle issues. By targeting products to a woman's current lifestyle needs, P&G can capitalize on the *betweenity* discussed earlier in this chapter. Again, products are made to order and packaged together, making life easier for the customer while making the business process cheaper and more efficient for the company.

Every business and every profession has its version of the fitting room—the competitive advantage that is underutilized or not perceived simply because things are still done the way they always have been. Not understanding this is causing major losses in many industries and businesses. This will continue to happen until they learn to see through alien eyes or the eyes of a child, identify their advantage, change their business to respond, and not compete against competitors' strengths.

Young people today truly see a different world. It is one of instant messaging and discussing personal issues on cell phones in public. They do their school projects online or in teams, the threat of terrorism is part of their daily routine, and they explore Mars electronically from their bedrooms. Their reality, from modes of communication to modes of work, is and will be startlingly different from the generations that preceded them. In addition, people of different cultures, religions, and genetic makeup will always have realities that differ from each other. The alien, too, would likely see realities different from any of these.

Seeing alternative realities more clearly helps you penetrate many veils—those that can cloud political issues, make you wrongly judge others' behaviors or beliefs, and lead you to believe that what you knew in the past shapes all you will know in the future. Seeing alternative realities with fresh eyes helps untrap your mind.

Start now. Pick up or subscribe to a thoughtful magazine that infuriates you and try to open your mind to its perspective. If you are into yachting, follow the world of bowling for a while, and vice-versa. Once a month, have your team at work explicitly state an assumption your business or company makes about its people or its customers and test whether that assumption is really the rule or a large exception to the rule. Train yourself to play a mental game. When someone makes a statement about the marketplace, try and switch figure and ground by asking, "What if it were the reverse image of that assumption?" So, if the perceived market were children, then grandparents could be a major target market. Not too long ago, it finally occurred to the banking industry that what it had assumed to be the "safest" market for mortgage lending—the married couple—was actually the most risky because divorce is the single-most responsible cause of mortgage default. Switch your perspective, and you could greatly increase your chances of success in the future.

2

TREND/COUNTERTREND

Sir Isaac Newton changed science with his laws of physics, one of which said that for every action there is an equal and opposite reaction. While Newton was not known for being a social scientist or market analyst, he would likely have been retained today as a high-priced consultant for his brilliant observations. For, indeed, in the world of human activity, every trend creates its opposite, or countertrend: Countertrends don't happen despite trends; they happen *because* of them.

For example, the developed world is entering the 21st century as the most secular (nonreligious) civilization in recorded history. Because many of the "whats" and "hows" of the world have been answered, many people feel they no longer need individual gods to explain or produce babies or corn or rain. Most of the major world religions have turned away from the many gods of paganism to one God (monotheism). Indeed, it could be said that the move from polytheism to monotheism was the first major downsizing and layoff in history. It is *because* of this growing secularism that, in the past several decades, so many in the world have turned to religion and spirituality. They seek to fill a void that arises from a need to believe in something beyond the material world. Even that countertrend contains opposing forces. New Ageism and Fundamentalism get stronger in opposition to, and to protest against, each other. The stronger fundamentalist Islam gets, the stronger fundamentalist Christianity gets to oppose it. And vice versa.

As another example, the trend toward modernity has, for thousands of years, caused its countertrend of antimodernity. This is increasingly (and desperately) expressed in rage and violence directed against both people and symbols of what the antimodernists hate and fear—such as the federal building in Oklahoma City, the World Trade Center in New York, the Pentagon in Washington, and a swinging nightclub in Bali.

As a third example of trend and countertrend, *disintermediation* has been a major trend in the marketplace over the past 50 years. This involves bypassing traditional channels for the delivery of goods and services, offering lots more options, choices, and sources of information. Now it has become so pervasive that its countertrend, *reintermediation*, is developing with great force. This means that new brokers, agents, and software programs, affinity groups and advisors, reference materials and consumer reports are all emerging to help you navigate in a disintermediated environment.

A fourth example is the increasingly overwhelming flood of information. This is such a powerful trend that its countertrend—negative information (having so much information that it subtracts from your ability to make wise decisions)—is an emerging reality. This makes everyone's job much more difficult. Not only are there more competing messages, but you grow increasingly skeptical as you find yourself drowning in information you can't easily validate.

These are some of the most obvious trends and countertrends. Of course, there are hundreds. This chapter explores six examples in depth to illustrate the point. The themes we cover are *No*

Responsibility Self-Reliance; The Sociology of Apology; The Emerging Diseases of Affluence; Technology, Thy Name Is Poetry; Consuming Versus Saving Safety; and The Decline of Community and The Rise of a New Consumer Durable.

Example #1: No Responsibility Self-Reliance

Indications are that we are moving into a future of increasing self-reliance. Divorce rates increased during the last 50 years throughout the developed world, lifetime employment is quickly becoming rarer (even in Japan), and company- and government-sponsored pensions and health care are withdrawn, diminished, or in jeopardy. An explosion of choices in the marketplace pushes decisions back onto you, and you are swept out into an uncertain sea of change, where the only lifeboats are the ones you make. Yes, you're increasingly on your own. But many people don't want that much responsibility.

It may be that self-reliance, the trend, is based on a trait that exists in a small minority of the population: *autonomy*, or the ability to fend for oneself. Some people thrive on autonomy, but most have a hard time being accountable for themselves, responsible for everything about and around themselves. The self-reliance future has begun to usher in its countertrend, the comfort of getting rid of responsibility by passing it on, opting out, or buying solutions in the marketplace.

Take personal finances, for example. Because we are no longer dictated to by community expectations, or universal ways of living through our life cycles, or prudent principles of old-fashioned banks, or forced contributions into corporate pension plans, financial self-reliance grew rapidly in the 1980s and 1990s. The marketplace was quick to offer a smorgasbord of choices—from auto leases and reverse mortgages to 401(k)s and junk bonds. Because there is always force/counterforce, the same period saw a growing countertrend—a shrinking from financial responsibility. When the two appeared in the same person, as often happens, it was manifested as a demand for entitlement without consequences—having one's cake and eating it too, as it were. For example, from 1994 to 1997, the height of that decade's glorification of financial freedom and autonomy, the number of Americans getting out from under their responsibilities by filing personal bankruptcies rose 73 percent. Many creditors were left holding the bag because they did not anticipate this countertrend.

In Japan in 1997, according to government statistics, more than 3,500 people killed themselves because of money problems, up 18 percent from the year before, as middle-aged male Japanese began to suffer from what psychologists call "restructuring-depression syndrome." They were caught in the movement toward individual responsibility, and they couldn't handle it. Their countertrend was to opt out completely. France's 4.5 million public-sector workers, according to *The Economist* (May 1, 1999), are a drain on that country's economy (forcing a tax burden of 46 percent of the GDP), but France cannot voluntarily reduce that number because people are reluctant to leave safe jobs. Europe, generally, has been struggling with its inability to get out from under the burden of the welfare state as a result of the backlash to the uncertainty of self-reliance. In high-tax economies that do not actively promote and nurture individual entrepreneurship—such as much of Europe—people find it increasingly difficult to compete on a global scale. So they begin the countertrend by resisting the changes. A trend/countertrend spiral is set in motion because the more countries and companies try to become lean enough to compete, the more workers and citizens want protection against the cuts. And the more protection is offered, the less competitive the country or company becomes, requiring it to push for further cuts. Businesses, globally, increasingly find themselves in the middle. They are caught between seemingly contradictory demands for both security and autonomy from their workers.

They are caught between the government's need for more money to pay for social benefits and growing competition, requiring cost-cutting.

Another area of growing self-reliance is health. More people seem to want control over their health, as seen in the rise in sales of diet and exercise plans and the growing popularity of alternative medicine. At the same time, people also expect technology and government to solve a lot of their medical problems. Paradoxically, the more autonomy there is, the more psychotherapy there is, with even online therapy developing mass appeal, because people need help with all the complexity confronting them.

Companies in the health-care business are profiting by responding to both the trend and the countertrend. Pharmaceutical companies, for example, market their products directly to the public now, capitalizing on the desire for autonomy. They also promise that more and more conditions, some of them not necessarily real illnesses, can be treated successfully with new combinations of chemicals. Yet the public's no-risk expectation, when they are forced to make their own choices, has resulted in skyrocketing pharmaceutical liability crises and jury judgments. This forces up the cost of health insurance—and gives rise to demands for nationalized coverage. Trend/countertrend.

In sum, while it is true that some major economic forces are spurring the world's people into more self-reliance, this is an uncomfortable state of being for many. It leads to numerous behavioral and attitudinal contradictions. Interestingly, for example, more young people are doing neighborhood and community service, but in the 1990s, less than one-third of Americans 18 to 24 exercised their responsibility to vote in the presidential election.

Trends and countertrends are powerful market movers. In the marketplace you can see that the void that scaled-down or withdrawn social benefit programs created is now filled with profitable opportunities in the coping and relief areas of coaching, therapy, management of personal resources, affinity groups, legal services, and the creation of new intermediaries in the information world.

In the workplace, the idea that everyone produces best in a completely self-reliant environment won't be productive unless it also acknowledges the countertrend. Despite some need for autonomy and a great need for respect, many workers might find the structures and benefits provided by traditional management a relief from the constant pressure to make more decisions and take more responsibility. Many people who work alone or at home say they miss the discipline offered by an office schedule and the interaction with others that keeps them connected to the larger world. That's why you see individual practitioners and work-at-homers wanting to connect with others, establish routines, and take courses such as time management to restore organizational discipline in a self-reliant world.

Products and services that enable the trend toward self-reliance, such as home computing and 401(k) plans, will be much more successful in the marketplace if coupled with the countertrend of warranties and risk-relievers. All organizations need to take into account the scapegoating (laying blame on someone else) that takes place, including lawsuits and public-relations disasters, when people, caught in the self-reliance trend, seek ways to shift their own growing responsibilities to others.

Example #2: The Sociology of Apology

The media and society put achievers on a pedestal. Then the counterforce sets in, and that leads to looking for achievers' feet of clay. Success is honored, but that honor soon becomes tinged with suspicion that standing out is somehow antisocial. Success has always aroused envy, but that counterreaction seems more violent today.

In the wake of the terrorist attacks on September 11, 2001, a lot of people in America and abroad blamed the U.S. for the events. Many even celebrated the attacks, including some in friendly nations. In Italy, for example, there were those who said that America asked for it by having dominated the world economy, power, and culture.

On some college campuses in the U.S., the focus was to look inward rather than outward, discussing "feelings" and seeing the attacks as a response to America's dominance in international trade and globalization. Many believed that since America had it coming, fighting back was wrong because it risked innocent lives. At the University of North Carolina, a teach-in called for an apology to millions of victims of American imperialism. Georgetown University sponsored a debate titled "Resolved—America's Policies and Past Actions Invited the Recent Attacks."

In fact, this reaction is only the most recent symptom of a countertrend that has been emerging for some time. The last decade of the 20th century in the U.S. was, as many observers noted, a time of escalating "winner takes all." From Wall Street to the baseball diamond, winning was everything, at whatever cost. Luxury goods and services were proudly flaunted by those who cashed in on the winnings, from the busy corridors of Silicon Valley to the gaudy mansions of Florida. The countertrend has now begun, and we are increasingly living in a time when those who win must either not win or apologize for their success.

Physical education classes have been gradually eliminating competitive sports to ensure that every child has self-esteem. Matt Labash, reporting in *The Weekly Standard* on an April 2001 symposium of the Journal of Physical Education, Recreation and Dance, says kids are taught to "set the bar low, then throw themselves a party for clearing it." This flies in the face of one of the oldest tenets of social psychology—that people try harder when they are competing with others. (It should be noted that since this countertrend began, more than twice as many children are overweight as 30 years ago.)

Business faces several serious issues. Competition among strivers in a business has often been a spur to creativity and accomplishment. Will young people with a negative view of competition provide the same high energy in the future? Will they still want to be better, or will they be content to be no worse?

Branding has been a major trend for over 100 years. Increasingly now, successful branding of products and companies is seen by detractors as bullying, as if success means taking advantage of weaker competitors. Today's executives, sensitive to their public image (and perhaps influenced by their own youthful experiences), fear that bully label. So the more successful modern businesses become, the more some executives seek to cloak themselves in a spirituality made up of ethical, meditational, and psychological views from many secular and religious sources so as to appear more humane. In this way, they can deal with layoffs, conduct transactions, and make money, not in triumph but in humility.

All this is leading to a schizophrenic approach to management, constituents, and the marketplace. The stock market has now extended its reach to the far corners of the world, and it is governed increasingly by impatient capital that punishes enterprises for not achieving stellar growth and gain by whatever means necessary, even at the expense of longer-term considerations. Yet, the sociology of apology rewards the underdog businesses and exalts those who claim similarities to the average guy.

The growth of legal liability globally is part of the desire to exact apology in the court system if it is not fully given in the normal course of operations. That causes public affairs functions in business to increasingly declare *mea culpa* (it's my fault). So, too, do the marketing, advertising, and sales operations walk a fine line between touting the organization's success and having it identify with the common person.

Human resources is increasingly pulled in two ways—one to design systems that weed out the underperformers, and another to help all employees be all they can be. The first is good for business; the second is necessary to ward off litigation.

In a world where the trend is toward believing that everyone should share in the win, perhaps no one will. If the countertrend grows even stronger and risk is avoided, because it is not seen as worth it, or it is thought to have no meaning, scientists and athletes, presidents and scholars will all seek refuge in blaming the system rather than taking on the risk (and basking in the pleasure) of winning. Given the human imperative, this is not likely to happen, and we will be in for a rough ride in balancing the trend toward rewarding the winners with the countertrend of the need for them to be humble and even apologetic.

Example #3: The Emerging Diseases of Affluence

The 20th century was one of great progress in health. As we embark upon the 21st century, however, we begin to be plagued with new illnesses and increased incidences of what had been thought to be controlled diseases, such as tuberculosis (TB). Late 20th century technology had indeed generated new remedies, but their very existence has created new challenges. In his book *Illness and Culture in the Postmodern Age*, author David Morris contrasts the trends in genetic testing and surgery with epidemics of alcoholism, obesity, chronic pain, and heart disease. Even children as young as 15 are reported to have heart problems, and in 1999 the Centers for Disease Control (CDC) declared 13 percent of children and teens in the U.S. to be overweight.

Advances in affluence and technology have clearly spurred the trend toward better health and health care. The old saying is that success breeds success, and it does. Throughout the world, people are for the most part living longer, healthier, more productive lives. The countertrend was inevitable. Some people, including scientists, claim that exposure to the electromagnetic waves present in high-tech televisions and computers, and cell phone microwave emissions, can affect living tissues in ways that might trigger biochemical stress. (There is as yet no conclusive proof that this is so.) Even exposure to light at night could act like a drug, disrupting your body's production of melatonin, the hormone that triggers a variety of biochemical activities and resets your biological clock. Recent research has pointed to evidence that increasing exposure to light at night—such as by shift workers and people on computers 24/7—could be carcinogenic. Interestingly, and perhaps to some extent a proof of this, as reported in *Science News* (October 17, 1999), blind people have lower rates of cancer than the sighted population.

The incidence of diagnosis of depression has doubled in the last 50 years. Experts predict that it will rank second in the world among disabling diseases by the year 2020, according to *U.S. News & World Report* (March 8, 1999). People are getting depressed at younger ages and with greater frequency. Nobody knows exactly what depression is, and 3 in 10 depressed people do not respond to treatment. Dr. Lawrence H. Miller, author of *Running on Ritalin*, estimates that between 5 and 9.5 million Americans are now diagnosed with attention deficit disorder (ADD), a disease that used to be called hyperactivity. Ritalin, used largely by white, suburban, middle- and upper-middle-class children, is increasingly being prescribed in astonishing quantities. Yet no one has paid serious attention to the probability that this set of symptoms is a predictable countertrend to the increasing amount of stimulation, information, and imagery young people's brains are subjected to at very early ages, after which they are in school systems that still teach the same slow verbal content.

Yes, affluence has led to better health, but it has also accelerated expectations. Now some have gone from wanting to "keep up with the Joneses" to "keeping up with the Gateses." This emerging luxury fever is a behavior that drives even responsible people to make themselves and each other worse off. People spend more because of the influential rich setting the pace at the top. Stress increases as consumer debt burgeons while the personal savings rate plummets. In his book *The Voice of the Earth*, Theodore Roszak asserts that being extravagant is a basic human need. In an age of pervasive media coverage of everything, the public is constantly exposed to breathless (and thoughtless) details of the lifestyles of the rich, famous, and notorious.

The impacts of an affluent society and culture on our health are more prevalent than ever. Prosperity, in addition to the benefits it brings us, also results in new behaviors that directly affect how our bodies handle disease. Chronic diseases, such as asthma, are increasing at alarming rates and are affecting a much wider spectrum of the population, possibly as a countertrend to the environment's becoming too clean, thus preventing infants' immune systems from getting the training they need. AIDS ravages the world as a direct countertrend to the development of formerly undeveloped areas and unfettered and easy travel. Diabetes is becoming epidemic as a countertrend to the luxury of having many more fats and sugars in our diets. Stress is expected to become the single largest source of health and disability claims in the developed world over the next decade as a countertrend to the lifestyles of affluence.

Businesses will face the consequences. The definition of disability, for example, will continue to widen; ADD is already considered a disability in certain situations. If the entire Prozac population comes under this disability umbrella, employers may find themselves with a large percentage of psychologically (in addition to physically) disabled workers. All this will greatly affect everything from productivity issues to health-care costs. The difference between customary and alternative medical treatment will change as people seek solutions to ailments that are not readily treatable by mainstream medicine.

Extravagance will persist, greatly enlarging the market for luxury goods and services. This will, of course, benefit businesses that know how to tap into it. But there may be unpleasant side effects. Some consumers with lingering guilt feelings might relieve these by blaming those companies for leading them into the extravagance—just as there is a tendency to blame advertising for "forcing" people to buy things they don't need. Materialism will lead to antimaterialism, manifested in everything from spiritual movements to terrorism.

It becomes clear, then, that a trend/countertrend relationship exists between affluence and technological advances and the patterns of emerging new diseases. Future advances in biotechnology will undoubtedly correct some of the ailments. Some day, for example, the 24/7 lifestyle may not be a problem from a biochemical perspective; maybe you will be able to take a pill to redirect your body's hormones if you are working at 3 a.m. Other maladies will arise. In the meantime, however, you face a transition period where the advantages of both technology and prosperity may be hazardous to your health.

Example #4: Technology, Thy Name Is Poetry

An amusing but important example of trend and countertrend is the emerging juxtaposition of technology and poetry. In the industrial era, most of the largest companies and brands were named after their inventors or founders or for the product or service itself. The giants of industry were named Radio Corporation of America, General Electric, American Telephone and Telegraph, Minnesota Manufacturing and Mining, International Business Machines, General Mills. In the post-industrial era, as technology allowed more companies to become more abstract and diverse, many of the names became initials (RCA, GE, AT&T, 3M, IBM). Then you began to see meaningless terms, sometimes computer-generated, as names (Exxon). Some names, such as Intel and Microsoft, were composites of ideas behind the products or services the company offered.

As we enter the next era, something fascinating is happening to company and product names. They are becoming *poetic*, in a kind of countertrend to the high-tech age. This is perhaps not so surprising at a time when people are beginning to move from the discipline of psychotherapy to the undisciplined avenues of spiritual soul-searching. In discussing the willingness of individuals to plunk down $60 an hour for philosophical guidance, Helen Kirwan Taylor, in a *Financial Times* magazine supplement, noted that while *science* can make you aware of the complexity of the world, *poetry* emerges to remind you that we all die, that we are all finite.

Apple Computer's ads in the first years of the new century encouraged people to "think different," using images of Picasso, Einstein, Chavez, Gandhi, and Martha Graham, although none of them ever used a computer. So, perhaps as a countertrend to high tech, here are the names of some high-tech enterprises:

- **Project Oxygen**—A new generation of fiber-optic technology that gives the communication industry room to breathe in its search for more signal space using wavelength division multiplexing.

- **Blue Mountain**—A supercomputer at Los Alamos (made by linking Cray computers) that can calculate 3 trillion operations per second.

- **Blue Pacific**—An IBM computer at Lawrence Livermore Lab that performs 3.9 trillion calculations per second.

- **Intersquid.com**—A computer company that gives away computers and charges for monthly Internet connections and service.

- **3-D Crunch**—A project by Silicon Graphics that analyzes protein sequences.

- **The Dark Aurora**—Believed to be a top-secret reconnaissance plane designed by Lockheed.

- **Amazon, iVillage, Netscape, Excite, Yahoo**—Major Internet-based NASDAQ issues.

It is increasingly clear that Generation X—and, possibly even more, Generation Y (those born since 1978)—in their search for meaning are attracted to terminology that is more image-laden than that of recent years. They are also increasingly comfortable with the marriage of trend and countertrend—technology and spirituality, poetry and complexity. Older generations would see this as a contradiction and would tend to assign more techy-sounding terms to techy undertakings. But for emerging generations, the connectedness of technology to the psyche may be an important part of their adaptation to the future. We all need to be aware of this melding of what John Naisbitt called "high-tech, high-touch." The more technology there is, the more its countertrend, humanization, becomes important.

Example #5: Consuming Versus Saving Safety

Every time humans seek to manage risk or reduce it, they wind up steadily increasing it. For example, bicycle helmets, knee pads, elbow pads, and such allow you to bike faster or skateboard more recklessly. Action and reaction. Almost like a tube of toothpaste: When you squeeze at one end, stuff that's less manageable oozes out the other.

Financial author Peter Bernstein, writing for *Harvard Business Review* in 1996, noted that the development of quantitative techniques for managing risk is allowing people to take more risks than they otherwise would. We operate according to a kind of risk-balancing effect: Changes that appear to make a system or organization safer in fact don't because humans seem to compensate for lower risks in one area by taking greater risks in another.

For example, antilock brakes allowed faster, more reckless driving. When the 55 mph speed limit saved lives, we upped the speed limit. The security of seat belts encouraged drivers to behave more aggressively, resulting in more (though usually less serious) accidents. Air travelers desire cheaper and more convenient flights, so safety advances have been partly offset by flying and landing planes in heavier traffic. Big used car chains reduce the risk of buying used cars, thus inspiring more buyers to take the higher risk of buying a used rather than new car. There are even wheelchairs designed for use in sports.

The advent of portfolio insurance encouraged a higher level of equity exposure than ever before. Even countries with low-risk pensions, such as the Netherlands, keep migrating into higher-risk arenas. Banks take greater risks because they've lost much of their traditional businesses to mutual funds and multipurpose financial institutions. And although even bigger banks created through mergers should be safer, the risk of bigger collapse is escalating.

Baby boomers' preventive health practices and vitamins allow them to take more lifestyle risks, such as mountain climbing, river rafting, and helicopter skiing. Despite their boomer parents' increasing focus on health, teens are becoming higher-risk because of lack of exercise, cigarette smoking, and alcohol abuse.

Genes inserted into animals and crops (to reduce risk of waste, loss, or disease) will increase environmental risk, just as chemicals have done, so there are attempts now to both strengthen *and* ease the stringent regulatory guidelines that have helped reduce that risk. As food technologies improved worldwide yield, disposable income rose in key areas around the globe. Now those populations are upgrading their eating habits, buying more meat, which creates a much higher demand for grains, leading to a higher risk future regarding food.

The end of the risk of the Cold War actually increased global risks by further increasing the number of refugees (a result of unchecked domestic and local wars) and loosing nuclear materials and dangerous knowledge into the free market.

The risk of lowered stock prices leads companies to downsize and revamp, but these risk-avoiding actions have only temporary effects on productivity and are not sustainable. In the process, these shrinking companies are at greater risk of corporate Alzheimer's—better processes, sleeker systems, and leaner workplaces erase valuable corporate memories without guaranteeing long-term competitiveness.

And contrary to another piece of popular wisdom, companies whose senior executives and directors own sizeable chunks of the enterprise (so they will take greater risks in order to greatly increase their returns) actually reduced their risk-taking. A 1996 study led by Peter Wright of Memphis State University found that below 7.5 percent insider ownership, risk-taking rises; over 7.5 percent, it falls as ownership increases.

Clearly, reduction of risk will continue to grow as an important business trend that will never reach its limit of possibilities because human nature keeps creating more and different risks out of the risks we learn to manage.

Example #6: The Decline of Community and the Rise of a New Consumer Durable

Some observers believe that over the past 200 years there has been a gradual decline in the sense of community as many in the world understood that term. Universally, dislocation of people (forced or voluntary), regionalization, and globalization have marched relentlessly across the face of the globe, affecting nations and peoples in profound ways.

Language is a central aspect of a community: Around the world, native languages are becoming extinct. This is significant because, according to Kenneth Hale of MIT, language reveals the importance a particular culture places on kinship and other relationships between individuals. It also suggests subtle, but potentially important, cultural community distinctions, such as whether a tree is considered animate. These are fast disappearing.

The U.S. has always expressed the ideal of assimilating communities of immigrants. Thus, many immigrant groups, such as non-Anglo-Saxon whites from Europe, have undergone a powerful pattern of conversion into the mainstream within three generations. Some intellectuals struggle with hyphenated community concepts, such as African-American, questioning the role of citizenship versus kinship versus community.

The growing percentage of singles in the U.S. population may also indicate a change in the traditional notion of community, which was built around marriage and family life. The share of never-married women 25 to 29 in the 1990s was 33 percent, triple that of 1970, according to census statistics. The share of men in that age group who never married climbed to 48 percent in the same period.

Psychologist Robert Jay Lifton's concept of the *protean self*—the constantly adaptable person—suggests that due to the breakdown of the social and institutional arrangements that traditionally anchored community life, people are learning to change their sense of self to reflect the flux of the times. Perhaps this is most evidenced by the hip-hop wannabe phenomenon, in which white kids dress and talk "black" because they want the same pride in color or ethnicity that an increasing number of minority teens exhibit.

So the assault on traditional ideas of community is leaving a gaping hole in the lives of many. With the destruction of community in the sense that we knew it, what will fill our need for community affiliation? What are the countertrends? Throughout the 1990s, authors talked about the "new tribalism." Conservatives push for family to be rewoven into the fabric of our lives. Post-9/11, many pundits and ordinary people, too, predicted a return to commitments to friends and loved ones. Yet for all the focus on family and friends, the coming years will be no less filled with dislocation, relocation, and rearranged affiliations.

However, one striking countertrend is arising from the changes in the historic sense of community—the commercialization of community. The marketplace abhors a vacuum. And the perceived absence of community is a vacuum. To create as well as capitalize on the countertrend, entrepreneurs, designers, professionals, and marketers are turning community into an emerging and important consumer durable-goods category. The wannabe kids represent big dollars to the purveyors of pop culture stereotypes. Christian Yellow Pages attract consumers to a new community of business (apart from the local directory), making being part of the Christian community a competitive strategy in some parts of the marketplace.

In fact, many traditional communities revolved around religion, and religion in many places is becoming a business. The sale of religious books in North America rose by 87 percent in the last decade and now accounts for about a tenth of America's total publishing sales. Importantly, a growing number of churchgoers see themselves as consumers—people buying services from their congregations. Many very large and successful megachurches are taking on a shopping mall culture, with coffee shops and concerts, bowling alleys and aerobics classes. Their leaders behave like entrepreneurs, using well-honed marketing skills to attract and retain "consumers."

New businesses, such as the Institute for Community Design Analysis, are springing up to help towns and cities reformat themselves into communities. "Defensible space" is a concept that focuses on lowering crime rates and reducing traffic by using walls, lighting, fencing, and shrubbery to manufacture a safe community. New towns, such as Disney's Celebration, are constructed to mimic nostalgic versions of community. Traditional neighborhood development is becoming the hottest new idea in suburban planning. Florida's Seaside—picket fences and all—and Kentlands in Gaithersburg, Md., are made for old-fashioned walking and talking. They market themselves to those who seek simpler virtues—beauty and community.

For those whose need for community is not based in geography, cyberspace is selling community, too. The Internet, the superhighway of cyberspace, is creating opportunities for human relationships, status, and sexual contact. People are becoming *netizens* (Internet citizens), and that includes hustlers as well as entrepreneurs. AT&T and other telecoms envision consumers and business associates seeking new relationships based on telepresence, which will create a new type of community, allowing friends and associates to enjoy the services of their choice as a group.

Employers are creating community through the use of personal development programs (PDPs), which might cost American employers up to $60 billion a year. Volvo, for example, involved workers in ongoing dialogues that made their activity an almost "total community" program. Nonprofits are leveraging their community service stature to make money by licensing their names (American Red Cross with bottled water and designer watches, the World Wildlife Fund with outdoor clothing, Veterans of Foreign Wars with Tetley coffee). These mini-communities are increasingly commercializing their standing in the eyes of the larger community.

Many more market and investment opportunities will come about as the decline of the old community will give rise to the new community. This new one will be open to investors, as well as to individuals who want to start new businesses.

So Newton Was a Futurist

Newton's Third Law that for every action there is an equal and opposite reaction is one of the most fundamental predictions of what will be. Trends and their countertrends lay down many of the paths by which we travel toward tomorrow. They constantly present you with paradox and contradiction, which you must accept if you are to see change for what it is. Rather than one straight line, they constantly cause parallel and branching byways. It is all about the multiple opportunities presented by the forks in the road. Businesses, institutional leaders, and individual people will have to become more comfortable with Yogi Berra's advice: "When you come to a fork in the road, take it."

For business, this is a critical point. Woody Allen once said that bisexuality was the greatest thing to come along since the wheel because it doubles your chances of a date on a Saturday night. So too do trend and countertrend. For example, if you make angel figurines, or candles, or books for journaling, or meditation guides, you can capitalize on the religious, the spiritual, and the secular.

The important thing to remember is that both trend and countertrend present opportunities for profit. At the fork in the road, businesspeople should not merely ask which is the best road to take. We should also ask how our assets and competencies can be used to our advantage on either or both roads. Executives at Victoria's Secret did this in the face of the trend toward unisex clothing. The founders of Southwest Airlines did this in the face of a trend toward airlines neglecting local routes in favor of hubbing. The promoters of sugary boy bands and young, sexy female heartthrobs did this in the face of heavy metal and punk music. Countertrends can make money. Creating them or riding them makes money. Ignoring them means leaving the opportunity to the competition.

Not realizing that every trend creates a countertrend will leave you confused and surprised by the unfolding events and changes ahead. Understanding the existence of countertrends will untrap your mind and allow it to process change much more accurately.

3

Substituting the
Spiral for the
Pendulum

It's true, as everyone says, that history advances in cycles. There have always been short cycles; there have always been long cycles. There have always been cycles of war and peace, business cycles, cycles of ascendancy and decline, cooling and warming climate cycles—the list is almost endless. Some folks may even remember the brief but extensive popularity of the *Kondratieff Wave* theory. It said that capitalist economies tend to have long cycles of expansion, inflation, and recession, repeated every 54 years. Both the ancient Mayans and the ancient Israelites believed in 50- to 54-year cycles of catastrophe and renewal.

This cyclical motion is usually described as a pendulum. The mental image we have of cycles is that, whatever the object of attention, activity goes in one direction for just so long—perhaps too long—and then it swings back, past center, to its original point, and then the process begins all over again. You have an idea of what "normal" weather is, and when you see the pendulum swing too far to the cold or wet, you expect it will swing all the way back at some point to hot and dry, with most activity being around the center of the arc of the pendulum's swing.

When a society's emotions swing too far to an extreme, you anticipate a correction and a swing back to center and then to the opposite extreme and then back again. When stock prices rise dramatically and then fall dramatically and then rise and fall, over time you expect the same conditions to prevail, causing the pendulum to continue swinging back and forth around some central point that represents true value. And when the political center swings to the left for some time, you expect it to swing back to the right for some time, and then left, and then right, and so on.

Because you have become accustomed to seeing cycles as pendulums that swing out and then swing back along the same arc, you can become trapped in that image. If you look through alien eyes, however, you can see clearly that things cannot possibly retrace their path back to where they have been. That is because the context has changed. Places are not the same, people are not the same, nothing is exactly the same as it was before.

The Heisenberg Uncertainty Principle says that even in a laboratory, you cannot precisely predict outcomes; all you can have is probabilities. It also says that you cannot perform the same measurement twice and get the exact same results the second time. It is impossible to replicate with absolute fidelity the exact conditions under which the first measurement was taken. Physics has proven that the act of observation itself changes the outcome.

Away from the laboratory, in the more amorphous and abstract worlds of social, economic, and political interactions, you can be sure that we'll never go back to precisely where we were.

But people have gotten used to the pendulum analogy. Comfort with it creates a kind of mental laziness, so that we actually see pendulums even where they don't really exist. A better model, as observation through alien eyes would reveal to us, is a *spiral*. Cycles do exist, but things never reverse themselves along the same path, and they never arrive back at the same place. They spiral up or down because the original point of departure is no longer there.

Example #1: The Social Fabric

In recent years, a number of marketers have noted what they see as a return to romance. They have observed in popular culture a more positive focus on romantic love, more people staying together, more belief in living happily ever after. During the last years of the 20th century, there was an increase in the marriage rate and a leveling off of the divorce rate in the U.S. Does that mean we will go back to the romantic ideal embodied in the love story films of the 1930s?

Even if we wanted to, we could not. Changed attitudes toward sex, changed roles of women in society and in the economy, the changed nature of relationships between men and women, wars, more education, and much more information, cynicism, and skepticism—all these mean we cannot possibly re-create, no matter how much we might try, the idealized romanticism of 70 years ago. Thus, while bridal gown retailers may see a renewed desire for traditional and elaborate gowns, stress management counselors and etiquette consultants can look for a boom in planning the wedding around stepchildren and stepparents, a product of the divorces and remarriages that have preceded many a modern wedding. Women who marry after their early 20s already have household goods, and frequently, so do their prospective bridegrooms. Often, these couples ask for experiential gifts rather than material ones. That opens up different avenues for advertisers and different markets for everything from spas to museum memberships.

Because change affects everything, the notions of living together out of wedlock, "starter" marriages, "starter" homes, and even "starter" children in the form of pets all create billions of dollars of shifts in consumer spending. As romantic love spirals continually onto new planes of relationships, businesses that neglect the newness and see only the pendulum swinging back lose out on all the possibilities created by shifts.

Recent years have seen an upsurge in religion, particularly in the U.S., but also among young people in other parts of the world. Does this mean our society will again be dominated by the unquestioning religious fervor that characterized America in its early years? No. One little fact can illustrate how different we are from that past. Religious adherents in America today, as surveys show us, are more tolerant of those who belong to other faiths than they ever were before. According to a recent Gallup poll, more than 75 percent of Americans believe that there is some truth to all religions. A more tolerant religious belief is not the same as the belief that drove the Puritans.

In addition, the religion revival is multidirectional. New sects are cropping up; new composites are created by putting together pieces from several religions—such as JuBu, a kind of Judaicized Buddhism. Throughout Latin America, Christianity is frequently being combined with traditions like voodoo. This is not, nor will it ever be, your great-great-grandparents' religion.

Believing in the pendulum has cost mainline religions a great deal in adherents and in dollars. By not recognizing the spiral, many have seen their erstwhile disciples split off to more conservative or more liberal sects, to alternative forms of spirituality, or to lay teachings that incorporate spiritual formats—witness the success of Deepak Chopra. The publishing business, the seminar business, specialty retailers (such as mineral and gem sellers), and even spas and gyms that offer yoga have all benefited from the spiraling of the trend back to religion and spirituality. None would have if they could see only a pendulum. Traditional houses of worship, and their efforts at money-raising, have suffered dramatically where only the pendulum swing was perceived.

Similarly, the renewed focus on family in recent years is seen by some as leading to a pendulum swing back to Ozzie and Harriet. It's not. With most married couples being two-earner households, with great advances in education levels and economic autonomy for women, with the redefinition of what we mean by family—people living together without being married, gay couples, so-called "intentional" families, a la *Friends* and *Seinfeld*—the very idea of family has changed. As it always has, by the way.

Conservatives have decried what they see as the deterioration of the traditional family. Also known as the nuclear family, it was always depicted as a father who goes to work and a mother who stays home to take care of the house and the average of 2.3 children. That so-called traditional family was in reality an artifact of the 20th century industrial world. In itself, it was a spiraling of family, not a baseline. Prior to that was the agricultural era family model—a multigenerational extended family in which all worked. The fact is, the family, like all societal institutions, changes in adaptation to changed circumstances. We may have once again swung around to valuing the family. But we do not travel along a pendulum.

Increasing numbers of successful women have no children. With housing prices so high and jobs hard to find, census data shows that four million Americans aged 25 to 34 live with their parents. In his book *Adoption Nation*, Adam Pertman writes that there are now five to six million adoptions in the U.S. alone, with increasing numbers among single and gay households. Many more children are born out of wedlock. Throughout Europe, the numbers are staggering as social stigmas fall away. As mentioned in Chapter 1, "Looking Through Alien Eyes," "illegitimate" babies account for almost two-thirds of the births in Iceland, half in Norway, and about a third in England, France, Ireland, and the U.S. Is this a pendulum swing back to the family that parenting magazines were originally designed for? Or what banks see when they issue accounts or credit? Or what advertisers depict when they want to exploit the return to family values? Or that political campaigners address when they run for office? Are housing developers, home maintenance companies, airlines, and institutions of higher learning paying sufficient attention to the new family in terms of design, pricing, accommodation, or innovation in product and service delivery?

Businesses that see themselves as family-based, such as life insurance, must adopt the alien eyes approach, or they risk becoming irrelevant. If they see their mission as serving and supporting families, they must see family as what it is today and what it may well be in the future. For in the world we are moving into, an increasingly democratized one, we decide for ourselves what our family is. Billions of dollars are at stake in the spiral from "old" family to "new" family, even as the shift is back toward family values.

It is increasingly clear that in the foreseeable future, there will no longer be *a* model of the family; there will be multiple models. If existing businesses do not accept that, consumers will find other businesses that will. The institution of family has spiraled upward and onward, while some businesses refuse to let go of the pendulum.

Example #2: Cycles in Business Oversight

Early in 1999, in response to public complaints by then-U.S. Securities and Exchange Commission chairman Arthur Levitt about the inadequacy of some audits of large businesses, the Public Oversight Board (at that time the self-regulating body for auditors in the U.S.) created a Panel on Audit Effectiveness. This panel, made up of eminent people from business, government, academia, and accounting, undertook, supposedly, an objective investigation of Levitt's charges and developed a comprehensive response to them.

Their undoing was in seeing this "return to governance" environment as a swing back on a pendulum that had swung too far in the direction of license and conflict of interest. In its final report, delivered in May 2000, the Panel said that *"While many specific recommendations are made for improvements in the conduct of audits and the governance of our profession, our report demonstrates that both the profession and the quality of its audits are fundamentally sound."* In other words, while there might on rare occasions be inadequate or flawed audits, this was a minor problem that could be remedied by *going back* to the basics of auditing.

As we all know, in 2002, along came the Enron, WorldCom, Tyco, A&P, Merck, and Xerox auditing debacles (among others).

The Panel appeared to believe that if auditors just went back to their old basic principles of auditing—really only a few minor readjustments—everything would be OK. But it couldn't be because too much had changed.

For one thing, there were formerly only a handful of dominant organization types. They tended to have set, prescribed, comparable processes and structures. Their operations generally conformed to widely-held principles. Thus, we could develop entire constructs of law, regulation, accounting, worker benefits—all the bits and pieces that added up to the social contracts between the organization and its stakeholders and the greater society at large. This was true whether considering family farms, the guilds, trade associations, merchant entrepreneurs, or megacorporations.

In the 21st century, however, it is clear that there will be no "typical" organization of any kind. Instead, whether small or medium or large, we are diversifying and multiplying and morphing into *hyborgs*—*hybrid organizations* that have inner and outer workings in common with few others, perhaps only themselves.

For example, operational structure today could include any permutation of

- Centralized versus decentralized control

- Virtual versus permanent versus contract employees

- Intangible versus tangible assets

- In-sourced versus outsourced work

- Wholly-owned subsidiaries versus majority stakes versus minority stakes versus joint ventures versus strategic alliances versus licensing versus leasing

- Local versus national versus regional versus offshore versus transnational versus global operations

Businesses less and less resemble each other or the models taught in business schools. They are more and more ad hoc and fluid, each one creating its own unique template, which can transform itself into something else as circumstances require. Auditing such organizations, especially when they engage in questionable practices, as Enron showed so clearly, demands an ability to think outside the box and a clear-eyed capacity to see the differences between today's and yesterday's business organizations.

Our comparing and controlling systems cannot go back to where they were. They will continue to be inadequate until we devise new ones that are calibrated to a unit of one. For example, just as there is talk of medicine's evolving to address each person's specific genotype (with individually timed and targeted pharmaceutical delivery and diagnostic processes), so too will management and technology and law and accounting principles be required to focus on the specifics of the hyborg rather than a generalized class of organizations.

Organizations will increasingly need to build, take apart, rebuild, and reconfigure their structures while simultaneously being able to respond quickly to feedback driven by success, not by processes. The *Lego-Bio* organization is an emerging model that combines the reconfiguration quality of Legos with the adaptability of a biological model. In such an organization, the pendulum is never an alternative. Operations are on continuing and multiple spirals.

For the accounting profession, thinking pendulum instead of spiral had disastrous consequences. Public outrage over accounting scandals forced even friendly legislators and regulators to expressions of concern and ultimately to stricter oversight. In June 2002, the SEC implemented an order requiring CEOs and CFOs of billion-dollar-plus companies to swear under oath that the numbers in their financial reports are correct. This, as the *Wall Street Journal* noted at the time, could subject the executives to both civil and criminal penalties. In July 2002, Congress enacted, and the president signed, the Sarbanes-Oxley Act, a comprehensive corporate fraud law that, among other things, imposed an independent regulatory authority on auditors. There is no pendulum here; there is no way to ever go back to the same point at which this all began.

Example #3: The Markets

Experts appear on TV shows and offer advice based on market cycles, believing that what occurred before will occur again, using the pendulum analogy. Few people have made fortunes based on expert panelists' advice. That's not because the cycle was called wrong. It's because most of these experts couldn't see what would be different this time around. For example, in 2002, many economists and pundits who saw recession were surprised when retail spending did not track with economic projections quarter by quarter. At the same time, we were beginning to learn that consumer sentiment is no longer as closely tied to purchasing behavior, as was previously thought. According to an article in the *Wall Street Journal* on April 8, 2002, neither the University of Michigan's Index of Consumer Sentiment nor the Conference Board's surveys had been predictive of consumer spending. Over the past 20 years, there has been little evidence of a relationship between consumer confidence, which might be driven by such factors as war, terrorism, and disasters, and consumer spending, which may be driven by cash flow.

It is entirely possible, some experts now assert, that depression as a result of economic downturn actually spurred spending on the part of some portion of the public, especially women. Consumer spending during the 2001–2002 slowdown years may have actually led to the validity of "When the going gets tough, the tough go shopping."

In neglecting to see the spiral, many retailers did not innovate or competitively attract customers with anything but price cuts. This could be, and often has been, a disastrous strategy. They saw the pendulum that the experts portrayed, but the consumer had moved on to wholly new adaptive behaviors in the face of economic hardship, a highly competitive marketplace, new information channels, and new spending categories. For example, the home improvement and home furnishings businesses profited greatly. So did Starbucks. So did video game manufacturers. The consumer's cycle spiraled, the experts clung to the pendulum, and the businesses that could distinguish between the two and strategize based on the spiral, are now in much better shape.

As you try to understand the unfolding future, it is important that you free your mind of the trap of the pendulum. When there seems to be a "return" to some former time or condition, make an effort to figure out what has changed in the intervening months and years— the social, political, technological, environmental, demographic, and economic events and circumstances that are true now but weren't true then. After that, let your mind's eye take in the new landscape. Then and only then will you begin to get the cycle right. Businesses can do this in teams. Individuals can do this alone or with people whose insights they respect. You can decide who can help you best do this. If any strategy is based on the process of a cycle, or a seeming return to an earlier condition, the trap of the pendulum can be seductive. The freedom to think in terms of spiral, however, can be far more visionary and far more profitable.

4

THE EXTREMES INFORM THE MIDDLE

Some years ago, we got a call from *Harper's Bazaar*, asking us to comment on the trend toward the "waif" look on the fashion runways—scrubbed faces, ankle socks, flat shoes, and childlike, innocent posturing. But at the time there was also a lot of the punk, nihilistic look as well—body piercing, spiked hair, and torn garments. So we said that the real story was the fashion designers' need to go to opposite extremes to get noticed in a world of hype and ever-present media messages. The reporter asked how she could place a business angle on that—"What can the fashion business do with that contradiction?" We said that in a couple of years, the woman on Main Street, having been repeatedly exposed to the two extremes and not being able to completely align with either, would chance a second piercing in her ear, a small rose tattoo on her back, and flat shoes. And that's what happened. Three additional purchases were made that wouldn't have been had there been a presentation of only one extreme, or none. Having its point of view continuously exposed to both extremes, the middle cautiously moved, and the fashion world cashed in. The dividends are still coming. Mainstream middle-class girls and women are sporting more piercings, tattoos, and flat shoes than ever.

From religion to politics to purchases, it is exposure to the extremes that moves the middle. For example, in the pro-life/pro-choice debate, only the most hide-bound proponents are exactly where they were at the beginning of the issue. Many feminists now believe that abortions should not be done after the fifth month of pregnancy unless the mother's health is at issue, and many Catholics, including nuns, have come out in favor of women controlling their own bodies. Meanwhile, the entire country was and is forced to think about an issue that was once only whispered about by a few. It could soon pale in comparison to issues of genetic engineering. To predict where the middle will wind up, it is essential to free your mind of one-sided traps and objectively consider both extremes, which ultimately inform the middle.

In the early 1800s, the German philosopher Georg Hegel proposed that societal change took the form of a dialectic—that there was always a thesis (an idea or proposition) and an antithesis (its opposite), and these eventually wound up merged into a synthesis.

As you try to understand the trends that will shape business strategies and personal choices in the future, this dynamic takes on great importance. In the early 1970s, an executive at the Prudential Life Insurance Company did an informal survey of fellow executives to determine who was quicker to embrace (or at least accept) the extreme new values that were emerging at the time—living together out of wedlock, experimenting with drugs (particularly marijuana), protesting government positions (notably the war in Vietnam), advocating for civil and women's rights, and so on. After looking at many demographic variables—age, sex, place of birth, education, income, marital status—he found that only one variable caused these otherwise conservative executives to have a favorable attitude toward the new values. And that was whether they had children of or near college age. The lesson of this research, we believe, goes way beyond the study itself and is just as valid now, 30 years later, as it probably would have been several thousand years earlier.

This is the *in-your-face* phenomenon. When something extreme is in-your-face, as it is when you have a child or a romantic interest who embraces something you have not known or seen before, suddenly your eyes are deflected from their lock on the ordinary, and your mind opens enough for even radically new ideas to take hold. Then, once the new is in-your-face, the rules change. Accept, or you alienate yourself from those you love, or the job you're after, or the neighborhood you want to live in, or the club you'd like to join, or the school you attend.

When AIDS first came to public attention in the U.S., it was considered the gay disease, fate pointing a moral finger at a subset of the population that engaged in a nonmainstream lifestyle. It was their problem, those people over there, not my problem, over here. But then something extraordinary happened. AIDS was killing Rock Hudson, and Elizabeth Taylor was taking the lead in getting the public to care. These were two close-to-the-heart idols of the very population that heretofore had condemned the sufferers.

Then it was a nephew. The neighbor's kid. A child's friend from school who got a blood transfusion. This distant scourge was suddenly shifting to in-your-face. The extremes that existed before—those who couldn't care less (in fact, who believed this was God's punishment) versus those who felt the nation should pull out all the stops and dedicate all its resources to helping cure this illness—were now what the middle paid attention to. The middle became informed, and the middle moved. There is no question that this country and others are in a very different place from where they began. And now, attention is focused on the Caribbean, Africa, and Asia, where the disease is destroying even larger percentages of populations. As the world shrinks, and over there becomes over here, in-your-face gets even more pronounced, the middle keeps moving, and nothing stays the same. In fact, once the middle has moved and incorporates aspects of the extremes, the extremes go further out, the process repeats, and the middle is ultimately informed and changed yet again.

This chapter explores four of the many examples of extremes informing the middle and why each affects you, business, and the economy. The following examples range from political governance, to technological advances, to free speech, to the evolving roles of men and women. To do this, we suspend our own biases and find the potentially legitimate points in each position so we might see where the middle will wind up.

Example #1: Corporate Social Responsibility Versus Free-Market Capitalism

Extremes of Corporate Social Responsibility	Extremes of Free-Market Capitalism
Multinational corporations are responsible for providing fair wages and safe working conditions for workers wherever they do business.	Corporations are responsible for maximizing profits for shareholders.
Big business and national governments have a responsibility to reduce the societal and environmental inequities caused by capitalist practices.	Local governments and communities are responsible for dealing with their own problems. Besides, Adam Smith's "Invisible Hand" concept will operate to see that free market forces will work for the good of humanity.
Industry should eliminate all wastes from manufacturing processes, except those that are useful, such as animal wastes. Ecology, based on James Lovelock's contention that the earth is a single superorganism (the Gaia Hypothesis), emphasizes the need to "reduce, reuse, recycle."	Industrial manufacturing processes should be efficient and profitable.

A middle informed by these extremes is calling for a more humane and compassionate capitalism. Free-market proponents, even including

Peter Drucker, become more receptive to government intervention, via regulation, legislation, and incentive, to ensure that businesses operate in a socially responsible fashion. It becomes important to many people, particularly the young, to work for companies that they see as responsive to their idealism. Businesses that want to succeed in recruiting the best and brightest publicly position themselves as socially and environmentally responsible.

Ideas that originally are considered too extreme to warrant attention are eventually absorbed in some way by the middle. For example, it was not too long ago that environmentalism was dismissed as a radical fringe movement. In the late 1980s, at an event held by a client of ours, a large financial services institution, we spoke of the increasing political clout of the environmental movement. The CEO of the company was outraged by this mere mention of what he considered to be "just a fringe movement." In fact, he was so incensed that he canceled our relationship. Fast-forward to 2003, when 10 of the world's key banks have signed on to the "Equator Principles"—environmental and social-impact standards to be considered when funding infrastructure ventures.

The "Third Way" politics of the early 1990s, as exemplified by Bill Clinton, Tony Blair, and Gerhard Schroder, were the outcome of a middle informed by the extremes of the Left and Right. The focus was on making the market economy more humane, reducing the societal and environmental inequities caused by capitalism, creating new welfare concepts that involved both compassion and responsibility, and encouraging new forms of global regulation.

The mutual fund company Pax World looked at the extreme positions on social responsibility and environmentalism in 1971 and created a socially responsible investment (SRI) vehicle that increasingly appealed to the moved middle—investors looking to make a profit while supporting a more humane capitalism. SRI funds have shown competitive yield in the ensuing years. Nike would have saved itself from a tremendous amount of negative press, not to mention lost sales, if it had taken notice of concerns about workers' rights in developing countries far earlier.

As the middle moves, accounting practices will likely have to reflect ecological and societal impacts as liabilities (or assets) not now recorded on the balance sheet. Manufacturing will be under pressure to move toward life cycle product management, which means factoring in energy and waste implications from production to disposal. Dell Computer is already doing this with its recycling program. And trade and professional associations will be on the front lines in dealing with new coalitions and power centers. They will not be able to take their constituents' or the marketplace's position for granted.

Once there were clear extremes: free market versus socialism, exploitation versus stewardship. Now there is a hugely moved middle, and everything economic will be affected.

Example #2: The Techies Versus the Luddites

During the early 19th century in England, in the beginning years of the Industrial Revolution, bands of farmworkers roamed the countryside, intent on destroying the new machinery in farming, which they feared would cause them to lose their jobs. Known as Luddites (named for Ned Lud, a deranged farmworker who began attacking machinery in the late 18th century), they were forerunners to those who came to fear that we and our ways of life would be replaced by machines and technology. Their position might be characterized as extreme technological fear.

Throughout the thousands of years humans existed, there were those who were the technology devotees. They used fire, the wheel, metals, gears, motors, invisible waves, atoms, and computer chips for what they saw as advancing the physical condition of humanity. Scientists and technologists have been key contributors to making great societies and thriving economies. Many people believe we owe everything to them, and all the problems we can foresee in the future will be solved by them. This position might be characterized as extreme technological optimism.

Again, it is important to list potentially legitimate perspectives of both extremes with an untrapped, unbiased mind in order to ascertain the movement of the vast middle. The list is lengthy, but here are a few of the key points.

Extreme Techies	Extreme Luddites
Technology will unite the world, overcome discrimination, educate universally, serve every need, and solve every problem.	Technology will put everyone out of work, machines will take over, we will suffer from an information glut, and values and morals will be debased as community and belief are circumscribed by globalized and dehumanized electronics.
Telecommunications technology allows you to work from anywhere at any time.	Distinctions between public and private life are eroded in a 24/7 world.
Enhanced surveillance capabilities will create a future in which crime and terrorism can be monitored and stamped out.	Technology enables criminal activity in offshore companies and finances, along with digital crime (hacking, identity theft, sabotage, fraud). Innocent people will be caught up in electronic surveillance.
The Internet will form a planetary intelligence that will connect to everything and make life easier and better for everyone. The Internet will create a world of "DotCommunism" and a better-informed, more engaged populace.	Virtual realities and implanted chips will remove your humanity and sense of self, giving control to machines and their makers. Copyright protection will be greatly undermined by the Internet.
Robo sapiens (a hybrid species of human and robot) will have an intelligence vastly superior to that of mankind.	Cyberpersonalities, whether electronic virtual assistants in the workforce or virtual romantic partners, will change human relationships beyond our ability to control them.
Genetic engineering will produce enough food to feed the world and deliver cheap medications to the world's poor, as well as cure most, if not all, diseases.	Genetic engineering will alter crops and other plants, and our bodies, in ways that will devastate the natural order and will create unanticipated and dangerous outcomes.

The middle, confronted by these extremes, is attempting to accommodate a little of both. For one thing, they are asking their governments to both foster *and* regulate the virtual world. The Council of Europe cyberspace treaty would create uniformity of law in the 41 member nations regarding hacking, fraud, and child porn. The

Hague Convention, governing 48 member nations, would hold an online store liable under laws of any member state. It will be interesting to see what global protocols will be devised as a result of being informed by extremes—one looking for standardization, and the other calling for diversity. Europe has effectively banned genetically modified foods, and opponents claim this has denied poor people access to the same food available to and eaten by Americans. The major food giants are being hit hard by customers on both sides, and the middle is beginning to move on this issue.

Surveillance devices allow electronic tracking of auto use to determine insurance premiums. It is already possible for companies to track someone's virtual travels on the Net, as well as someone's virtual location when using a cell phone. But who will draw the line, and how? A number of bills have been introduced in the U.S. Congress in response to consumers' demands for control of their private data and accountability from the companies that gather it. All this is happening while more people embrace the Net and cell phones and tracking systems such as OnStar.

Most people want social interactions with computers to mimic the social rules they follow offline. Socially attractive values such as honesty, approachability, and trustworthiness are necessary to build rapport with users. Psychologically, people enter the world of the computer and give it the same respect due another person. They expect to get that respect back, and they are angry or hurt if the computer doesn't follow the rules. Smart interfaces are moving away from indifference and toward emotional experience, using courtesy, empathy, flexibility, inventive uses of language, praise, flattery, and politeness.

Children are becoming as attached to computerized toys as they are to a live pet. Japanese men are subscribing to relationships with virtual girlfriends who are realistic, emotional software programs. Thus, the definition of a loving tech interface relationship, with all of the protocols involved, is already evolving.

You, like your peers, are going online but attempting to protect your identity. You, like your peers, are beginning to think about when you don't want to be reached on your cell phone. You, like your peers, rely heavily on e-mail but are learning how to get out from under the tidal wave of spam and messages. You, like your peers, are making the changes and are somewhat accommodating the extremes as you seek balance in your own life.

The techies and Luddites will continue to hurl considerations, objections, lawsuits, scenarios, and political threats at each other as technology marches on. But through it all, the middle, hearing what the extremes have to say, and seeing what the extremes envision, will be much more informed and will pick and choose from new technology, new behaviors, and new forms of relationships. The middle will move.

Example #3: Free Speech Versus Censorship

Extremes of Free Speech	Extremes of Censorship
Anyone should be allowed to say anything via any medium to any audience.	There are limits to what can be said in any venue, and the community and the government should be allowed to set them.
Vulgarity and crudeness are the prices we must pay for freedom of expression. The public, whether it's one person or one hundred million people, has the absolute right to decide for itself what it should communicate, watch, enjoy, and do. It is perfectly okay for Icebox.com, an incubator for edgy shows, to push the envelope with tasteless, offensive characters. It is okay that the Internet currently has some 2,300 hate sites. It is okay that one of these, Stormfront.com, went into the web hosting business so that extremists could evade Europe's anti-hate laws.	The language and the imagery of a society gone awry should be stamped out. Censorship should be applied to TV, the Internet, and the media to protect our values and morals and to save our culture from incivility.

(continues)

Extremes of Free Speech	Extremes of Censorship (Continued)
Democracy will be strengthened by complete disclosure and total free speech.	Democracy will be jeopardized if national security is compromised. For this reason, we must restrict free speech where government matters are concerned.

So how does this move the middle?

Virtual voyeurism, abhorred by conservatives and fundamentalists and supported (at least in concept) by cultural libertarians, is on the rise. In the first years of this century, we have been overrun by reality TV shows like *Big Brother* (in which 10 ordinary people live in a fully wired house for 100 days, during which everything—*everything*—they say and do can be seen and heard), *Survivor*, and *The Osbournes*. Teens hook up cameras to their computer monitors so that strangers can watch them via the Internet. MTV's Tom Green, who has a big youth following, did a TV special on his operation for testicular cancer. People have given birth, with every detail shown, on the Internet. Blogging (a term derived from web logging)—posting one's thoughts, ideas, and experiences on the Net on the assumption that other people will (or should) be interested in them—is all the rage. Ralph Nader's Consumer Project on Technology petitioned for Internet suffixes such as ".isnotfair" and ".suck," making it easier for people to vent about what they don't like.

On the other hand, Wal-Mart (the biggest seller of books, music, and videos) does a thriving business by refusing to offer entertainment it believes will offend its customers. Christian bookstores and religious and spiritual media are among the fastest-growing segments of the publishing business.

The extremes protest each other's positions, and the middle is forced to pay attention. Eventually, in the typical household, *The Simpsons*—once considered the outer bounds of disrespect and incivility—comes to be seen as pretty tame. Reality shows that get phenomenal ratings in their first seasons become boring, and explicit displays of sexuality in the media are shrugged off as not nearly as damaging as exposure to violence—which, in itself, has also been pushing the boundaries in the news and in entertainment.

There is constant debate over how much of the government's data, decisions, and doings should be revealed to the public. Some believe none, and others believe all. As revelations and crises come and go, the middle is constantly moved. Exposure to the sexual misdeeds and substance abuse of presidents is now part of mainstream awareness. Data obtained through the Freedom of Information Act (an act once considered highly radical and unpatriotic by some) is used fairly frequently by left and right alike. Michael Moore's 2004 film *Fahrenheit 9/11* is hotly debated by both sides and may eventually set the stage for a new form of nonfiction film that will reshape the traditional documentary. The middle will come to embrace these films as edutainment (a combination of education and entertainment), finding yet another medium through which to gain access to information formerly undisclosed.

All major enterprises have, or will have, at least one (and probably more) rogue website about them. These sites, often created by disgruntled employees or dissatisfied customers, provide commentaries and information about the targeted company. The content can range from unwanted revelations to scandalous criticisms. Some companies take legal action against such sites—in most cases, a vain exercise. Shrewder businesses monitor the sites and look for potential new ones. They prepare and distribute reasoned and reasonable responses that present their positions and try to effectively counter outrageous charges. More companies will have to develop this approach as the Internet continues to evolve into a modern version of the ancient Roman Forum, in which opposite camps vent their frustrations and expose their emotions on every issue to a middle that finds this increasingly acceptable.

The debate over free speech has raged in the U.S. since the founding of the Republic almost 230 years ago. At times it becomes almost unbearably intense, as it did during Senator Joseph

McCarthy's heyday in the 1950s and as it has today with the fierce arguments over national security and constitutional rights. As terrorism and concerns about it increase, the disputes will get both hotter and louder. In the process, the middle will hear, carefully evaluate, and adjust to the extremes, changing its position as it believes the times warrant.

Example #4: Traditional Versus Nontraditional Gender Roles

If we look at traditional distinctions between men and women, they tend to cluster around what you might call the "six Bs"—*brawn, breadwinning, brazenness, broncobusting, breeding,* and *beautification.* If you exhibited a great deal of any of the first five, you were extremely macho. If you were at the opposite end of the spectrum, you were extremely feminine. But in the modern world, these extremes have become unpalatable to the middle. Those who defend the "real" male and those who romanticize the "real" woman don't make sense to people who do neither.

Extremes of Traditional Gender Roles	Extremes of Nontraditional Gender Roles
Men are defined by their *brawn*— their ability to use physical power for economic and social advantage. Women do not exhibit raw physical power if they want to be liked and accepted. Men without great strength and assertiveness are not great men.	The physically weak nerd can be macho in a society where brain power counts more than brawn in economic success. Strong, athletic women are participating in boot camp fitness classes and pumping iron in gyms.
Men are the *breadwinners.* Women stay home and take care of the family.	Women are becoming the major or only breadwinners in their households. Househusbands are on the rise.
Men are *brazen*—aggressive, competitive, and self-assured. Women are demure and restrained.	Women in movie roles and rock groups are as brazen as men. Violent crimes committed by women are rising. Men who show their softer, feminine side are becoming more common.

Men are *broncobusters*. They are better able to tame the engine of their era, whether it is a horse, car, or computer.	Women in the U.S. are purchasing more cars than men. Women tame computers as easily as men and have historically been major inventors of and innovators in software.
Men are the dominant determiners of *breeding* and are defined by their virility.	Hormonal research reveals that men as well as women have estrogen. Male menopause, marked by declining testosterone, is recognized. New technologies allow for reproduction that circumvents intercourse or low sperm count. Human reproduction via cloning would eliminate the need for men altogether.
Women pursue *beautification* because good looks and youth are the keys to success. They ultimately also guarantee the advantages women can give their offspring.	Men are pursuing good looks and youth, as much as (if not more than) women. *Metrosexual* is a recently coined term to describe hip, urban, heterosexual men who are exploring and experimenting with what used to be traditionally feminine pursuits.

Constant exposure to these extremely opposite descriptors is moving the middle. Brainpower in the modern era accounts for far more than manual labor in economic success. Technology is enabling physical parity for the disabled: Sports competitions that feature wheelchair athletes are extremely well attended. Globally, military displays of might are not changing the world so much as the *new* new world order, which is based on negotiations and "soft power." (Anyway, remember that Golda Meir, Margaret Thatcher, and Indira Ghandi all led their countries in war.)

The ability to rescue someone during an emergency, a very manly thing, is another case of strength giving way to technology. For example, drivers using cell phones with satellite positioning capability can summon outside help quickly and effortlessly. And the heroes of 9/11—the police, firefighters, and emergency service workers—did include women.

Women are increasingly heading up businesses big and small. Great global corporations are now run by women, who typify the shift in economic status of women around the world. *Newsweek*, in reviewing the social crisis gripping Russia at the end of the last century, reported that Russian men are suffering from alcoholism because they feel their pride and power diminished. Male life expectancy there has dropped dramatically, to a 15-year difference (58 years for men versus 73 years for women). The divorce rate is 76 percent. While Russian men respond with sexual harassment and sex discrimination in the workplace, countries such as India, Egypt, and Bangladesh register more acid attacks on women. Almost everywhere, as women are bettering their lot, they are becoming the major or only breadwinners in their households, leading to serious inroads into this expression of macho and backlash by extremists.

The modern version of horsepower has been the automobile. The car for a long time has been a symbol of men's independence, prowess, and mechanical know-how—in short, a metaphor for macho. Women now account for 60 percent of all new U.S. car sales. Women have headed the Canadian divisions of Ford and GM. The average guy can no longer repair a new car; this can be done only by technicians who can work with the myriad of computerized parts. And the future portends more automation of driving.

The most modern engine, the computer, was both created and tamed by men and women alike. According to the National Museum of Women's History, in 1977 the Defense Department named its computer system ADA in honor of Ada Byron, who designed the punch-card program for computers in *1843* and first formulated the *garbage in, garbage out* principle. Admiral Grace Murray Hopper created the basis of modern computer software by 1957 and helped develop COBOL. The Silicon Valleys of the world are equally populated by both sexes. No doubt women's participation in the computer revolution (and their historical advantage at keyboard typing) takes the edge off any macho associated with this work engine.

The working out of gender extremes will continue to have significant impact on business. Nurturing, caring, and stewardship are principles of what some consider a more feminized management style. But now "masculine" managers are charged with running organizations staffed by independent workers who demand the kind of respect and personal attention that reflect both the masculine and feminine styles of management.

Advertisers and marketers can continue to attract revenue based on the extremes having moved the middle:

- Nike has taken advantage of the newly informed middle of athletic women, as exemplified by its website "Play Like a Girl," taken to mean play like a female athlete, because girls, too, play pickup ball with boys in the "hood." Women are the fastest-growing market for outdoor outfitting.

- Beautification with makeup, fragrance, earrings, and cosmetic surgery is now (as it was ages ago and in other cultures) something more men do. When basketball star Dennis Rodman started wearing eye shadow, Estée Lauder and Chanel began catering to men for hydrating, cleansing, exfoliating, and self-tanning. Nail polish makers are courting the male mass market; male beauty salons are on the rise globally. Recent research by Japanese cosmetics giant Shiseido indicates that 65 percent of Japanese men under age 30 bleach their hair, 38 percent have their eyebrows shaped, and 32 percent have applied a facial pack.

- A majority of American men no longer do their own household repairs and upkeep (painting, plumbing, electrical, lawn). Instead, they call in outside help or use Home Depot or Lowe's to help do these traditionally macho domestic chores. And women have become a major market for home repair and alteration. So both Lowe's and Home Depot, recognizing the trends, positioned themselves as good places for the new woman. Some statistics point to women now being their major market.

- Pfizer's Viagra, along with its recent competitors, is a recognition by the pharmaceutical industry that easing up on taboos regarding gender roles represents great market potential.

The woman on Main Street likes her jewelry, her beautiful tattoo, her athletic shoes, her pickup truck, and her bikini underwear. And the guy on Main Street is focusing on interior design and fashion beyond his high-tech toys, does regular weightlifting at the local gym, gets an occasional pedicure, collects teddy bears, and wears earrings. The extremes informed the middle, and the middle has moved.

How to Study and Use the Extremes

You must appreciate the extremes to understand and anticipate the future because that will be where the middle goes. And, to some extent, the backbone of a true democracy is the ability of the extremes to scream equally loudly at each other. Without that, the middle either would be dictated to by one extreme or would never change. The problem is that most of us find one extreme more appealing, so we reject, even ignore, the other. By accepting the fact that *both* extremes offer some validity or value, it becomes easier to reduce your bias and set about figuring out which aspects of the extreme are valid enough, pleasing enough, powerful enough to change the ever-evolving middle.

If the outcome of a particular debate is central to your business or your personal life, list the potentially valid points, whether or not you like or agree with them, for each extreme. You can bet the future will be shaped by some common ground in the middle—a little from one side, a little from the other. Free your mind from the trap of one-sided bias, and you will manage your business better, see new opportunities, be happier in your personal life, be a better citizen, and eventually be a more adaptive person altogether—far better positioned to deal with, and even shape, the future.

Part II

ORGANIZATIONAL TRAPS: INSTITUTIONAL BIASES AND BLOCKS TO RESPONDING TO CHANGE

While observing the British army on maneuvers just prior to World War II, a visiting American officer noticed something he thought was peculiar. As he watched an artillery battery deploy, with the men dismounting from trucks and preparing their cannons, he turned to his British escort and said, "I notice you have seven men on each gun crew, but six do all the work while the seventh man just stands at attention. What's his function?" The British officer replied that gun crews had always consisted of seven men, but he didn't know why the seventh man did nothing. He promised to look into it. The next day, he called the American and reported that the seventh man had held the horses.

When we look at our own organizations—whether businesses, governments, schools, or anything else—how many seventh men do we see? How many customs, practices, and processes have become rigidly embedded in our structures and are continued simply because they have always been there and no one thinks to question them?

In this part of the book, you take a close look at four techniques that help you see your own organizations through alien eyes and let you break the chains of unchallenged tradition. The underpinnings of these techniques are *Efficiency Breeds Vulnerability*, *The Multiplier Effect of New Distribution Channels*, *Entropy*, and *Integrity Begets Quality*.

5

EFFICIENCY BREEDS
VULNERABILITY

Trekking through the rainforest of Gamboa, in Panama, one comes across countless miniature freeways and highways composed of millions of ants. Each ant carries a tiny piece of leaf going in one direction, while an equal number scurry in the opposite direction, having already relieved themselves of their load at their home base, and are now hastening back to pick up yet another piece of leaf. What the ants do with these leaves (they make compost from them) is not the issue here. Their football-field length 20-lane highway is, as we eco-conscious tourists try desperately not to step on the ants intent on their laborious workaday commute. The guides are amused by our concern. They tell us to go ahead and not break our necks trying to get around or over the ants. If you step on them, it doesn't matter. There are thousands more right there to back them up, and a few hundred gone will not affect their task.

A number of scholars are currently examining how the swarming of ants (and bees) might be relevant to organizational management and personal behavior. There are numerous theories about why these insects perform so well at laborious tasks. As the guides point out, a key is *redundancy*.

Nature is amazing. Everywhere you look, from the floor of the forest to the innards of the human brain, redundancies abound. Brain research on stroke victims shows that women recover more quickly than men do from the effects (such as speech impairment or paralysis) because their brains are more interconnected, creating the redundancies necessary for another region to kick in and augment the damaged portions.

In a stunning scene from the movie *Spartacus*, slaves chained to the oars of a massive boat are forced to continuously row to a drumbeat that slows or quickens, depending on the needs of the ship's commanders. Dozens of men push and pull in seemingly endless, monotonous rhythm, and when one falls ill, he is discarded and replaced with another. In the early industrial revolution, workers in factories, too, were considered cogs in a wheel that were redundant and replaceable.

Today, in a much more highly efficient world of rockets, chips, telecommunications, and biochemical breakthroughs, many individuals are still replaceable parts in a larger operation, but there are far fewer of them because labor is expensive and machines are cheaper. As a consequence, the potential long-term benefits of redundancy are passed up in the interest of *efficiency*.

Efficiency is usually defined as operating with little waste of energy, effort, or material. It is generally measured as the ratio of an entity's output energy to its input energy. Agriculture was a more efficient economy than that of the hunter-gatherer. One fixed home replaced multiple dwellings; foraging far afield for food was eliminated; machinery, animals, and tools were developed and harnessed to relieve humans of their physical labor; and even the crops themselves were grown using knowledge of best practices for highest yield with decreasing input.

Industrialization brought further efficiencies to the economy. Cities sprang up to concentrate workers and enterprises, eliminating the time, cost, and energy required to connect far-flung people to the centers of work and commerce. Buildings became taller to maximize land, infrastructure, and material use and to further shorten the distances that dwellers and workers had to travel. People were enticed to empty their cookie jars and overturn their mattresses and put their money in banks. By efficiently aggregating people's funds, banks better leveraged their assets and provided them with higher returns and safer repositories.

Energy systems became massive, with centralized command, control, and generation systems to more efficiently feed the ever-extending grid. Automation marched on, from dumb machines to smart computers, in the never-ending search for more efficiency in the economy. The end of all this is still beyond our sights, stretching into the everland of tomorrow.

Efficiency unquestionably brings benefits. More and better goods are produced at a lower cost, and this is a boon to consumers. However, everything has a price, and the price of efficiency often is increased *vulnerability*.

You can see examples of efficiency, and the vulnerabilities it creates, all around you.

Example #1: Acceleration Through Electronics

Electronics enabled even greater advances in efficiency. Unifying systems brought almost unimaginable speed to commercial transactions. But in their wake they also brought multiple vulnerabilities. Australian criminologists Peter Grabosky, Russell Smith, and Gillian Dempsey say that the effectiveness of transactions in cyberspace offers increasing opportunities for certain criminal activities:

- Stealing funds electronically
- Extortion

- Defrauding Internet services

- Online security fraud

- Deceptive advertising

- Theft of intellectual property

- Industrial espionage

- Identity theft

Perhaps an even scarier eventuality is system paralysis. A networked world, particularly one that is increasingly wireless, is subject to electromagnetic interference (EMI). Criminals use EMI devices to render alarm systems useless. Militaries are rapidly developing EMI-based weapons that will destroy an enemy's command and control systems. Cases have been reported of cars immobilized by high-voltage lines under roads. In one instance in 2001, when the *USS Carl Vinson* arrived at Bremerton, Wash., EMI emanations from it made thousands of keyless cars' locks stop functioning.

Example #2: Efficiency in Government

Human political history is a seemingly endless striving for efficiency. We created governments to take away the tangled web of individual conflicts, behaviors, and standards; to protect us with more concentrated strength; and to orchestrate monopolistic utilities so that everyone's needs could be met, even at the farthest fringes of communities. From feudal lords in their massive moated castles to Washington, D.C. with its Capitol building and Pentagon, the entire history of government, like much of the rest of the world, is a move toward efficiency.

But not all went with that flow. America's Founding Fathers were brilliantly different. They had a healthy fear of all that efficiency brought with it. They agonized over how efficiency concentrates power and how power is invariably abused. They agonized over the fact that efficiency speeds up decision-making, and sometimes the most important decisions are made over long periods of time with maximum reflection and input. They agonized over the fact that different peoples and cultures perceived different realities and had different credos and beliefs, while efficiency required—indeed, demanded—conformity.

So they designed the U.S. government with the stroke of caution (or genius) known as the "balance of power." Power was shared by three branches of government—the executive branch, the judicial branch, and the legislative branch. All this makes for competing bureaucracies and a great deal of inefficiency, but it has protected this country from military coups and takeovers and frequently (but not always) from rash and disastrous decisions. It has also allowed for great diversity of thought and expression (guaranteed in the amendments to the Constitution).

To the extent that government is made more efficient—for example, if all the branches are dominated by the same party and all the dominant players in that party have the same point of view—things move along faster, and more gets done. But will this create enormous vulnerability if the efforts are wrong-headed or ill-fated? That is the concern this country faces in the first years of the 21st century. This was the central question that the designers and signers of the Constitution mulled over and addressed in 1787.

Example #3: Warped Speed

In his book *Working at Warp Speed: The New Rules for Project Success in a Sped-Up World*, Barry Flicker claims that the more labor-saving and time-saving devices we produce, the faster things move and the busier we become, so that we're working at warp speed but getting nowhere fast. The relentless push for efficiency has led to everyone's running on overload. It has resulted in poorly defined goals because they are designed too quickly, so as to pander to current pressures without being given the time and thought necessary to attain a long-term vision. People are given unrealistic completion dates ("I need this yesterday") based on unchecked assumptions. A sense of urgency results in poorer, not better, communication, a reduced or omitted planning effort (seen as being too costly and resource-intensive), lack of support from other departments in any organization because they are also on overload, and constant fire-fighting (it seems less wasteful of resources if no action is taken until a crisis occurs).

The Continuous Linked Settlement (CLS) bank has revolutionized international currency exchange. It settles foreign exchange trades among the largest banks, thereby reducing the risks of uncertainty as to time of payment. But this process increases other risks the banks face. One has to do with liquidity. Banks must make their payments when the CLS schedule dictates, not when it is convenient for them. The other has to do with concentration. If the system goes down for any reason, such as EMI, the whole currency-trading business ($1.5 trillion a day) is paralyzed.

In 1988, the U.S. Navy cruiser *Vincennes* was involved in a regrettable incident in the Persian Gulf. The *Vincennes* is an Aegis-class ship with a highly advanced computer control system designed for extremely quick decision-making. When its radar spotted an approaching plane, the computer concluded that it was hostile. When the plane was 9 miles away, the computer ordered a missile to be fired, bringing the plane down. On a pre-Aegis ship, the slower technology of a sailor with binoculars on the wing of the bridge would have determined that the plane was a commercial airliner, and that tragedy would not have happened.

Not only have we forgotten how to use binoculars, but we have become instruments of the instruments designed to serve us. We are highly vulnerable to the speed that eliminates our senses, reason, and experience. We have somehow forgotten that Captain Kirk was always more triumphant than Mr. Spock.

Business offers numerous examples of the same outcomes. Marketers working at a major food company client of ours two decades ago were becoming increasingly concerned about the effects that bar-coding technology was starting to have on them. Market data had come to them monthly, giving them ample time to analyze the information and make reasoned decisions on product distribution. They were now receiving the information weekly, and soon they would be getting it daily. They were inundated, and as a result, they were acting quicker and more impulsively, on the basis of snapshots rather than the motion picture of consumer behavior. Importantly, they were not receiving more information; it was just coming to them more quickly.

There's no doubt that instant feedback has been a boon to many a company in stocking and restocking warehouses and shop floors, and even in the manufacturing process itself. But now, instant feedback (information that modifies events by immediately sending back data about the results of those events) is becoming the mantra of corporations and national economies. *Forbes* reported in October 2002, that about 100 corporations, including IBM, Microsoft, and various smaller companies, were establishing high-speed information feedback systems, or "real-time enterprise computing." Automobiles are making use of that feedback technology. Amazon.com uses instant-feedback loops, and so do credit card companies, supermarkets, and department stores—all to profile and ultimately choose for the consumer. The *Forbes* article says that, as fast feedback loops become more pervasive, you will be faced with more moments of risk and vulnerability as you surrender to machines your world of choices and experimentation, and potentially your ability to learn from the choices you make.

There was no market for the Walkman until Sony introduced it. And it took a while before the market caught on. Portable and private entertainment is now a way of life. Chances are, efficient instant feedback would have dissuaded Sony from continuing its offering.

Politics by instant feedback polling has been robbing us of deep thinking and informed judgment. We have moved from ponder to pander, with all that entails. The roaring success of the U.S. economy in the 1990s encouraged other nations to strive for what seemed to be American efficiency, especially in their utilities (transportation, communication, and energy systems). Highly efficient economic systems are highly vulnerable; the whole system, rather than just some of its parts, can become too weak. So the speed of stock market reaction now takes its toll on European investors.

Nicholas Fraser, author of *The Voice of Modern Hatred*, wrote in *Harper's* in 2002 that scandals on Wall Street were one of the most potent forces leading to harsh comments throughout Europe about America's hypocrisy in having sold Europe on privatization. The U.S. drive for efficiency, in creating the vulnerabilities that ensue—from fraud to mismanagement to uniformity to exclusion of unprofitable customers—is, according to Fraser, one of the key elements in the global backlash against the U.S.

The Continuing Importance of Redundancy

In the end, while efficiency appeals to many as a desirable objective, it is a powerful predictor of the fallout that can occur unless it is accompanied by redundancy and diversity. The consequences leave nations and organizations, companies included, highly vulnerable to downtime, collapses, backlash, criminal activity, natural or man-made disaster, and even blight (such as computer viruses). The major impetus behind the push for biodiversity is that nature was wise in creating so much variation. A genetically uniform crop or animal is far more vulnerable to a single disease than a population with a variety of adaptive traits.

Diversity in business is important for just such a reason. Conformity or one mistake or breach can bring down a whole company or the systems on which it depends. Along with backup sites and systems, executive thinkers need a diversity of backup brains, or the efficiency of the executive suite will be continually vulnerable to crises that will occur with all its stakeholder groups. Companies have even hired convicted hackers to help understand their systems' vulnerabilities.

In each case, efficiency helps us see the future because it becomes inevitable that there will be financial collapses, serious interference with communication systems, $50 billion natural disasters in concentrated coastal areas, power outages, building collapses, terrorist targets, and pandemics of disease that spread quickly in concentrated populations. From smog and congestion to breakdown of intimacy, efficiency has its costs. They are all predictable.

In sum, the dangers of efficiency for businesses are as follows:

- Concentration of *space*, which creates the vulnerability of high-cost destruction. After 9/11, financial firms in downtown Manhattan saw the wisdom in inefficiently placing their functions and people in scattered locations.

- Concentration in *time*, which creates the vulnerability of rash decisions, overload, and burnout. Companies that ruthlessly pare payrolls and require more output from their remaining workers risk increased error rates and actually lower per-person productivity.

- Concentration of *systems*, which creates the vulnerability of intrusion, shutdown, and ripple effects. Computer hackers, with their viruses and worms, can do serious harm because everyone is driving along the same information superhighway.

- Concentration of *conformity*, which creates the vulnerability of uniformity, leaving the mind, body, or system open to crippling attack. When we asked some bankers in the early 1980s who they saw as their strongest competition over the coming decade, they all named other banks. Not one of them cited GE Capital or Vanguard or any of the other emerging financial institutions that would so quickly and massively intrude on the banks' turf because the bankers all thought alike. Congressional reports on the CIA in 2004 severely criticized the groupthink that prevented the agency from challenging its assumptions.

- Concentration of *power*, which leads to the vulnerabilities of abuse and the obedience that prevents renewal and creativity. In his masterful retelling of the King Arthur legend, "The Once and Future King," T. H. White metaphorically has Merlin turn the young Arthur into an ant. Over the entrance to the ant colony is the slogan "Everything not forbidden is compulsory." Unthinking repetition of mandated tasks, with no deviation or originality permitted, may work well for ants, but it is deadly for an organization of human beings.

In today's world, with everything on a larger scale and happening more rapidly, efficiency is clearly a predictor of vulnerability. We are constantly told to back up our systems, diversify our portfolios, and have Plan B ready should Plan A fail.

This is sage advice. Free your mind from the trap of believing that efficiency is the most important goal, and you will be smarter about the redundancies that will ensure a safer, more productive future for yourself, your government, and your business.

6

THE MULTIPLIER EFFECT OF NEW DISTRIBUTION CHANNELS

Among the most fundamental changes the U.S. economy has seen is what economists call *disintermediation*—bypassing traditional delivery channels to distribute goods and services. It began in the late 1950s in the financial world. People took their money out of banks (their traditional intermediaries for savings) and shopped around for higher rates of return elsewhere. This spurred the growth of mutual funds, reshaped life insurance into a more sophisticated financial instrument, and led to the invention of real estate investment trusts and other tax-sheltered investments. Eventually it led to shopping on the Internet for the best mortgage and CD interest rates.

Disintermediation has come to affect every other business and profession, not just finance. In some cases, this means eliminating the intermediary, or broker, or retailer, or professional. In other cases, it means finding a substitute. For still others, it means going directly to the producer. In the future, it might mean *becoming* the producer.

Disintermediation, then, is about introducing new and alternative channels of distribution—whether for information, money, health care, clothing, or whatever. The mental math most people do when a new distribution channel comes along is subtraction. They tend to fall into the trap of believing the new will *replace* the old. Not necessarily. In the case of distribution channels, this has never been true. In fact, what usually happens is not even addition—it's multiplication. Until you escape the trap of subtraction, you will never see the great benefits that come from thinking about future opportunities in a world of multiplication.

What is important to remember is that each delivery channel, to succeed in a world of increasing choices, must seek its own strength and not attempt to compete against the specific advantages of other distribution channels.

Example #1: Media

When radio was introduced, everyone in the family congregated in the living room to "watch" the radio. That's why, when TV was introduced, it was widely believed that radio would be finished. Radio did suffer for a while, until it shed itself of its murder mystery series and variety shows and concentrated on what it did best: music, talk, and news—in short, all the things people wanted to hear but didn't have to see. Then, together, radio and television strengthened each other, and from that came spin-offs of political analysis, music sales, celebrity paraphernalia, magazines, and so on.

When VCRs came along, there went movie profits—or so it was thought. Instead, the movie studios made a great deal of money on tapes. Some movies that failed in initial distribution (such as *Austin Powers*) were so successful in rental that they spawned sequels. In international distribution, where traditional movie houses are not always available, tapes filled the need and, in the process, greatly increased the market. Profitable new opportunities sprang up around peripherals in the children's market when kids watched the same tape (such as *The Lion King*) dozens of times, clamoring for books, records, and toys, which are sold through a number of channels, from Disneyland to catalogs to Toys-R-Us.

As the 21st century begins, there is still "cave painting." Artist LeRoy Neiman goes to the Olympics, splashes some oil on a canvas, and sells the original for tens of thousands of dollars. The copies go for thousands. Coffee table books that feature the art go for about $100.

But if you wanted to see a photo of the event, you wouldn't buy a Neiman. You might, instead, buy *Sports Illustrated*. If you wanted to *see* the event, you wouldn't do either. You would watch it in real time or see the video. And if you wanted only the *results*, you would do none of the above. You would read the paper, or dial a phone number, or go on the Net, or watch a news headline broadcast, or listen to the radio—multiplication, with each channel finding its own advantage and creating even more new options.

Example #2: Print Versus the Internet

When the Internet started to publish articles in magazine format, there was great concern in the publishing industry that paper magazines would disappear. What actually happened was the introduction of hundreds of new magazines that depended on the existence of the computer and the Net, from *Home Office Computing* to *Computer Retailing Weekly*. What many of the pundits missed was the strategic (and, in some cases, unperceived) advantages of hard copy as a distribution vehicle for larger written works. For one thing, pulsed images (computer) are less user-friendly to the brain than fixed images (on the printed page) over an extended period. The brains of today's humans are more comfortable with printing the page or reading the article in a real magazine. The magazine, with its feel and visual gloss, satisfies different mental and sensory needs than does the computer screen or the computer printout.

Another important factor is how memory is stored. The human brain stores information in several ways, and they are different for short-term and long-term memory. Short-term memory is stored in a mental file cabinet that can weed out the files quickly when their immediate function is complete. Long-term memory, on the other hand, is shunted to another set of mental files. The reason for this is that we have reference points and context that help store long-term memory. This is called *colocation*. For example, if you wanted to remember a newspaper article you read two months ago, you would first subconsciously recall which section of the paper it appeared in, whether it was on the left or the right, if it was a full page or half, whether it had a photo, if it was near an ad, and so on. In other words, you would colocate the information you want to retrieve with all that accompanied it.

This is one of the reasons that, when you crammed for exams the night before taking them, you tended to forget soon after the test all that you learned. That's because it was all a jumble of short-term files, with no context or color or entertainment value or sensual gratification or stimulating reference points. Having none of that, your brain couldn't care less if the stuff got discarded. Interestingly, we sometimes do remember what we got *wrong* on the test. That's because those items were singled out, challenged our ego, forced us to reflect and relearn, and were isolated in a richer contextual pool surrounded by the unhappy reality of points off the exam.

With respect to the brain, it is pretty clear that print and computers serve very different functions. Publishers need to understand those differences and leverage them rather than ignore them. The Internet will become the premier distribution channel for short bursts of news and items of interest, but the print format will be better for the "larger"—larger topics, larger retention. The most vulnerable print channels, therefore, are newsletters and textbooks. The former are not read in lengthy format, and the latter are rarely used by people other than academics, except to pass a test. The multiplication of hard copy and online possibilities will, however, create hundreds of new opportunities for newsletter and textbook publishers, from chatting with the authors to interactive workbook exercises to comparing notes with other readers to researching in further depth anything briefly mentioned in the original material. *Not* subtraction—*multiplication*.

Example #3: The Campus Versus Online Learning

The Internet poses the probability that the most knowledgeable and entertaining teachers/authorities in the world can teach courses to everyone, anywhere, at a fraction of the cost and with greater quality than most professors and teachers on most campuses for most subjects. The advent of Net-based education—*distance learning*—has raised questions about whether it will replace the traditional academic institution. Keep in mind, however, that different distribution channels have different advantages. The old doesn't disappear; instead, the landscape generally consists of the new and the old coexisting.

In fact, envisioning a talking head (no matter how entertaining) teaching a course in biology or archaeology is an example of the educated incapacity discussed in Chapter 1, "Looking Through Alien Eyes"—knowing so much about how education *was* done that we cannot see it differently. The new channels of interactive technology will allow people of any age to learn, rather than be taught, by actually *being* there and *doing* that. Using virtual-reality gaming technology, you will be able to become a white blood corpuscle, fight off invading microbes, and learn more about the bloodstream than 10 classroom lessons could provide. Using similar virtual-reality projection systems, you will be able to participate in an archaeological dig and acquire more understanding and appreciation than any lecturer could impart.

Furthermore, given the multiplier effect, there is no reason that universities can't go into retailing, setting up environments in which shoppers can *experience*, through virtual reality, the course content and then buy books, tapes, artifacts, clothing, and anything else that extends the experience in knowledge beyond the delivery site.

What the existing form of higher education—the campus—can provide that the new forms cannot are socialization, multicultural interaction, independence, and various rites of passage into adulthood (such as learning how to do one's laundry).

Of course, for those who cannot afford the money or time for the campus option, online courses will proliferate. So will combinations of the two. In fact, a lot of what goes on in many campuses now is already online.

Example #4: Retailing

Retailing, clearly, is often seen as a major victim in disintermediation. But it needn't be because of multiplication. Not only does the anecdote in Chapter 1 about clothing and fitting rooms apply here, but so do dozens of other considerations. Take mattresses, for example. One Sunday evening, about 10 years ago, one of us came home to an apartment whose roof had leaked and damaged a bed. In prior years, that would have meant a trip to the department or bedding store the next day, and then waiting days for delivery. But now there is 1-800-MATTRES(S). That number was called, and arrangements were made to deliver a new mattress the next morning, between 6 and 8 a.m., and to remove the old mattress at no cost. What's wrong with this picture? Nothing. Except this: If a woman is engaged to the man of her dreams and they are setting up a home and buying furniture, she would be very unlikely to dial 1-800-MATTRES(S). Instead, she would drag the fellow into a number of bedding and department stores to try out mattresses. This would heighten and legitimize the experience and the choice. Different delivery channels, different advantages. So now, the 1-800 companies that sell mattresses also have showrooms. Multiplication: telephone, traditional stores, Internet, catalogs—new choices, overlapping players.

Example #5: Health Care

Health care is a prime example of professional disintermediation and multiplication. Fifty years ago, there were three major health delivery channels: the general practitioner, the hospital, the pharmaceutical company. Then, more doctors became specialists. People wanted specialists, so they had several doctors, not just one: the internist, the gynecologist, the cardiologist, the orthopedist, the pediatrician. These did not subtract from each other; rather, in the process, all got richer because people consumed more medical care overall. So doctors referred their patients to each other.

Hospitals went through this also. Costs and management issues forced third-party payers to put pressures on them to reform, and mergers and acquisitions occurred. In the process, hospitals became "cutthroat," and outpatient alternatives sprang up. This spawned a host of responses by hospitals, including offering childbirth classes, stress reduction centers, and all kinds of wellness boutiques. Multiplication.

Pharmaceutical companies reflect the same upheaval. Some are licensors of intellectual property or brands, others own discount distribution outlets, and still others publish catalogs. Advertising directly to the consumer, bypassing the doctor, has led to an enormous upswing in drug purchases, much to the horror of those tracking the escalating costs of health care.

Along with all these came do-it-yourself home testing kits (for everything from pregnancy to insulin levels), spas, diet books and centers, storefront clinics, multidoctor corporations, and channels for alternative medicine (chiropractors, homeopaths, acupuncturists, nutritionists, aromatherapists). Multiplication.

Choices and Options

The last decades of the 20th century might well be called the Choices Era. In a hundred years, the American economy had gone from Henry Ford's "The customer can have any color car he wants, as long as it's black" to Burger King's "Have it your way." Options of all kinds proliferated, and consumers reveled in the new power to get what they wanted, when they wanted it, and how they wanted it. In retailing, we went from department stores that dictated the terms of the transaction—this place, these hours, this merchandise, these prices— to Amazon.com and eBay, with customers deciding what, where, when, and even how much to pay.

Distribution channel choices seem to be multiplying exponentially in every aspect of life, from the most mundane (choosing a supplier for your electricity) to the most life-changing (choosing a hospital). Everything in between requires making choices, as people custom-order, or build, their own computers, decide which cell phone service plan delivers what they want, and probably even one day choosing what delivery system for gene therapies they want for themselves, their children, and even their babies in utero. Certainly, how you get and send information will explode into endless hybrid options.

Consumers will face both boons and boondoggles. The multiplication of telecom competitors resulting from deregulation is a case in point. Competition roused (some) telecom companies from their monopolistic stupor, making them develop new products and services and even lower prices. On the other hand, you are now condemned to endless marketing calls and incomprehensible junk mail from those same revived phone companies.

How Multiplication Can Help You See the Future

People are fast becoming *mediapeds*—media on two feet. The revolution in telecommunications and computing is permitting low-cost transfer of information and ideas to many people. Currently, the number of people online worldwide is well over 250 million. More importantly, we are witnessing the rapid convergence of the Internet with TV, telephone, radio, and CD players. The number of mobile phones surpassed land-line connections by 2004. They can provide you with constant access to local and global information no matter where you are. Within a few years, more phones than computers will be connected to the web. Eventually, more *things* (like bathroom scales and Barbie dolls) than humans will be connected to the web.

Internet appliances, like cell phones, will be everywhere. Networks will form, linking cell phones, digital assistants, and all other types of handheld peripherals. In effect, omnipresent communication will result, enabling you to be in constant contact with miniature, wireless, highly personalized networked computing, and with computers embedded in your clothing and body. Wristwatch-like devices will furnish data about your current health status. Microchip implants (electronic capsules) imbedded in you could replace credit cards, keys, passports, and documents. They could also send messages to computers that control intelligent buildings. Software will assist creative artists, and anybody will be able to write music from his or her brain waves using "cybernetic music-creation systems." Your calendar will scan for related information online and offline. "Scentography" could release online scent data as smells to the computer user to enhance entertainment and reality. Within the next 50 years, neural implants will augment all your senses and provide virtual sensory experiences. Chips will extend your brain's capacity and suppress inputs from your real senses when virtual reality is required, replacing your senses with signals appropriate for the virtual environment.

Thus, the way in which you will be constantly attached to media images will affect your brain and your very self. You may see a major shift in how you experience life and your relationship to it. More people are already living vicariously by watching on TV and the web how others live and make choices—entertainment meets media meets voyeurism. And they are relying more on the "third voice"—online, pop-up video—to further mediate that which is already mediated.

The possibility of advertisers narrowcasting messages right into the brain, activating a buying response, may be looked on as "theft"— the expropriation of human attention. Short of that, "ambient advertising" will offer talking billboards, computers secreting aromas, and man-made 3-D environments on streets that consumers will have to walk through as they go from one place to another.

As for the individual, multiple channels present the opportunity for multiple identities. The search for "Who *am* I?" can now be "Who *are* I?" In the '60s and '70s, many young baby boomers set off to find themselves. They went to Nepal and Peru (the really smart ones went to Paris) in an effort to get away from how their circumstances defined them. Identity was, for almost everyone, *found* identity. In other words, it was determined by external factors over which they had little or no control: who their parents were, where they lived, their schooling, their race and religion, their family, and other affiliations. This tyranny of circumstances determined, in the eyes of others, who they were.

In revolt, the young boomers wanted to determine their own identities, to go from a found identity to a *made* identity.

A generation later, that transformation is now easily possible, even without travel to some distant place. Technology is the enabler. The Internet is a delivery channel that can allow you to multiply yourself—to be whoever and whatever you want to be at any time. You can be one other person, or you can be a dozen other people. A famous cartoon from *The New Yorker* depicted two dogs, one at a computer keyboard and the other seated on the floor. The first says to the second, "On the Internet, nobody knows you're a dog."

This multiplication of possible identities, while scary for some people, can be extraordinary for others. It can also create serious problems for business. Market research can become a nightmare. How do you categorize people who are as shifty and elusive as an

NFL running back? How can you predict consumers' behavior when you don't know who they will be tomorrow? New ways of tracking and forecasting consumers will have to be developed.

Attention Is the Monetary Unit

John Perry Barlow, one of the founders of the Electronic Frontier Foundation and a former writer of lyrics for the Grateful Dead, wrote some years ago that "In an information economy, *attention* is the monetary unit." If he did or said nothing else, he deserves to be remembered for this profound insight. The multiplying of delivery and communications channels, and the geometric expansion of information that these have made possible, mean that people today are living in the midst of the information equivalent of a California freeway at rush hour. A constant flow of information and distribution channels bombards them. For example, it is estimated that the average American is subjected to more than 2,000 marketing messages a day.

Clearly, the key to success in such an environment is the ability to get people's attention. If you decide not to watch or hear a General Motors commercial, your will is more powerful than the more than $3 billion that GM spends on advertising every year.

The tension created when new distribution channels arrive to compete with existing ones will always begin by causing uncertainty and confusion. But when the dust settles, those who are smart enough to figure out what their channel does best, and what best to do in an era of multiple channels, benefit, and the pie gets bigger for everyone. A complete substitution effect has never happened, nor is it likely to.

7

ENTROPY

The Second Law of Thermodynamics is based on calculations proving that as systems become more complex, the energy in them dissipates over time, eventually leading to a disordered state that requires more energy to control than the energy originally invested. This is *entropy*. Imagine a newly built house. After some time, the carpeting and windows need cleaning and eventually replacing. Later, the exterior and roof need refurbishing and eventually replacing. Even later, the masonry and foundation need repair and overhaul, along with the plumbing. Ultimately, it becomes so costly to maintain the house that it is cheaper to tear it down and rebuild.

The business world is not exempt from entropy. *Benchmarking*—identifying the best business practices and the companies that embody them—is a perfect case in point. One company does something spectacular that succeeds because of its culture and its point in evolution. Other companies try to emulate that by studying the process and grafting it onto their own operations. But because it didn't naturally spring up in the acquiring company, a great deal of energy must be expended over time to maintain and support the adopted practice. Eventually, the effort begins to stagger under its own weight, and it takes more energy to keep it going than it did to adopt it in the first place.

Bringing in star performers from outside can also result in entropy. According to an article in the August 2004 issue of *Inc.* magazine, research done by Harvard Business School professors showed that star performers usually don't do as well when they move to another company. Their previous success depended to some extent on the fit of their talents and their previous employers' people and resources. When the stars begin to fail at their new employer, they tend to drag down the level of performance across the organization. One small company cited in the article, The Wildflower Group, found that not only did the failing outsider become sullen and resentful, but so did others in the firm. It then began to take more energy to maintain the imported talent than to successfully grow the company's own.

You can predict much of the future by seeing entropy set in. To escape the entropy trap, organizations have to work at being more innovative, nimble, and unafraid of experimenting with the new that can arise from their own revisioning.

Example #1: Taxation

Taxation is a good example of an entropic system. The U.S. tax code, now several thousand pages long, requires increasing outlays of energy—accountants, tax lawyers, appraisers, IRS agents, investments in computers, audits, and so on—to maintain a system that is performing its original function less and less efficiently. In the modern world, taxation not only pays for government services; it also is intended to even out income ranges and redistribute wealth. Thus, we have the graduated, or progressive, income tax, and the high rates of taxation on inheritance. Over time, massive amounts of energy go into undermining these intentions of taxation, resulting in a diffusion of the system's energy. In addition, many changes in recent decades have further drained the energy of tax systems, as discussed in the following sections.

Intelliwealth

Tangible assets are generating less wealth than the leveraging of ideas and knowledge in this emerging economy. The U.S. trade surplus of intangible intellectual property is growing by $25 billion a year. American global royalties and licensing revenue topped $37 billion in 2000, according to the Commerce Department. Tourism and gambling rank first and second in many areas of the U.S. as a source of income. Yet we have not been innovative enough in figuring out how to tax intangibles in ways that adequately reflect their growing role in the economic equation. So we are spending more and more energy to keep the old system afloat.

Massive Personal Wealth

The wealth transfer in the U.S. between 2005 and 2052 may be at least $40 trillion. There is strong sentiment for abolishing the federal estate tax that currently raises $28 billion a year and creates windfalls for charities, estate-planning services, and accountants. The enormous growth of wealth has led to mass purchases of $10 million mansions and ocean liner traveling homes. CEO compensation is reaching nine-digit figures. The United Nations reports that multinationals and wealthy individuals are avoiding taxes by increasing offshore deposits, which by 2000 amounted to about $7 to $8 trillion. Underground (tax-evading) economies are growing, such as the one in Canada, which is fueled by a growing national antitax coalition and a growing brain drain to the U.S. The European Union will continue to lag behind the U.S. economy unless it cuts its high marginal tax rates to permit those who take financial risks to keep the rewards.

All this becomes a drain on the tax system because, for example, along with the massive wealth comes massive debt. The emergence of the global shareholder created a potentially disastrous global gambling casino, as we saw in 2002. Japanese government debt is rising, and the same is true for U.S. personal debt (margin debt has tripled over the last five years). Tax policy was frequently used in the 20th century to encourage debt, and this will raise important issues for the 21st century.

Another troubling trend in the U.S. is the escalating cost of a college education. While there is talk of free education, or low-cost education on the Internet, youngsters are graduating with a great deal of debt to pay down even before they enter the workforce. This debt will, in effect, be a tax on them at the very same time they are asked to contribute more to the burdensome retirement rolls of an older population. Unless we innovate here, this too will diffuse energy from the original system of taxation.

The Online World

Europe is lavishing energy on figuring out how to collect value-added taxes on products sold and distributed on the Internet, leading to potential drains on the system as more firms ignore tax rules and run their Internet sales operations from offshore tax havens. The Internet allows for the increased globalization of crime, a major nontaxed portion of the world's economy and a great drain on the system. Whether related to underground or legal activities, the lack of Net boundaries will create dilemmas for tax jurisdictions, as well as questions about who is taxed to pay for the new energy needed to start and maintain the global entities required to oversee or control all these transactions. Serious efforts aimed at new controls will be far more productive than continually slapping band-aids on the festering old ones.

Encouraging Investment

Europe knows it must cut tax rates to lure investors, since venture capital has become so critical to economic success. Foreign venture capital is moving into Japan, including more foreign takeover bids, as that country's markets become more accountable and transparent. India is simplifying excise tax procedures to help businesses escape from red tape and corruption-eroded profits, and venture capital there is getting more favorable tax treatment, all in an effort to ward off entropy.

It may very well be that in the 21st century, we will see a major shift in the underlying goal of taxes—away from redistributing wealth and toward encouraging wealth creation. Even the Green Party in Germany advocates cutting taxes on business to spur start-ups and protect small investors. In the move to encourage wealth creation, we will have to reinvent various aspects of tax systems around the world, in part because we're not always sure of cause and effect, even in less complex economies. For example, in the U.S., the home mortgage interest deduction has been used to encourage home ownership, but Canada, with no deduction, has a similar home ownership rate. And many taxes have had unintended effects, such as the marriage penalty, which has led some older persons with more traditional values to live together out of wedlock.

Global Aging

A rapidly aging Europe is facing a pension crisis. In Spain's aging population, only 5 to 15 percent have any kind of private retirement savings. Aging populations will force rethinking about tax policy with regard to encouraging continuing work, not overburdening younger workers with social costs, and spurring economic growth rather than stagnation. (See Chapter 10, "Demography.")

The tax challenges posed by all the factors just discussed are unprecedented. They range from unregistered cross-border money flows, to accounting for pricing and repricing of options, to questions about how to tax nonquantifiable assets and benefits, to how to keep productivity up, to intergenerational equity.

Clearly, for tax systems to escape from the stranglehold that entropy now has on them, innovation and creativity are desperately needed. The new economy and demography of the 21st century will call for major reinvention of taxation and taxpaying. Simply protesting taxes and patching the systems will not solve the long-term problems and may lead to taxes that will have a stifling effect. For example, the many who now seek to escape taxation by doing business on the Net, or relocating to an offshore tax haven, could lead to a web (no pun intended) of global taxation that could be punishing, irrational, and even more incomprehensible, with costs of interpretation and compliance shooting into the stratosphere. More and more energy will be needed to maintain the existing tax systems, which is why many now feel it is time to consider tearing them down and rebuilding.

Example #2: The Internet

The Internet is an example of a system that became a disordered state in a remarkably short time. The energy at its core, information, has become so abundant and indeed overwhelming that ever-larger amounts of energy are required to maintain its usefulness. It has become like the wordy person who, when asked what time it is, tells you how to make a clock.

The Internet may ultimately ease and expedite commercial transactions, but right now, for many if not most people, it is difficult. The much-heralded e-commerce auction economy requires that participants be well-informed; purchasing a car now requires a good deal of online research. Many people don't finish e-commerce transactions, apparently, according to a study done in 1999 by Yankelovich Partners, because they can't find all the information they need.

Information is highly fertile. It reproduces itself geometrically, and it soon overwhelms the human capacity to manage it. Advances in technology are accelerating and exacerbating this problem.

In olden times, people of means had a key servant who relieved them of the burden of dealing with such matters—the *steward*. It is becoming clear that in the coming years, the steward—whether electronic or human—will be important in helping people overcome the entropic drift of the Internet. The reliable, knowledgeable servant who knows what's best for you and your family and makes electronic communication efficient will be a treasured possession in the 21st century.

Another such valued servant will be the *navigator*—someone who helps you find your way through the maze of information. A navigator will be what Merlin was to the young Arthur, wisely selecting from all the available information whatever is necessary for surviving and thriving.

Stewards, navigators, and other *learned intermediaries* will be increasingly necessary until chip implants carry us to the next state of human development, where we will not spend more energy propping up a system that was supposed to reduce our energy input.

Example #3: Addiction to Adrenaline

As a society, we in the U.S. have become addicted to adrenaline. The multiplicity of options, to everyone's surprise, has led many not to fulfillment but to *boredom*. It takes more and more stimulation (energy) to keep people interested. The levels of excitement and danger must escalate; witness the growing popularity of extreme sports and so-called adventure travel. American children are experiencing what some observers call "scheduled hyperactivity." Their play time is increasingly overloaded, competitive, and goal-oriented, with more energy poured into getting the same energy output as prior generations.

The same is true in business: More and more energy is invested faster and faster to get positive outcomes:

- More effort is spent on reacting to the technologies that create fierce competitive challenges.

- Entrepreneurial fever is fast taking hold, even in France, where 12 percent of French students surveyed in 2000 wanted to start their own firms as soon as they graduated, and another 40 percent wanted to be entrepreneurs at some point, giving up the traditional safe, secure life of government service.

- Fast action and return are the scoreboard, not long-term business success. Every day, in every way, executives in highly competitive and growth businesses seek or are exposed to excitement of unprecedented magnitude, and the more exposed they are, the more and faster they need to seek it. There is no question that, as with all addictions, not only are they becoming dependent on their need for thrills, but they also must seek out higher levels to get the same stimulation, whether related to conference format or business strategy. This means, of course, that they must pour in more and more energy via their people faster and faster to maintain the level of excitement they crave.

Raising and managing young people weaned on this addiction is becoming a source of serious concern. Students easily dispute or reject a task at hand; they have high expectations of technology and are disappointed if it doesn't immediately perform to their expectations. Their need to experience thrills is marked by their immaturity in doing so. Much costly technology mischief is caused by youngsters around the world seeking thrills (such as the Love virus, initiated by teens in the Philippines in 2000). The classic children's stories have become slow and boring. In the Harry Potter books, magic occurs in every paragraph, and there is a constant unfolding of surprise and creativity. Interactive technology allows youngsters to become constantly involved in the action and the shaping of outcomes.

Tradition is falling victim to the need for excitement. Even though about two-thirds of all couples in the U.S. live together before marrying, weddings and honeymoons are planned to be unique and eventful, with lifestyle gifts replacing household items. The rise of what *New York Times* columnist David Brooks calls the bohemian bourgeois (bobos) points out the contradiction that the more we have, the more bored we are. Consumers want "experience," even when they shop, and brands are having to reposition themselves away from the product and toward a lifestyle, reflecting more aspirational dreams and expectations. The energy bar keeps getting raised, and traditional ways of doing business have to invest more and more energy to prop up their weakened competitive positions.

Complexity and Entropy

Entropy means, ultimately, that systems and organizations become less and less efficient, and people constantly work harder to attain efficiency. It also means that things break down more often and more easily. For example, some 60 percent of "smart machines" with built-in computers—cars, cell phones, VCRs—use off-the-shelf software. Such software contains up to 15 bugs per thousand lines of code, according to the Software Engineering Institute. So the machines occasionally malfunction because it takes less energy for software firms to do post-release corrections. Furthermore, there isn't enough energy (skilled programmers) to make the software right the first time.

Machines can process data in billionths of a second (nanoseconds)—and will soon be able to do so in millionths of billionths of a second (femtoseconds). But human beings require significantly more time to process information. And in today's world, for many if not most of us, time is an increasingly rare commodity. Technology, much of which is meant to make our lives easier, often does the opposite.

For example, a new cell phone may come with a 156-page manual. (Hey, it's just a telephone!) One of the most popular digital watches comes with a 36-page manual. Thousands are returned because owners can't figure out how to adjust for daylight savings time. These "advances" can sap our energy, and they produce more disorder than order in our lives. As a consequence, in efforts to reduce or eliminate entropy, people do not, cannot, or will not use enough energy to fully master their new tools.

The extraordinary increase in information has overwhelmed the energies of the education system, which cannot accommodate it, and the entropy here is creating a *know-how gap*. There is a growing gulf between what young people learn in school and what they need to function effectively in the workplace and in a world in which societies and organizations are increasingly complex.

Add to all this what happens when organizations mature. They become bureaucratic. Entrenched managements devote more and more of their own and their organizations' resources to self-preservation and maintenance of the status quo. They become not only resistant to, but hostile to, change. In the process they become more vulnerable to crime and incompetence. We have recently seen this manifested in organizations ranging from the Roman Catholic Church to the FBI.

An increasingly important shaper of the future will be how well we identify—and think about how to counter—the signs that we are becoming entropized. Among them is what could be called *"The Bridge on the River Kwai* Syndrome." This is what happens when a company reaches the point where its rules and procedures become more important to it than its customers and employees are (as is true of many financial services companies). This is also what happens when a community worries more about maintaining its traditions than what energy these may drain from creativity, progress, comfort, and well-being. Entrepreneurialism and competition thrive as older systems fall victim to systems harnessing new energy, not yet affected by the ravages of entropy.

"Why?" can be perhaps your most helpful counter to entropy. Each time you encounter a customary routine that you automatically follow, in your work or your personal life, ask yourself, "Why?" Why am I doing this? What purpose does it serve today? Is there a better way to do it? Does it need to be done at all?

Countering the mental trap of entropy can be difficult because it requires you to think and ask at times when you might prefer not to. It might mean you have to do the following:

- Give up many "sacred cows" and start over. Authors have to face that with each book they write, sometimes eliminating or redoing chapters that require too much wasted energy to fix or that are inappropriate for the book.

- Pick your fights more wisely. The power of your opinion dissipates when you fight or complain about too much. Focus on what is *really* important, and try to fix that.

- Lose the fear of experimenting, particularly with less significant things. Often young people are better at using new technology because they do not read the manual. They are not afraid of failing once or twice as they figure things out. Older people are often so afraid of failing that they spend too much energy trying to get even fairly unimportant matters right the first time.

- Be more aware, active, and informed politically. Entrenched politicians count on entropy so that their ineffective activities will not be challenged.

- Give up relying solely on the best practices of others in running your business. The energy required to maintain ideas that don't necessarily fit comfortably with your organization may eventually be more than the energy it took to copy them in the first

place. Often it is better to look to your own strengths and innovate accordingly. Starting new with what is best for you and
your customers will take less energy, in the end, than constantly patching on someone else's successes in the hope that they
can work for you.

• Stop trying to fit every opportunity or challenge into an old
  framework. Making it fit can use up far more energy than
  broadening, shifting, or replacing your framework.

8

INTEGRITY BEGETS QUALITY

During the 1980s, and into the early 1990s, Total Quality Management (TQM) was the Pet Rock or hula hoop of the business world. Most big companies—and nonbusinesses as well—proclaimed fervent belief in Quality. Multitudes of books on the subject were rapidly produced and made lots of money for their authors. New and established consultants benefited from the willingness to spend whatever it took to get to the pinnacle of the Everest of quality. Award programs, such as the Malcolm Baldrige Award, established by the U.S. Congress in 1987, bestowed accolades on organizations that epitomized success in achieving quality. Today, TQM lives on in such programs as Six Sigma, which gained some popularity when it was espoused by GE's former CEO, Jack Welch.

Unfortunately, as we pointed out in the preceding chapter, entropy has often taken hold of the process. Many companies that tried to enforce quality only by borrowing strategies, formulas, and pronouncements from others wound up spending enormous amounts of wasted energy with little or no eventual improvement in their competitive standing.

That is because TQM had an inherent mental trap: It was essentially a statistical approach. You tried to reduce the number of errors or flaws to a minimum, and it was about the product or service by itself, not so much the employee/worker or the customer. TQM let you predict that your product would be better, but not necessarily the essential nature of your overall organization—that is, the employee morale, customer delight, ethical choices, and general well-being and success of your organization. Professor Tony Simons of the Cornell University School of Hotel Administration, in an article in *Harvard Business Review* in 2002, showed how such simplistic quantitative approaches fail. In the early 1980s, many companies rushed to sign on to a quality program called "Quality Circles." In fact, it was adopted by 90 percent of Fortune 500 companies. Eighty percent of them abandoned it within five years.

Quality is not merely a matter of statistics. Rather, it is a moral issue. In today's environment, you cannot impose behavior, top-down, on an enterprise. You can lead only with top-down examples and values. These must be founded on *integrity*—respect for, and open, honest, and fair dealing with, all stakeholder groups, especially employees. *If true integrity exists, quality is a natural by-product.* It requires no additional or wasted energy in the system, thus avoiding entropy. Professor Simons' research shows that the ultimate result will very likely be a more productive and profitable organization.

During the height of the craze, we (somewhat tongue in cheek) proposed a 30-second TQM program that we were willing to offer free of charge. It was a very simple program, consisting of only three examples of true quality, embodied in three quotations:

- Professor Emeritus Ted Levitt of the Harvard Business School wrote, "The purpose of any business is to get and keep a customer."

- Jerome LiCari, R&D director at Beechnut Baby Foods, left the company before a major scandal broke. When asked why, he said, "I thought apple juice should be made from apples."

- The Golden Rule, which paraphrased what Jesus Christ said in His Sermon on the Mount, "Do unto others as you would have them do unto you."

In all seriousness, a program based on these statements of principle can be effective in guiding a company toward high quality in its products and services and in its relationships with its customers, employees, and shareholders. This is true whether a company has three employees or 30,000 and whether it has three customers or 30 million.

Example #1: Getting and Keeping a Customer

At a time when almost everyone, from CEOs to consultants, is preaching a service gospel, a kind of "customer apartheid" seems to be emerging. Based on statistical analyses, customers are categorized according to their profit potential. The good ones get more and better service; the others get less service and, indeed, may even have to pay for service.

Some consultants are encouraging this trend. They contend that businesses should concentrate on building sustained relationships with their top customers. And they advocate mining data to profile the customer. This means they see customers as producing or nonproducing assets, with the nonproducing customers becoming a kind of untouchable caste, unwanted and unencouraged.

Underlying this development is a profound value shift in many parts of the nonsocialist world. The '50s and '60s ushered in a time of strong belief in egalitarianism—that everyone should have equal opportunity, that there should be a level playing field. But, as legal scholar Ronald Dworkin points out, even the left has moved away from egalitarianism. In the U.S., welfare reform, based on the premise that all people should be productive members of society, was pushed by a Democratic administration.

This value shift seems increasingly to be reflected in how businesses look at their customers. Service is usually seen as a controllable cost, an investment that should get maximum returns. Thus, many companies are outsourcing their call centers to other countries, or using advanced technology to shift much of the service workload to the customer. As the computer has enabled a reduction of staff, things that workers used to do are increasingly being done by customers. We have all had the experience—a very common one now—of calling to place an order (or lodge a complaint) and then plodding through an often detailed voice mail menu. And when your particular need is outside the available electronic options, the process can become even more time-consuming and laborious. We now must program our own phones, connect our own communications systems, or search for half an hour for help in a large store.

In a private conversation with us some years ago, the eminent pollster Daniel Yankelovich observed that American consumers have gone from being uninformed and passive to being informed and assertive. In the process, they have become more sophisticated. It therefore becomes easy to predict that, as we increasingly recognize we are doing more of the work, we will demand something in return. Or we may decide to cast our lot instead with organizations that serve us rather than ask us to serve ourselves. You don't keep customers by making them work harder, unless they truly get what they want and it's something they can't get elsewhere. Focus on statistical quality alone does not take any of this into account.

Despite years of focus on quality, in most companies, Marketing and Customer Service are still two different departments. Indeed, they are often so disconnected from each other that they might as well be in separate companies. Wrong as wrong could be. To ensure a more effective future, they should be two closely connected parts of the same department. Customer Service should instead be called *Aftermarketing*. Just as Marketing's purpose is to *get* customers, Aftermarketing's purpose is to *keep* them. And that is—must be—a marketing function.

We all have our own horror stories of feeling put upon by organizations that say they want us to do business with them.

One of us, Brown, was a long-time customer of some major financial institutions. Because he is an older, single man, he wanted to minimize the delays and hassles likely to result should he die or become incapacitated, so he decided to execute a power of attorney. He discovered that he couldn't do this merely by filling out one form. Each financial institution would accept only its own form.

He filled out all the forms, had them notarized, and submitted them. Some time later, he received a letter from one of the companies—Fidelity—accompanied by another power-of-attorney form. According to the letter, the form he had just submitted was no longer valid, and he needed to complete and submit the new form. The difference between the two forms, by the way, was not immediately apparent.

He called Fidelity's Customer Service number. A pleasant young man, in response to his complaint, told him that they would accept the first form. End of story? No. Two weeks later another letter from Fidelity arrived, along with another copy of the second form, repeating the request that he submit the new version. He again called Customer Service and spoke to the same pleasant young man. This time, however, he was told that he must use the new form and that Fidelity would not accept the first form.

He asked to speak to a supervisor, who also told him that Fidelity insisted he resubmit the new form. Whereupon he said that he had filled out the one form they had sent him, and he had no intention of filling out another just to satisfy some unintelligible bureaucratic requirement. And, he said, Fidelity could either accept that first form or close out his accounts and send him his money.

If you were Fidelity, faced with such a demand from a customer, what would you have done? What would anyone who understood Professor Levitt's fundamental principle do? Fidelity closed the accounts.

Getting and keeping a customer should be a major focus of anyone doing business. Falling into the trap of managing quality does not address the issue of keeping the customer, which is far more important in ensuring a successful future.

Example #2: Apple Juice Should Be Made from Apples

Trust is the glue that holds societies and organizations together. Without trust, everything grinds to a halt. Even a highly lawyered society like ours depends on trust for most of the many transactions we all engage in every day.

Many surveys point to a prevailing lack of trust today, which is reflected in a variety of ways, including a kind of paranoia, especially among the young. This is increasingly evident in popular culture. Younger people seem to have a greater willingness to believe in conspiracies, often because that is a way to create a sense of coherence and rationality in what is seen as a complex, chaotic, and irrational world. People in their young adult years are what we might call the "Oliver Stone generation," since Stone's stock in trade is movies obsessed with conspiracies.

Recognizing how important trust is, some people and organizations are trying to restore it. They focus on strengthening their brand names—devoting more resources to making sure that the promise of quality is honored. If their products and services lack quality, they can anticipate that their customers will exhibit less loyalty and more willingness to switch to other providers of goods and services. But, as we said earlier, focusing on quality only, without understanding human behavior and expectations, is a seductive trap that can get a company in trouble.

The Nordstrom department store chain established a policy saying that customers could return any purchase any time without explanation. L.L. Bean has had the same policy even longer. In both cases, the company is telling customers that *their* reaction to the products is the true and ultimate test of quality. The companies, in effect, are saying not that they stand behind their products but that they stand behind their customers. If the customers say it isn't apple juice, the store's answer is, "If you say it isn't, it isn't." That definition of quality goes far beyond statistical measurement. It's a definition of quality that speaks volumes about the companies' underlying integrity.

Example #3: Do Unto Others...

Integrity and trust are central to a company's relations with its employees. With all their quality controls, reengineering, downsizing, and other attempts at adaptation, organizations have too often been heedless of the impacts on the psyches of their people. As a consequence, ill will and lack of trust are everywhere now. The social contract is seen as broken.

A lot of what goes on today destroys rather than creates trust. In businesses, much of what transpires erodes relationships with workers—not sharing gains from increased productivity; use of contract workers (and outsourcing), leading to less mutual obligation; the "buy and burn" method of exploiting people, especially in high-tech industries; "virtual" organizations that don't have the face-to-face interaction needed to establish trust.

With technology and long hours a given in most organizations, a split is taking place in the working world—one that runs down the fault line that cleaves two distinct *value sets*. One value set, *Slash and Burn*, is fast-paced, generates fast bucks, and leads to rapid growth and profit, but with early burnout, lowered morale, low tolerance for diversity, and quick bursts of creativity dulled over the longer term, leading to quicker turnover. The other value set, *Stewardship*, is more patient with people, is more caring with longer-term relationships with the marketplace, is concerned about the role one plays in the community, and looks for good, but more modest, rates of return.

In the future, both these models will exist. You may see your own organization as fitting one or the other.

Although Slash and Burn companies achieved some level of quality in the past, that may no longer be so in the future. Since it is the employee, after all, who delivers quality, the organization founded on integrity may be the higher-quality future performer. Human resources strategies and policies must increasingly be aimed at creating a credible new social contract, one that focuses on a new relationship based on mutual integrity—honesty, equity, openness, and fairness. These are not quantifiable. They do not conform to theories of quality management, but they will likely lay a much firmer groundwork for future success.

Quality will come to mean a continuing and growing emphasis on responsibility, both institutional and individual. Employing organizations will be expected to exercise stewardship responsibility for their people's current and future well-being. While it has been talked about for years, it seems that the 21st century will be the time when the idea that businesses should treat all stakeholders equally may really move from concept to practice. The result will be that traditional quality measures will become subordinate to indicators that an organization is an all-around good performer.

Surface Social Responsibility Is Not Integrity

It is now widely believed that businesses should report to the public on their environmental performance—which, of course, should be commendable. Ten years ago, almost none of the world's 250 biggest companies did so; now more than 35 percent report.

Morality and responsibility are in. The major business scandals of 2001 and 2002 didn't create this trend; they accelerated it. We have long expected that an integrity ethic would become a major part of the 21st century value system, and now it appears to be happening in a big way. You cannot survive for long in the next decade if you want to keep your customers but you focus only on your product's quality. In 2002, according to the *Wall Street Journal*, defense lawyers reported that they were finding jurors more suspicious of business executives and more cynical about business ethics.

We must note, however, that one thing became clearer as a result of business scandals: *Doing good matters only if you do right*. Enron was, by all accounts, an exemplary practitioner of good corporate citizenship. It supported the arts and gave generously to help its communities meet pressing social needs. Tell that to its shareholders and employees. Among other results of the Enron catastrophe is likely to be a new look at the theories and practices of corporate social responsibility. Indeed, there is evidence that good service is a stronger determinant of corporate reputation than philanthropy.

The fact is, reputation (the third down in the football metaphor discussed in Chapter 14, "Football Meets Shopping") is not a simple matter. It is a subtle, complex, and often confusing issue. Today's more-skeptical and better-informed public views business in ways that cannot easily be addressed by one-dimensional approaches, such as focus on quality or throwing around buzzwords like corporate social responsibility.

Perhaps because well-intentioned social responsibility doesn't necessarily result in approval, critics of it have emerged again. David Henderson, formerly the chief economist for the Organization for Economic Cooperation and Development (OECD), argues that corporate social responsibility does more harm than good. He says it raises costs and prices and reduces profits. This is another version of what conservative economists said in the 1970s and '80s. But the earlier arguments were based on ideology; this new one appears to be more pragmatic and, therefore, may be more powerful.

At a time when the public is bombarded by many messages from business, some of them contradictory, people make decisions based on what they want to believe. Criticism of business is mounting, and the result is a decline in public favor for business management. It would be a serious mistake for business to believe that good deeds alone will build good will.

In fact, the term "corporate social responsibility," with its faint aroma of *noblesse oblige*, probably should be discarded. Perhaps a better concept is *corporate citizenship*. All of us, as citizens, have public duties that we perform, not for profit but for community cohesion and betterment. These range from paying taxes and serving on juries to mowing our lawns and curbing our dogs. Businesses should recognize that they have citizenship obligations as well, a concept that goes far beyond the public relations activities implied in the term corporate social responsibility.

Companies will have to address first whatever real problems they have, in the marketplace and in the workplace. That can help create an environment in which good corporate citizenship can be appreciated for what it is—the backbone of quality—rather than being seen as self-serving or an attempt to whitewash.

When Marxism collapsed along with the Soviet Union, capitalism was elevated to an uncontested position. But from the beginning there was a backlash (trend-countertrend). All during the boom days of the 1990s, corporations enjoyed great favor with all income segments of the public. Capitalism and unfettered management in the stockholder interest were seen as socially responsible because they spread the wealth in ways that became the envy of the world. But the antitrust suit against Microsoft, brought on by its seeming monopoly in the face of its less-than-sterling quality, was the first sign that the golden age of championing the entrepreneur and executive might be facing harder times.

Stewardship and Integrity

Stewardship, or the longer-term focus on community, the environment, and stakeholder groups, will continue to evolve and emerge as an important counterforce to unopposed capitalism. This ethic will in all likelihood again pick up great steam in the U.S. But it will probably emerge strongest when the leading edge of the baby boom begins to retire around 2011. At that point, boomers will start paying attention to the legacy they leave to the world. Although 6 years might seem like a fairly long time, it is not. Given the short-term pressures on the bottom line and stock performance, it would take that long for a corporation, institution, or profession to slowly develop and solidify its image of stewardship in the eyes of the world. Single actions, even big ones, are seen as marketing ploys. Only long, steady attention to stewardship places a company or profession in a good light with the public and regulators. And only investing in the long term this way can ensure a true image of quality.

Some years ago, one of us was an adjunct lecturer at a graduate school of business, teaching a course on business and society. The students, all working full-time, were not only bright but decent. Yet, when given exercises about potential problems facing companies because of wrong, illegal, or immoral behavior, their focus—unanimously—was on how to protect the company and its executives. Probing them afterwards revealed that they all believed, based on their experiences at work, that this approach would help them get ahead. In other words, what they saw around them led them to conclude that they had to suspend or ignore their own moral codes if they wanted to succeed.

We thought at the time, and we still think, that was a damning indictment of the prevailing values within business. Events since then have shown what can result. The costs to businesses that have slighted the importance of integrity to emphasize quality have been staggering.

Executives who want their companies to be quality companies in the future must understand that they can never achieve that unless they begin with, and base everything on, integrity. There has never been, and there will never be, a hot theory or system or process that can create sustained quality in an organization that lacks integrity.

It is not likely that you will achieve integrity by focusing on quality. But it is highly likely that focusing on integrity will engender quality.

Part III ————

SPRINGING THE TRAP: SEEING THE BIG PICTURE

Now that you have begun to overcome some of the biases that have trapped your mind, it's important to look beyond the particular issues you focus on and see the big picture. Sociology courses generally don't focus on math. But societal events and trends frequently conform to mathematical concepts.

The *Law of Large Numbers* is one of those constants that, because it is always in the background, tends to be ignored. But its importance cannot be overstated. In a society of 100 people, social control is easy. If the society consists of a million people, control becomes much more difficult. Expand the population to five or six billion, and you can see how impossible it is to ever fully prevent crime, deviance, and terrorism.

No social, political, or economic trend can be fully evaluated without factoring in *Demography*. Solutions to environmental concerns, for example, are impossible without taking into account how everything in the environment is affected by numbers and movements of people—and by economic factors related to that.

It has been said that human society doesn't have problems; it has dilemmas. Problems can be solved; the best we can hope for dilemmas is that we keep them from getting worse. But that may be because we think too small when considering solutions. The *Lowest Common Denominator* offers a larger approach to dealing with apparent dilemmas that could present better prospects for turning them into solvable problems.

9

THE LAW OF
LARGE NUMBERS

A 2002 article, "The Odds of That," in the *New York Times* Sunday Magazine caused quite a stir. Author Lisa Belkin said that people are always finding conspiracies or supernatural coincidences where they may not exist. She quoted Stanford statistician Persi Dianconis, who pointed out that, given the fact that there are 290 million people in the U.S., 290 times a day a one-in-a-million shot will occur. Belkin's article resulted in our receiving phone calls from friends and associates across the country asking, "Isn't that what you guys have always said?"

Well, yes, we have. But we didn't discover this. Neither did Dianconis, nor did Belkin. The Law of Large Numbers has been around for a long time. We learned it in high school. So did you. But few people, once they leave school, appreciate the importance of this fundamental mathematical law in putting events into context.

The definition of the Law of Large of Numbers is this:

In repeated, independent trials with the same probability p of success in each trial, the chance that the percentage of successes differs from the probability p by more than a fixed positive amount, $e > 0$, converges to 0 as the number of trials n goes to infinity, for every positive e.

This law translates as follows: The larger the number of trials, the higher the probability of a statistically projected outcome. For example, if you toss a coin, the probability of heads is always 50 percent, and it remains so for each toss. If you toss the coin 10 times, you might get heads three times and tails seven. If you toss 100 times, you might get 60 heads and 40 tails. But if you toss 1,000 times, you are likely to more closely approach 500 heads and 500 tails.

The Law of Large Numbers, conservatively extrapolated, also leads us to understand that the larger the number, or the more time that goes by, the higher the probability of *any* occurrence, statistical or random. Thus, if you had one nuclear reactor and one year went by, a nuclear accident is far less likely than if you had 100 nuclear reactors over the course of 25 years.

Example #1: Critical Mass

Another acceptable conclusion we can draw from this law is that the larger the sample, the more likely a critical mass is to develop around outlying probabilities. Let's use 1 percent of the population as an example. If a group of 100 people has one violent individual, the other 99 will be able to control the one. Keeping the percentage the same, in a group of 1,000 people, 10 could be violent. The other 990 could probably control nine of the 10, but one is likely to succeed in creating terror. Bump the number of people up to a million, and 990,000 might be able to control 9,000, but 1,000 will succeed in wreaking havoc. There is no need to tell you what to expect in a world of several billion. Once the number of wrongdoers reaches a critical mass, they strengthen each other even more than just the constant percentage would indicate. In other words, although the percentage remains the same, the strength of the deviant mass begins to multiply. The Internet is now available to further strengthen the connection of these individuals, magnifying the potential for havoc.

Author Howard Rheingold calls groups of people who use high-tech communications devices to act in concert, whether or not they personally know each other, *smart mobs*. Demonstrations in all countries are increasingly made successful by the ability of outlying people to connect with each other and pass on information, plans, and positions. By bumping up the number of protestors from a few in many scattered places to many in one network, the probability of action is much greater. Rheingold compares the magnitude of this change to that of the time when humans first settled into villages and formed nation-states. The Law of Large Numbers says that, when aggregated this way, probabilities of events actually occurring are greater.

Bob Metcalf, the inventor of Ethernet and the founder of 3Com, incorporated the Law of Large Numbers in his "Metcalf's Law," which states that a network grows more powerful as more people connect to it. There is also the law called the "fax effect," which states that, although fax machines were around for decades, it was only when enough people had them that you could take faxing for granted. What was the point of your having a fax machine if nine-tenths of those you needed to communicate with did not? But once three-quarters had faxes, faxing became a way of life.

This is all about *critical mass*. Once you bring up the numbers to where you have critical mass, probabilities of everything increase, as does the aggregation of those effects.

Example #2: Peer Pressure

Societal and organizational behaviors, long believed to be learned and cultural, are in reality subject to mathematical and physical laws. The Law of Large Numbers, for example, combined with a fascinating field of study in physics, reveals the genesis of what has come to be known as peer pressure.

Whether we're talking about molecules, financial data, or the flocking of birds, when units are alone they behave one way, but when influenced by others they aggregate, even if that means moving far from their original position. Jayanth Banavar of Pennsylvania State University and his colleagues used simple diffusion to model this phenomenon. Banavar employs the metaphor of a random walk, in which the direction of each step is governed by chance, such that, although a crowd might begin at the same point, over time it becomes evenly scattered in all directions. But then add the key variable—*drift*—to the diffusion equation, and the outcome changes. In the case of walkers, drift means that people are more likely to go in the directions in which they spot other people. If the drift is strong enough, it overcomes diffusion by the increasingly powerful tendency to aggregate. In statistics, this distribution pattern is called *fat-tailed* because the aggregate of people, particles, data, or animals can end up far from where they started. In opinion and polling research, this is known as the *halo* effect—when one or two answers to critical questions begin to infect all the surrounding or similar questions, such that the answers begin to clump together rather than separate into discrete assessments, one question at a time. In politics, this is called the *bandwagon* effect. It describes what happens when one candidate begins building critical mass; it is what enables him or her to attract more supporters. This is also the crux of Malcolm Gladwell's theme in his best-selling book *The Tipping Point: How Little Things Can Make a Big Difference.*

Physicist Eugene Stanley of Boston University found the same *fat-tailed* distribution in his work. He said that such distributions govern bird populations, the economic productivity of nations, and stock prices. Banavar says the tendency to aggregate—in social systems known as peer pressure—could help in our fundamental understanding of everything from ants and bacteria to people buying or selling stocks or donating to charitable causes based on what their peers do. The larger the number of players, the greater the influence, creating an inevitability as to the outcome.

Sociologist Duncan Watts, author of *Six Degrees: The Science of a Connected Age*, says that a product's success can be driven by an *information cascade*, whereby increasing numbers of people buy the product because they see that other people are buying it. (This concept is also known as *swarming*.) Clearly, the larger the number of people buying the product, the more likely this effect is to result. That is because, as Watts and others point out, large numbers increase the likelihood of observable—and perhaps even predictable—group behavior.

Example #3: Bell-Shaped Curves

Another sidebar to the Law of Large Numbers is the principle of the bell-shaped curve. Also called a normal distribution pattern, this is the sorting of any population into a spectrum, with the extremes at the ends and the bulk in the middle. The population could be people, data, events—anything. With only a few in the sample, you are not likely to get a smooth sorting. But the higher the number in the sample, the closer you come to the bell-shaped curve.

If you have a population of five people, one might be very short and three might be very tall, with one average. You could have them stand in line, in size order. If you draw the curve of their height distribution, it will look something like Figure 9.1.

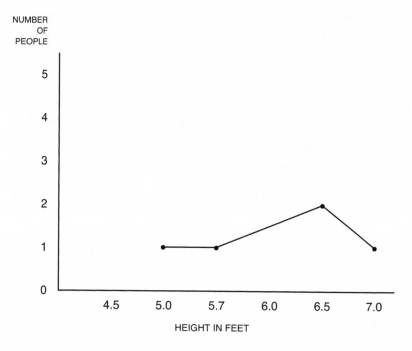

Figure 9.1

But if you put 1,000 randomly-selected people from a single society (because some societies tend to have taller or shorter populations
than others) in size order, you will likely have several who are very
short, more who are somewhat short, many more who are a little
shorter than average, a lot who are clustered around average height,
many a little taller than average, some who are somewhat tall, and a
few who are extremely tall. The curve will be bell-shaped, as in
Figure 9.2.

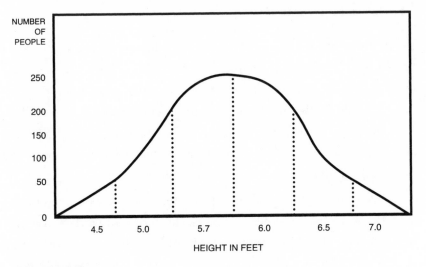

Figure 9.2

The Law of Large Numbers, therefore, dictates that you are far more likely to approach the normal distribution of a bell-shaped curve with a larger sample size. Bell-shaped curves are critical to understanding forces for societal change because, as we discussed in Chapter 4, "The Extremes Inform the Middle," the extremes of the curve inform and reshape the middle. This enables us to predict with some degree of certainty the likelihood, for example, of a deviant group's becoming mainstream. For instance, now that divorce rates are near 50 percent, when you add divorcées to those who are never married or widowed with at least one-third of their life remaining, you conclude that it is lifelong marriage to the same person that has become the alternative lifestyle. Long-term, long-lasting marriages are not the mainstream, so they move toward the extreme, and the populations within the curve shift significantly.

What Lies Ahead

In the future, we may expect to see accelerated mainstreaming of gay households, multiracial households, unwed motherhood, seniors cohabitating out of wedlock, ministers of alternative religions, practitioners of alternative medicine, computer geniuses, and so on. The Law of Large Numbers determines that once a critical mass is achieved, it attracts more to it, meaning that what was once the extreme is more likely to move closer to normality.

This is an important factor in projecting the value of niche markets, the trajectory of political causes, the future of worker discontent, the potential for corporate theft and sabotage—in short, just about everything you need to know or could be confronted with in a large and well-connected world of diversity. It is why terrorism will never go away, nor will heroism. It is why niche markets, even though they may be small percentages of the population, can be viewed by the savvy marketer as mass markets. This is because, in a very large population, the numbers become more important than the percentages. That is why, for example, the luxury market is attracting so many players today. The well-to-do are a relatively small percentage of the total population. But in the U.S. alone, a small percentage of 290 million people can be a large number—and a very lucrative market. Others have become attracted to the behavior and values of that market. It is also why human resources executives and insurance companies will be presented with the challenge of accepting rather than rejecting behaviors and lifestyles that were previously deemed unacceptable.

In contrast to the luxury market is the huge population of the rural poor, a group traditionally neglected by marketers. The fact is, there are more poor people in the world than rich people. Hindustan Lever in India has built brand loyalty by reaching out to this segment, offering soaps and products and the opportunity for these consumers to choose good brands and value—things that the poor want, just as the wealthy and the middle class do. Marketing quality products to the poor indicates respect for them, another factor in building brand loyalty. Hindustan Lever estimates that by 2010, 50 percent of its sales will come from the developing world. Small purchases by vast numbers of poor people, as Hindustan Lever has discovered, can add up to big sales and big profits.

Money and respectability are irresistibly drawn to each other. When a fringe segment, by virtue of its growth to an acceptably large number, becomes attractive as a market, it's on the way to becoming legitimatized. As a consequence, it develops clout. Magazines, financial and consumer products, and advertising all begin to pay attention, as has been the case with the gay community. This, then, can influence politics, as the same gay community did when it focused attention on HIV/AIDS and successfully directed a reallocation of medical research funds. Using that as an object lesson and leveraging the Internet, other concerned people exerted political pressure to attract attention to and push for support of their own causes. Even though many of these causes involved small percentages of the population, their actual numbers were enough to affect public policy.

The Law of Large Numbers is a simple, basic mathematical principle that, when remembered, helps reduce your surprise at unfolding trends or events. When used, it can free your mind to envision, create, and leverage opportunities in your professional and personal lives.

10

DEMOGRAPHY

In a 2002 article about demography, *The Economist* quoted the philosopher Auguste Comte, who said, "Demography is destiny." Demography is certainly one of the most critical determiners of future trends and their direction. For example, as you saw earlier in this book, the world population is aging to an extent that has never before happened. As of 2002, 600 million people in the world were older than 60. One million people turn 60 every month, and it is projected that, by 2050, some two billion people will be over 60. Because of below-replacement-level birthrates, for the first time in human history there will be more old people than young.

This will inevitably lead to a series of critical outcomes. Public and private retirement plans will be seriously strained, and retirement itself will have to be rethought. Many children in aging countries will find that, with no siblings or cousins, their closest relatives will be their parents. Homogenous cultures will be forced to accept greater immigration. These inevitabilities will lead to political and social upheavals, to products and markets never before as potent and needed, and, in many cases, to innovations that will create enormous opportunity and challenge.

Example #1: Demography and Islam

In the immediate aftermath of the horrific events of 9/11, millions of words were spoken and written about why it happened. The causes ranged from religious fanaticism to U.S. policy (or lack of it) in the Middle East, from "the clash of civilizations" to poverty, from lack of economic opportunity to American imperialism. It may well be that all are, at least in part, valid explanations. But one causal factor not thoroughly hashed over was demographics. And that may be the most important driving force of all.

In their landmark 1971 book *The Imperial Animal*, the aptly-named anthropologists Lionel Tiger and Robin Fox said that "The central question for any social system is 'What do we do with the young males?'" That haunting question is particularly pertinent as we look at the issue of relations between Islam and the West, beset as they are with fear, hostility, suspicion, distrust, and resentment.

To begin with, young males in almost all species, as anthropology studies and your own observations can tell you, are naturally competitive, aggressive, territorial, and even violent. Testosterone runs rampant in them, and societies throughout human history have struggled to control their fervent energies and to direct those into channels that benefit society rather than damage it.

With this in mind, let's look at the demographics in the Muslim countries—particularly the Arab countries—as compared to the West. In Egypt, as of 2002, 54 percent of the population was under 25. In Saudi Arabia, 60 percent. In Afghanistan, 61.8 percent. In the U.S., on the other hand, 35 percent of the population was under 25. In Japan, 26.5 percent. In the UK, 32 percent. In Canada, 32 percent.

According to the U.S. Census Bureau, the median age of the U.S. population in 2000 was 36. It will be 38 in 2015 and 39 in 2030. In Western Europe, the median age in 2015 will be 43, and in 2030 45.

In just one Muslim country, Pakistan, the median age will be 24 in 2015 and 29 in 2030.

The 22 Arab countries currently have a total population of about 280 million people, pretty close to the current U.S. population. A big difference, however, is that more than one-third of the 280 million Arabs are younger than 16. By 2020, it is estimated that the Arab population could be as much as 460 million. The fertility rate—the average number of children born per woman—is 6.1 in Saudi Arabia, 6.9 in Afghanistan, and 5.5 in Pakistan.

Compare that to the West. Most of the developed countries are experiencing a *baby bust*. Italy's fertility rate is 1.2. The replacement rate would be 2.1. Spain, Greece, the Czech Republic, Norway, Russia, and others have similarly low fertility rates. This means that their populations will decline. Today, some 64 countries, with about 45 percent of the world's population, have below-replacement fertility rates. As a consequence, they will see significant population declines. This includes not only European countries, but a wide range of others, such as Japan, Iran, Sri Lanka, and Korea. If nothing changes, Italy's population will dwindle to 8 million by 2100, and Germany will lose 85 percent of its population by that year. By 2050, Japan's population will decline by 14 percent, and its median age will be 49. Russia's population could decline by one-third. Only the U.S. among major industrial countries can anticipate a population increase. That is because, although our birthrate is fractionally below the replacement rate of 2.1, we have the benefit of more immigration. For Latinos in the U.S., a rapidly growing segment, the birthrate is almost 3.0. But our growth rate is nothing compared to that of the Arab countries.

What does it all mean? Factor in some other considerations:

- More young men in Muslim countries are going to college.

- Economic growth in Muslim countries is not keeping up with population growth, meaning that more young men—including the college-educated—will lack economic opportunity.

- The increasing availability of communications and information technology in Islam is facilitating the spread of and recruitment to radical ideologies. Less fiery brands of Islam cannot really compete because the young will choose fire over ice far more often than not—and not just in Islam, as the growing attraction of young Americans to more fervent religious expression shows.

In July 2002, a multinational group of Arab scholars, under the auspices of the United Nations Development Program, issued a gloomy report on the state of the Arab world. Titled "Arab Human Development Report 2002," the study was an unsparing look at the desperate need for both economic development and political liberty in Arab countries. Teenaged Arab males interviewed for that study seemed without hope. Almost 50 percent of them expressed a desire to emigrate, mostly to North America and Europe. As one commentator said, the report shows how dismal the prospects for young men are in the 22 Arab states.

Perhaps the most frightening factor is something we see emerging from Palestinian despair. Throughout history, a significant deterrent to war has been the unwillingness of mothers to lose their sons in battle. Not too many years ago, it was the growing resistance of Russian mothers that forced the Soviet Union to end its war in Afghanistan. But some Palestinian mothers applaud and encourage their sons—and even their daughters—to become martyrs. If this mind-set should spread to other parts of Islam, in the context of the factors just enumerated, the consequences could be unimaginable.

All in all, then, no analysis of the future of terrorism can be useful if it does not take into account the overwhelming importance of demographics.

Example #2: Why the Number of Youths Matters

Getting back to the question of what do we do with the young males, changes in warfare will also have a growing effect in the future. Countries have always utilized the aggressive energies of young people in soldiering and fighting. As war becomes more technical, some observers question whether pushing buttons will satisfy young males' urges to violence. In this connection, those who condemn the violence in video and computer games may be overlooking how such virtual activities might effectively substitute for real violence.

Businesses will have to be increasingly alert to the possibility that the aggressive and competitive instincts of young males could be manifested in sexism and sexual harassment. Past instances of that on Wall Street show how real the problem can be, particularly in businesses that have macho traditions.

The difficulties many organizations are finding in the team approach may be, at least in part, related to the need young males have to win—and to be seen as winning. The cooperative approach, while it can have some value to the organization, does not always lead to superior performance by young men whose urges are competitive.

One point of concern for all organizations is the impact of budget problems on public education—in particular, the cutback in extracurricular activities such as athletics. This reduces the opportunities for young males to have positive outlets in team sports. That, in turn, can lead to exacerbated workplace problems and heightened costs in crime and vandalism, such as computer hacking and theft. It would be worthwhile, it seems, for businesses to allocate some of their financial support to neglected extracurricular programs.

Many older people see the involvement of young people in religion as desirable and positive, both for them and for society. As we noted, however, young people often bring to religion a fervor and passion that can develop into a crusade mind-set that can lead to more culture clashes, both internally and globally.

Another very serious youth issue is the growing male-female imbalance in China and India. In both countries, sex-determined abortions and female infanticide have resulted in large surpluses of young men in the 15-to-34 age segment. China has 13 million more males in this category, and India has 16 million. Both governments have become alarmed at the explosive potential of this imbalance. They are stepping up recruiting in the police and military and using these young men as export labor. It will not be enough. Waging wars may be one way for these countries to reduce the internal threat from this excess of young males.

Example #3: Asian Demographics

China and Japan have a complex and changing relationship. To begin with, let's look at some basic population statistics. China's population in 2002 was 1.28 billion, a figure projected to reach 1.45 billion by 2020. Japan's 2002 population was 127 million, with a projection that it will be 122 million by 2020. The key here is the likely decline in Japan's population, which, when combined with the aging of that population, portends major problems. A 2004 study by the Japanese Institute of Life Insurance showed that the Japanese are increasingly postponing or even avoiding marriage. Fifty-four percent of Japanese women in their late 20s are single, up from 31 percent 20 years ago. Half of single Japanese women age 35 to 54 claim to have no intention of marrying. The median age in Japan in 2000 was 38.6, one of the highest in the developed world. In 2020, it will be an astonishing 45.1.

In China, on the other hand, the corresponding numbers are a median age of 29.9 in 2000 and 37.1 in 2020.

In 2002, in spite of a decade-long decline, Japan's economy was the second-largest in the world, behind only that of the U.S. China's economy was, as near as anyone can tell, the third-largest. While Japan's economy sat becalmed, entangled in weeds for over a decade, China's moved ahead rapidly. There is a rivalry here, one made much more intense by deep suspicion and distrust between the two countries, much of it rising from their 20th century conflicts.

Will China continue to grow and flourish? Will it overtake Japan and economically dominate the Far East? Will Japan slide into decline and mediocrity? Will it be forced to submit to China's economic, political, and military might? Clearly, demographics will strongly influence the eventual outcome. The many businesses rushing to establish themselves in China attest to how important the demographics are.

Example #4: Immigration

Another demographic factor deriving from the population imbalance (young versus old) between the developed Northern countries and the less-developed Southern countries is immigration. Vast numbers of young people desperate for economic opportunity will move north. This movement, like that of army ants, will be inexorable. They either move or starve. While many, if not most, developed countries do their best to limit immigration, no one can successfully prevent it. Indeed, some observers feel that if controls were too effective, the result would be a worldwide explosion of violence.

Clearly, the North needs more workers than can come from its native populations. But no country, not even ones with relatively liberal immigration policies, such as Canada and the U.S., wants to be inundated. There is a need for effective policies that mitigate the worst effects of immigration and encourage economic development in poor countries. Business can do its part by helping create jobs and higher incomes in the developing world.

Other factors also contribute to the immigration dilemma.

Environmental problems, such as the spread of deserts caused by overuse of farmland and lack of rain, are also creating refugees. At least 25 million people may already have been uprooted by such problems (perhaps more than from wars and oppression), with an additional 900 million people living in environmentally marginal areas. Lack of potable water or its opposite, extreme flooding, both represent potential causes of conflicts in the future and likely causes of even greater refugee flows.

Another contributing factor is food. While optimism continues about our ability to feed the world, primarily through technological developments, there are also causes for concern that we may be facing a food crisis. A particular area of concern is the possibly huge impact of China's switch from a grain-based diet to one based on meat consumption. Its raising of livestock will mean greatly increased inroads on their croplands and diversion of grains to feedstock. This could lead to China's need to import vast quantities of grains, driving up the world's grain prices and further depriving and destabilizing poorer countries.

Urbanization represents yet another problem area. For the first time in history, more than half the world's population lives in cities. The enormous tides of people moving into Third World cities are creating a great health hazard. Rapidly growing cities are becoming disease vectors, creating situations (and costs) that their countries are unable to deal with, and these diseases are fast intruding on the developed world.

Clearly there is a great need for a concerted global effort to come to grips with the underlying political, economic, and social problems that are making migration such a seemingly intractable issue. Failure to do so will result not only in a bigger and ever more costly problem, but in a growing potential for conflict—and in the spread of rabid xenophobia.

Example #5: Aging

Let's take a closer look at some aspects of aging and how they will deeply affect our future. As mentioned earlier, the number of people 60 and over in the world is expected to reach two billion by 2050. For the first time in human history, there will be more humans over 59 than under 16. By 2050, one fifth of the older population will be 80 or more. The Potential Support Ratio (PSR)—the number of people aged 15 to 64 for each person 65 or older—is expected to be four, down from nine in 2000.

The economic concerns that will arise from this are almost too much to contemplate. How will societies be able to provide the economic and health-care needs for massive older populations? Countries that treat their older people generously, such as those in Europe, will not be able to go on doing so without drastic economic and social changes.

The graying of the world will even affect the commercial rivalry between the European Union and the U.S. By 2050, according to *The Economist*, Europe's population, now over 450 million, will have declined to perhaps 360 million. The U.S., with a current population of about 290 million, will have anywhere from 400 to 550 million people. Most tellingly, according to the Census Bureau, the median age in the U.S., after peaking at 39 in 2030, will be 38 in 2050. In Europe it will be 52.7. The economic, social, and political implications of this are staggering. The pension burden in Europe will be like an immense anchor, holding back the economy.

Many older people will have to change from being economic drains to being economic contributors. Ways will have to be found to compensate for, or limit, their heavy use of health-care resources. Immigrations from less-developed countries will become ever more necessary.

Our 1993 book, *Office Biology*, explored the fact that an aging workforce will require a different workplace. For example, as people age, their eyes change. The average 60-year-old person needs three times as much light to see an object as does a 20-year-old. The eye's lenses become thicker, and this tends to make glare more of a problem. Night driving is an issue the automobile and insurance companies will have to be increasingly concerned with. The ability to differentiate among shades of color diminishes; the lens, the cornea, and fluid in the eye yellow as you get older, and this changes perceptions of colors and shades. Blue and green, for example, become more difficult to distinguish.

Hearing also declines. Over time, the ear loses its ability to detect higher frequencies—particularly those of about 1,000 cycles per second (one kilohertz). The human voice can cover a spectrum ranging from under 100 cycles per second to more than 8,000. The ability to hear much of this spectrum begins to fade as people age. (Men, it should be noted, begin to experience appreciable hearing decline on average six years earlier than women. Because women and children speak in higher frequencies, they are the ones who become more difficult for aging people to hear.) It is sobering to consider that the ability to detect speech well across the sound spectrum can be 5 percent less for people in their 40s than for people in their 20s. Yet no one wants to admit, sitting in the boardroom or conference room, that he or she is having difficulty hearing.

Aging bodies in the office, like those of aging athletes, tend to be less able to handle stress and strains. They suffer injuries more easily, and they recover more slowly. Ergonomic design, intended to make the workplace both less injurious and more comfortable, will have to have an age bias in the future: What will be best for an older workforce? What will reduce muscle fatigue and lessen chances of developing musculoskeletal conditions such as tendonitis, carpal tunnel syndrome, and ligament inflammation? Ergonomics, a consideration much needed in product design, will also have to factor in the differing effects of color and noise on older workers.

Let's not forget menopause. Female baby boomers are becoming menopausal by the millions. Many suffer debilitating symptoms, which can affect them on the job. More than that, the sheer size of the market will drive pharmaceutical research, particularly because of the continuing controversy surrounding the 2002 announcement that the widely used hormone replacement therapy was potentially more harmful than helpful.

The future impact of aging on housing patterns is also likely to be profound. The 20th century movement of older people southward in the U.S. might not continue. It would appear, for example, that many retirees are choosing to stay where they are. This is leading to what gerontologists are calling Naturally Occurring Retirement Communities (NORCs). So large apartment developments, such as New York City's Co-op City, and suburban communities are having to add the amenities that older people need or demand—senior-care centers, home health care, educational programs, and so on. Eleven percent of the elderly currently reside in nursing homes or assisted-living complexes. By 2030, there may be well over 60 million older people in the U.S. whose care will impose high costs on communities around the country.

Companies that understand the need to accommodate these facts about aging will benefit from consumer gratitude. Making print on dials and in manuals larger and clearer works well for younger as well as older customers. Putting better lighting in restaurants, or even giving diners a small flashlight in dimly lit ones, will help get consumers to come back again.

Age and Relevance

Most importantly, we will have to see the aged in terms of their *relevance*. With improvements in health and longevity likely to continue, if not accelerate, it will be absurd to go on thinking that anyone over 65 has outlived his or her usefulness.

The aging population is healthier (and, in many cases, wealthier) than ever before, they have more work and life experience, they are eager to remain active, and they expect to live longer. But they will have a difficult time defending their relevance.

Marketing messages increasingly portray older people as more attractive and vibrant than in earlier eras. But they also usually show these people in leisure activities or in retirement. These messages reinforce the irrelevance of elders to the serious business of day-to-day life. They are made to feel as if they are drains on the health-care system and in competition for public funding with the needs of the young. Their role as storytellers, recounting history and experience, becomes less relevant in an age of immediacy. In many businesses, they feel marginalized because their technical skills are often outdated or insufficient, and they find themselves (if they are still working) taking orders from people half their age. Recruiters shun them. Meaning will not be their issue—relevance will. Many will retreat into believing that their role as grandparents is the cornerstone of their relevance. But a significant number will not have grandchildren or won't have them close enough to sustain their relevance on those terms alone.

As baby boomers, in particular, become the healthiest and wealthiest cohort ever to move into old age, they will demand and command respect in the marketplace. That will require businesses to find new ways of looking at older markets. Companies will have to stop thinking about walkers and wheelchairs for the older markets and look instead at what's cool, desirable, sexy, and fashionable.

Conversely, auto manufacturers have to take into account that, as people age, they become less flexible. Therefore, automakers need to make their vehicles easier to get into and out of—without making them look like cars for old people. Auto manufacturers have avoided making cars more suitable for older people because they fear that younger buyers will reject them. Meanwhile, seniors looking for more age-friendly vehicles bought large numbers of golf carts, none of which were made by the big U.S. auto companies, which thus missed out on this big and growing market opportunity. Many seniors, because they want something that's both comfortable and sexy, customized their golf carts to be flashier and faster.

Advertisers must vigorously reject the stereotypes that so offend today's youthful old. TV and print ads too often still depict crotchety or semi-senile old people with nothing to do except gossip or chat—or discuss in great detail their embarrassing physical decline. Advertisers need to recognize that most older people are healthy, vital, and active.

The travel and entertainment industries, too, will have to become more accommodating to their wants. Hotels should see that older people get rooms close to elevators. Restaurants should recognize that loud noise is hard for older ears to take and impairs the ability of older people to have conversations. Airlines, railroads, and cruise lines should provide more comfortable waiting areas. They also should more actively promote their senior-discount policies and arrange more tour packages that cater to older travelers' desires for learning and adventure.

The health-care industry will be under increasing pressure to provide products and services that are wellness-focused, not just illness-focused. These will range from plastic surgery to pills that control or elevate moods. Additionally, insurers will be under increasing pressure to pay for it all.

The public sector may come to recognize elders for the assets they can be because they may be willing to work for less pay in jobs that are perceived as public service. For example, the military will increasingly be engaged in intelligence rather than combat, so people should be able to enter the military at 50 and work 20 years before retiring. The same is true in the private sector. Because one in nine baby boomers is projected to live to be 100 years old, writing off people over 50, and certainly over 60, will lead to major social dysfunction unless this issue is faced soon.

Jonathan Swift said that everyone wants to live a long time, but nobody wants to get old. We are facing a future in which it may well be possible to age without getting old. It will be a world very, very different from what we have known before.

Example #6: "Ymigration"

For four centuries, America has been absorbing peoples and cultures from all over the world, and our history has been one of large-scale immigrations. In the past 150 years, the U.S. has been the recipient of not only the oppressed, the venture seekers, and the economically disadvantaged, but also the best and brightest minds and talents of the globe. Asian and European scientists have been pouring into the U.S. Foreigners are awarded 60 percent of the doctorates in the physical sciences and 30 percent in the life sciences. One quarter of biotech company founders and CEOs were born abroad.

It is quite possible that, for the first time, the U.S. will begin to see a significant proportion of its own emigrate from the U.S. Generation Y, the population segment born between 1978 and 1995, may be the first generation in U.S. history to have many of its members leave these borders to pursue large chunks of life, if not all of it, overseas.

Following the low-birthrate years of Generation X, Generation Y, which is comparable in size to the baby boomers, will continue flowing into the U.S. workforce over the next 15 years and change the ratio of available jobs to available workers. Their debt levels upon college graduation will be enormous. (Current graduates are averaging in the $40,000 to $70,000 range from private universities and $20,000 from public, and tuitions are rising faster than ever.) Because of the size of this group, they will be far less likely than Generation X to find readily available high-paying jobs to offset those loans. Overseas, the picture is different. Countries in Europe must encourage immigration as they witness the depletion of their workforce and an increase in the pension rolls. Italy will have to add 4 million people by 2025 just to stay at 1995 replacement levels, Germany 14 million, France 2 million, and 35 million total for the entire continent. To keep the ratio of workers to retirees at the 1995 level, Europe needs 135 million more people by 2025, and it will have to compete aggressively for the talent currently heading to the U.S. There are now 1.3 million more jobs in information technology in Europe than there are qualified workers. Certainly, outsourcing some of these jobs to countries such as India or China will resolve part of the problems. Just as clearly, youthful Americans may see much better opportunities in the depopulating world and begin to take advantage of them.

Example #7: The U.S. Becomes the Southern Hemisphere

Demographic trends show that the U.S. will increasingly feel the Latino influence. Already the largest minority, Latinos will have more impact on U.S. culture and politics. In places such as Los Angeles and Houston, over half of all children under 14 are Latino. In 2002, more than half of all births in California were Hispanic. Over time, Americans' connections of family and tradition, formerly heavily European, will shift more and more to Latin America and, to a lesser extent, to Asia. Europe will become more remote and perhaps less important to the fabric of life in the United States.

Example #8: The Burgeoning Global Middle Class

Demographics is not just about population. It's also about such matters as income distribution, education levels, and class.

What could be one of the most revolutionary driving forces of the early 21st century may be the growth of a global middle class of vast proportions. Some observers predict that, by 2015, there will be nearly two billion middle-class people in the world.

While this number may seem impossibly large, it isn't really. China now has at least 100 million people—and probably more—that by Chinese standards are middle-class. By 2015, a conservative estimate based on present patterns of economic development would be 200 to 300 million. India may well have an equal or larger number. Latin America, long a region with a small upper class, a small middle class, and a vast poor population, is seeing, in fits and starts, a solid and significant growth in the middle class. By 2015, there could well be another 250 to 300 million of them. Add Europe, North America, Indonesia, Iran, and all the other developed and developing countries, and the two billion figure is not at all unreasonable.

Keep in mind that middle class is not just about income; it is also, and perhaps more importantly, about a set of values that create the bourgeois mind-set. These values include optimism, belief in freedom and opportunity, materialism, a better life for one's children, ambition, and the importance of education.

Consequently, there will be an acceleration of aspiration. Middle class used to be a goal in the U.S.; now it's a launchpad from which to get rich. It took more than 100 years in the U.S. for there to be a widespread belief that middle class is a stepping-stone to wealth. But it won't take anywhere near that long in the rest of the world, simply because we live in a time in which everything is speeded up, as if we were in a centrifuge.

It has been—and still is—customary for some intellectuals, radicals of both the right and left, and members of elite castes to sneer at the middle. This "bourgeoisphobia" overlooks the fact that the middle class is the engine that powers both capitalism and democracy. The middle is the source of economic energy and innovation, and it's the mainstay of democracy. Countries such as Cuba, North Korea, and Venezuela that view the middle class as an enemy force and that repress it or drive it out can kiss economic development goodbye.

Think, if you will, what this will mean for global economic development. The middle class is a voracious consumer. It wants. It wants houses, it wants cars, it wants vacations in nice places. It wants furniture and clothes and restaurants to eat in. It wants to acquire, it wants to save, it wants to invest. It wants its children to have better jobs.

The future market for goods and services around the world—from cars and houses (and second homes) to clothes and jewelry to food and wine to exercise equipment and self-help courses—will be immense. Economies that are prepared to respond to this tsunami of demand will prosper in ways they cannot now imagine.

With the explosive growth of the global middle class, the market for what we have traditionally seen as luxury goods will be many times larger than what it is now. And that will further change how we will define luxury (see Chapter 11, "Compromise Versus Lowest Common Denominators").

Example # 9: Women

For many years in American business, a fierce argument—which, unfortunately, is still around—has raged about whether women are sufficiently represented in management, especially senior management. In 2004, class-action lawsuits were brought against America's largest employer, Wal-Mart, and one of the most prestigious Wall Street firms, Morgan Stanley. Female employees claimed that the companies discriminated against them in promotions to management positions. Advocates for women say there is still a glass ceiling. Male executives say it's not discrimination; it's because there aren't enough qualified women.

That argument will be made moot by demographics. For the 2001–2002 academic year, enrollment in American colleges was 54 percent female. In the future they will inevitably rise to the top because the majority of managers will be female.

Example #10: Marketing to Children

Historians and sociologists have labeled the 1960s a revolutionary decade. And so it was. But in some ways, the 1950s may have been even more revolutionary. It was in the '50s that television began its radical alteration of American society. One thing TV did was, for the first time ever, market directly to children. Always before, marketing to kids had been aimed at parents.

Children became a market. What happens when a population segment becomes a market? Well, for one thing, it is empowered. It becomes aware that it has power. So, in a way, parents are right to blame TV for how rotten their kids are. The late prominent futurist Herman Kahn once said that you can't raise a kid who's got a lawyer. Similarly, it's harder to control a kid who has spending and market decision power.

TV could also be blamed for the skepticism, cynicism, and irony so characteristic of young people, starting with the baby boomers. It used to take a while for kids to learn that their parents had lied to them about Santa Claus and the Tooth Fairy. They learned almost instantaneously that adults on TV lied to them. In the '50s, one of the big advertisers to children was a cereal called Maypo. Kids saw the ads and clamored for Maypo, repeating its slogan: "I want my Maypo!"

The parents, of course, bought it. The kids hated it. What a lesson. That could very well be how youthful opposition to the Vietnam War in the '60s began.

An important point, as was stated in Chapter 9, "The Law of Large Numbers," is that seeing any population segment as large enough to be a market empowers that group as it has never been empowered before.

Example #11: Where People Go

Throughout the world, people are migrating to urban areas and sea-coasts. The urbanization issue has been widely and frequently discussed, as have the problems attendant upon it, such as poverty, disease, sprawl, and so on. But the coastal issue may, in its own way, be equally troublesome.

Currently, more than half the people in the U.S. live in coastal regions. It has been estimated that, by 2025, 75 percent of Americans will be coastal. This raises a host of concerns:

- Pressures on the ecosystem

- Preservation of wetlands and marine life

- Increased housing costs

- Controlling tourism and traffic

- Transportation bottlenecks around access to beaches

- Impacts of global warming

- Increasingly destructive impacts of tropical storms, such as hurricanes

As coastal areas around the world become more crowded and as global warming threatens to raise sea levels, these issues will become more contentious unless we begin now to address them better than we have been.

Caveat on Demography

Having absorbed all this, you should also know that long-range population projections can often be wrong. Any number of changes or discontinuities can, over a long period of time, significantly alter rates of population growth or decline. Demographers for years predicted large and perhaps unsustainable population growth rates for Africa. Then came three unanticipated factors: AIDS, a decline in the birthrate across the continent, and almost constant, brutal war throughout the continent.

In another example, Japan's forecasted decline in population is based not only on the aging of that society, but also on its traditional xenophobia, making it unlikely to offset the decline by encouraging immigration. But there are indications that may change. In the year 2000, there were more than 36,000 marriages in Japan in which one partner was not Japanese. Although this might not seem like a lot by U.S. standards, it is six-and-a-half times the number of such marriages in 1970. This could signify an increased willingness on the part of Japanese to accept outsiders.

Beware of Extrapolation

Several years ago, one of our retailing clients retained another— much larger—consulting firm to prepare statistical projections for the next five years. One of its projections was that there would be, for the foreseeable future, a significant shortage of workers. The consulting firm said that this would be particularly true for the kind of entry-level jobs our client was most interested in. We challenged that finding for two reasons:

- It was based on the number of Generation Xers and did not sufficiently account for the advent and size of Generation Y.

- It assumed an unbroken upward trajectory for the U.S. economy.

Because the consultants used only straight-line extrapolation of current trends, they were wrong. Generation Y, 71 million strong, is the largest cohort since the baby boom, even though it is a smaller percentage of the population than the boomers are. The consulting firm's mistake was making the percentage much more important in its calculations than the numbers.

These cautions aside, you should not slight demography and its importance in shaping our future. Indeed, no look at the future can hope to come close to validity unless it factors in and constantly monitors demographics. This is one of the most important ways to open your mind so that it can grasp the big picture of what is to come.

11

COMPROMISE VERSUS LOWEST COMMON DENOMINATORS

This is one of our favorite thinking techniques because it debunks one of the most revered mental traps. When you are confronted with alternatives that are at odds with each other, you believe it is best to seek a compromise. However, the reality is that when you think about what compromise is, objectively and honestly, it is generally not the best possible approach to problem solving. That is because it speaks to a negative outcome ("I'll give up something because the other party is also giving up something") or a midpoint between two possibilities, satisfying neither. Any compromise is likely to be a lose-lose solution.

In marketing, for example, compromise can be deadly. If two market segments want opposing product or service features, the marketer often offers a little of both, but not all of one. The competition can see what was left unsatisfied for one of the two segments and can then satisfy those consumers completely, gaining control of much of that market.

In politics, compromise can lead to discontent and perpetuation of antagonisms because no one is completely satisfied with the outcome. In labor negotiations, it can lead to a continual revisiting of the contract. In trade or professional associations, it can lead to loss of unhappy members. In regional conflicts, it can mean endlessly simmering hostilities.

Constantly looking for compromise, on a grand scale or even a trivial scale, is therefore not a good mental habit. Consider a couple in a typical New England suburb, thinking of painting their house. The man wants to paint it green because he likes earth tones; the woman wants to paint it yellow because she likes cheerful colors. If they compromised, they would paint the house chartreuse—halfway along the yellow/green spectrum. But no couple in its right mind living in that area would do that because the result would be neighborhood animosity and a lowered property value. Instead, the couple might go to a paint store, thumb through hundreds of samples in a relatively short period of time, and decide on terra cotta peach, which is *both* an earth tone *and* a cheerful color, satisfying each party completely.

In the business and political worlds, as well as in your personal life, you are frequently confronted with choosing between green and yellow. How often do you settle on chartreuse, hoping (believing) you can get away with it?

There is usually a better way to arrive at solutions. When you first learned fractions, and you had to add 1/5 and 1/7, you were taught you couldn't solve the problem until you had a denominator of 35. That's because 5 and 7 do not talk to each other as fractions. But 5 goes evenly into 35, and 7 goes evenly into 35, and then everything works. Thirty-five is the *lowest common denominator*. You did this math correctly all through school to pass exams, but now that you're in the real world, you forget the math and gravitate toward expediency. When confronted with 1/5 and 1/7, the tendency is to use 1/6 (halfway between the two) and then wonder why the solutions inevitably fall apart after some period of time.

In life, as in math, you must pay attention first to the denominators, not the numerators. The numerators in life are the surface things people say or request; the denominators are the real needs or expectations they have. Using the case of the couple painting the house, you can express the equation this way:

Him: **Her:**

I want to paint   I want to paint
the house green.   the house yellow.
(numerator)   **(numerator)**

_____   +   _____ **= X (the solution)**

I like earth tones.   I like cheerful colors.
(denominator)   **(denominator)**

The wrong solution, the compromise, is to find the midpoint between the two numerators (chartreuse). The right solution, the lowest common denominator, is arrived at by multiplying the two denominators (earth tones × cheerful colors) and finding, for example, terra cotta peach, into which earth tone and cheerful both fit.

For some reason, the term _lowest common denominator_ (the simplest or smallest concept into which all factors evenly fit) has come to mean in the minds of most people the worst possible compromise. Yet, it is the furthest thing from that. It is not a compromise. It is the _strongest_ chance you have for a successful solution.

Finding any common denominator requires a fresh look. You can do this only by shifting your focus away from surface indications and statements, but that's difficult because the obvious is where we tend to fix our gaze. Perhaps the best illustration of this is the man who sees a crying boy on the street corner at night looking for something.

"What's the problem?" asks the man.

"I lost my quarter," sobs the boy. The man offers to help look, and after 10 minutes, he asks the boy, "Are you sure this is where you lost your quarter?"

"Oh, no," answers the boy. "I dropped it across the street."

"Then why are we looking here?"

"Because this is where the streetlight is."

Use this story as your guide to seeking common denominators. Do *not* look where the light is; rather, look where the quarter was lost.

Example #1: Employee Diversity

One clear example of how all this works can be seen in the issue of workplace diversity. When diversity initiatives are proposed in organizations, they tend to focus on where the sight line is easy: black and white, male and female, young and old, ethnic minority and majority. However, let's examine the point of wanting diversity: It offers, among other things, a wider variety of knowledge, a richer context for strategy, a greater representation of the views of the public at large. This is different from nondiscrimination (or equal opportunity) initiatives. The latter are imposed by legal or societal pressure and are aimed at population quotas. The former is desirable for greater levels of operational success.

Approached this way, if you reexamine what is really meant by diversity, it comes down to different thinking and behavior. But this is what most organizations do not want; they want conformity—like-minded people who get along with each other. So they can far more easily tolerate people who *look* different than people who *are* different. A company woman will go a lot further than a typical woman. She still faces a major hurdle, however. When you delve beneath the surface even more, you come up with the real problem: *In advancement and promotion, the higher you go in any hierarchy, the more comfort takes precedence over competence.*

What makes people at the top most comfortable is a commonality of viewpoints—the same world view. For decades, on the surface, objections about women reaching the top focused on the fact that their desire for motherhood would impair their commitment to the job. In fact, a significant proportion of women trying to get to the top sacrificed having children for that privilege. So it was never really about motherhood; it was about what happens when you drop the m—*otherhood*. It is, after all, others who are underrepresented at the very top—minorities, very short people, women, those who are physically disabled, and, above all, those whose thinking diverges sharply from that of their peers.

Once you understand that acceptance or rejection of otherhood is the real problem regarding diversity, the lowest common denominator is the culture of the organization. Does it embrace a variety of thinking and behavior styles? If yes, people of any color, age, sex, or belief could qualify as long as they are competent and complement the mix of people already on board. Does the culture reject alternative ways of thinking and behaving? If yes, the way one thinks and behaves has to be calibrated against the norm, first and foremost, and then people can be hired, regardless of their physiology, so long as they conform to the culture. Where recruitment for diversity has strayed into obvious physiology and focused on appearance—that is, the compromise solution to the diversity dilemma—it has led to resentments, failures, mismatches, financial strains, and poor public relations.

Now let's see how the math works in an old-line, traditional-culture-based organization:

Management:

We need to a hire a more demographically
balanced workforce. (**numerator**)

We don't want to shake up our comfort zone.
(**denominator**)

Workers:

Despite our different beliefs and physiology, we deserve to be a part of this company. **(numerator)**

We don't want to be uncomfortable in the workplace. **(denominator)**

To add management's view to the workers' view, you would have to multiply the denominators (no shaking up of management's comfort zone × no discomfort on the part of employees) to get the lowest common denominator: Hire only those people who fit in with the company culture. Then and only then can you turn your attention to the issue of demography and make a concerted effort to achieve diversity of race, sex, age, and ethnicity.

The math works differently, however, in a company that values diversity of thinking and viewpoints. In this kind of company, the example works as follows:

Management:

We want a more diverse workforce. **(numerator)**

We feel there is value to the organization in different ways of thinking and viewing the world. **(denominator)**

Workers:

Despite our different beliefs and physiology, we want to be accepted and respected as part of this workforce. **(numerator)**

We want our different points of view to be tolerated, listened to, and factored in. **(denominator)**

The way this type of organization would solve the diversity issue is, again, to add these viewpoints together. To do that, it must first multiply the denominators (there is value in diverse perspectives × we have different points of view). To achieve its diversity goals, then, this organization would resolve to remove whatever obstacles exist in the organization to a diversity of opinion, expression, or strategy. Then the organization can hire the best and brightest of any sort, probably getting to demographic diversity a lot faster than the prior traditional organization.

In each of these cases, while the surface issues (numerators) of diversity seem to be the same, the denominators are sufficiently different and require wholly different solutions.

Example #2: Majority Rules

One of the most widely accepted examples of compromise is the idea that the majority opinion should prevail. This is not necessarily how everyone sees fairness. In fact, Lani Guinere, Bill Clinton's nominee for U.S. Attorney General, was rejected in 1992 because of her nonmainstream ideas about this very topic, even as she was nominated for being both female and black.

Conservatives felt that Guinere's record showed she went too far in yielding to minority interests. In a later interview, Guinere said that her record did not reflect that she was a liberal so much as it reflected that she was a mother. When children get into heated disputes with each other because they don't all want to play the same game, most mothers do not say, "Take a vote, and what the majority wants you will all abide by." Rather, they generally say, "OK, kids, take turns." Mothers know instinctively that, by taking turns, *all* participants are satisfied. When the majority rules, some of the kids—perhaps the same ones all the time—are left out or have their needs or wants (or what they can add to the mix) overlooked.

Let's assume that on this particular day the children's preferences look something like this:

Child #1:

I want to play a board game. (**numerator**)

I want to play with others. (**denominator**)

Child #2:

I want to play a board game. (**numerator**)

I want to play with others. (**denominator**)

Child #3:

$$\frac{\text{I want to play ball. (\textbf{numerator})}}{\text{I want to play with others. (\textbf{denominator})}}$$

Child #4:

$$\frac{\text{I want to play online games. (\textbf{numerator})}}{\text{I want to play with others. (\textbf{denominator})}}$$

The majority rule, or compromise, would be to allow all the children to play, so long as they played inside, either board games or online. But the lowest common denominator would accommodate all the children by recognizing that, whatever they did, they were playing with each other, either inside or outside the house. By making them take turns, each child gets exactly what he or she wants, and each also learns to accommodate what the others want. Not only does this make for a more satisfying solution for the parents, it also lays the groundwork for a more hospitable society.

Mothers know that taking turns is a great lowest common denominator, so it is no wonder that Guinere and others like her—executives, professionals, politicians—are frustrated by the insistence in many situations on majority rule. "The test of democracy," wrote philosopher John Mortimer, "is not that the majority should always get its way but how far minorities are respected."

Example #3: International Conflict

Whenever we discuss the intrinsic weakness in compromise, we are asked about the Middle East, or Ireland, or India and Pakistan. We believe that these seemingly intractable conflicts actually prove our point. Some of the most brilliant minds of the past half-century and the most delicate negotiations have failed to ensure permanent solutions. Compromise after compromise has led to the reopening of tensions because some group has not been satisfied.

In each case, the negotiations and the media tend to focus where the spotlight is instead of on the real nature of the conflict. Sometimes this expediency is because there is a confluence of forces beneath the surface, and they make an overwhelmingly complicated equation (somewhat like adding $1/5$, $1/9$, $1/x$, $1/33$, $1/y$, and $1/1000$). So compromises are much faster than finding the lowest common denominator. Sometimes, the lowest common denominator is politically incorrect (such as one party completely conquering and eliminating the other—a solution that has played itself out many times in the past). When the opposition was completely erased, the winner had long-term success. When the opposition was only partially erased, the winner eventually faced more conflict and challenge, and occasionally, an overturned victory.

We are not suggesting that nations or populations be wiped out because that is an unacceptable common denominator. So we look to the alternative: Take each component of the equation and satisfy it rather than model an answer to the whole.

For example, take the Middle East. Longer-term solutions would be possible if each subset of issues that made up the whole were approached with finding a common denominator. Take water. It is important for Israel not to give up access to water, and fresh water will become a major source of global conflict in coming years. Ensuring a way for everyone to have guaranteed access to fresh water is more important, ultimately, than which side has people living where. Given the enormous amount of money poured into the tensions arising from the Middle East conflict, wouldn't it make more sense to divert some of that money from arms and toward solving the water problem?

Example #4: When the Denominators Are 4 and 8

When you add 1/4 and 1/8, an interesting thing happens. The lowest common denominator is 8—both 4 and 8 go evenly into 8. Yet 1/8 is smaller than 1/4; in fact, it's half the size.

In the marketplace, the instinct is to compromise by catering to majority rule, or the single largest market, assuming that enough of the rest of the market will fall in behind the greater portion. The same is true regarding attracting voters. Math tells us differently.

Consider, for example, Ralph Lauren's long-term success in the fashion world (despite cyclical ups and downs). Many designers come and go, but he has had three decades of staying power. Perhaps you can find the clue to why in his store (popularly known as Ralphingdale's) on Madison Avenue in New York City. The store has a masculine look—lots of wood and brass and brick and rustic settings. Yet the majority of people who shop there are women. Women feel comfortable shopping in a beautifully appointed male environment. Men, however, do not feel at ease shopping in a feminine environment. They will go into Victoria's Secret, but most of the time it won't be by themselves. We have no research on this, but from observation and anecdotes, designing with compelling surroundings for men (in this case, the minority market) also serves to attract women (the majority)—and it doesn't work the other way around. The smaller population is the lowest common denominator.

Some years ago, J.C. Penney was exploring the creation of a catalog for arthritis products. The company had decided to put an attractive older woman on the cover because over two-thirds of the arthritis market is older women. But we suggested that the company use, instead, a handsome older man, a younger woman, and a child (some of the other one-third of the market, albeit smaller shares). The reason? An arthritis catalog that features an older woman on the cover would probably not appeal to younger men, or younger people generally. On the other hand, an older woman would have no problem shopping from an arthritis catalog whose cover featured men and younger people. Politically incorrect? Well, maybe. But psychologically correct? Probably.

About 20 years ago, a middle-aged male math teacher in an inner-city high school mentioned to us that the upscale magazine *Brides and Your New Home* was the bible of inner-city high school girls, the great majority of whom were black and Hispanic. The then-editor-in-chief, Barbara Tober, didn't know that these minority youngsters probably accounted for a large part of her newsstand sales because her readership data was heavily skewed to subscribers, who tended to be white and upscale. This male teacher, with no educated incapacity in the area of bridal magazines, was able to see what an alien could see: For Hispanic girls, their quinceañera ("sweet 15" birthday party) was a significant rite of passage that included, for many, the hiring of limousines, "bridesmaids" with matching dresses, elaborate parties, and expensive gifts. For them, a bridal magazine was the perfect template for their own event. For the black young women, the upscale wedding arrangements and peripherals such as those featured in the magazine were highly unlikely to be a part of their future, so the periodical pages represented their aspirations and fantasies, much as romance novels do for romance-deprived women.

So it may have been then (and may still be) that low-income minority teens make up a significant portion of that magazine's market. But, importantly, the question is: Should Tober have acknowledged this large hidden market and addressed it in some of the magazine's content (the compromise strategy)? Or should she have ignored them and gone with her known market? Definitely the second, since her known market in this case was the lowest common denominator. Her publication was aspirational. If she compromised that one bit, she would have lost not only her target market, but also the potentially even larger one she was actually paying no attention to.

Upscale market:	Downscale market:

I buy this bridal magazine to give me ideas. **(numerator)**

I buy this bridal magazine to give me ideas. **(numerator)**

$$\frac{\text{I buy this bridal magazine to give me ideas. (numerator)}}{\text{I want to be a success with people I admire. (denominator)}} + \frac{\text{I buy this bridal magazine to give me ideas. (numerator)}}{\text{I want to feel like the upscale people I admire. (denominator)}} = X \text{ (strategy)}$$

I want to be a success with people I admire. **(denominator)**

I want to feel like the upscale people I admire. **(denominator)**

The solution to satisfying both markets is to completely satisfy the upscale market. When you multiply the denominators (succeeding with upscale peers × feeling like upscalers), you in no way acknowledge a downscale readership.

Example #5: What's in a Definition?

Providers of luxury goods and services are delighted that the upscale market has swelled to previously inconceivable proportions. There are millions of millionaires in the U.S. alone. But what these companies are struggling with is how, as luxury items increasingly go mass market, to attract the new consumers. They tend to think the critical issue is pricing. Wrong. If you believe luxury equates with money, you have a hard time differentiating yourself when money is plentiful. Some people pay full price for first-class airline tickets, which could mean thousands of dollars for a round trip. However, because of frequent-flyer miles and more available dollars, these people are crowded by no- or low-fare travelers. Thus, domestic first-class flying is frequently no luxury. It often feels as much like a cattle car as economy class. Sometimes there's more room to stretch out in the half-empty coach section than in the packed first-class section.

The reason luxury has been equated with expensive is that money wasn't always so plentiful for so many people. Suffering from the educated incapacity of "luxury equals high cost," luxury goods manufacturers and sellers are compromising by raising prices, having sales, raising prices, having sales, and getting stuck in a vicious cycle that, in the end, does not solve their problem.

Consider the facts:

Fact 1:

A great many people have a great deal of money. **(numerator)**

Everyone would like to have the scarce things they believe could greatly improve their quality of life. **(denominator)**

Fact 2:

Many more people have access to high-priced goods and services, so these offerings are not as exclusive as they once were. **(numerator)**

Everyone would like to have the scarce things they believe could greatly improve their quality of life. **(denominator)**

If marketers paid attention to only the numerators, they would jack up their prices, or go to more limited distribution, or choose from a host of other compromise strategies that would attempt to get beyond the problem of remaining exclusive while still catering to the growing number of the affluent. However, if they cast their lot with the denominators—which, when multiplied, lead to the simple conclusion that perceived quality of life is more the issue than price—a whole new collection of strategies emerges.

The lowest common denominator here is, once again, to completely redefine the issue. Rather than equating luxury with cost, luxury should be defined as *scarcity*. That which is highly desirable and scarce is today's luxury, regardless of price. Thus, anything wanted that is in limited distribution is still a luxury. But anything that saves time also is a luxury. Whatever reduces stress is a luxury. Quality relationships and trusted associations are a luxury. Access to high-quality medical care, or excellent service in a commercial establishment, or competent and helpful people in bureaucracies, are luxuries. Seen this way, many companies that were not in the luxury business can now be, and many that were will lose ground if they don't shift to the common denominator, which is desirability plus scarcity, independent of price.

Here's another example of redefining the playing field to achieve a common denominator: In the early 1980s, Union Mutual Life Insurance of Portland, Maine, found itself in the middle of a battleground, with nuclear energy at the center. Pro-nuclear forces and anti-nuclear forces were poised to battle each other, via a referendum on the ballot, over whether to shut down the Maine Yankee nuclear facility. Union Mutual, one of the three largest energy users in Maine, had an economic stake in keeping the facility open. The company could have done what any major player in such a situation might have done, and indeed used to do—employ its financial, advertising, political, and employment muscles to influence the local media, politicians, and its workforce to lobby, and vote, pro-nuclear. But whether the company won or lost, it would be remembered in a negative light for having done that. In the long term, pushing the issue would compromise the good citizenship the company enjoyed in Portland and in the Statehouse.

So the company didn't compromise either its reputation or its stand on the issue. It didn't go halfway or partway. Instead, it redefined the issue.

The company created a resource center on nuclear energy, including many books written on the subject, pro and con. It made this available to all who were interested. It held seminars and debates, to which it invited some of the most knowledgeable people on nuclear energy—for and against—and opened these not only to their employees but also to the general public. And the company took out ads in papers, stating that it was in favor of Maine Yankee's remaining open and explaining its economic rationale. More prominently, the company challenged everyone in the state to get out and vote on this issue on Election Day, *whatever* their position. The company proclaimed this to be one of the most important citizenship issues of the decade and that every voter was responsible for making his or her views known. In effect, it said that democracy was as important as, if not more important than, where one stood on this issue.

Done. Just like that. The issue was no longer nuclear energy, but *citizenship*, a common denominator that united all sides. Win or lose at the polls, Union Mutual won a lot of points in the state. In the end, Maine Yankee stayed open, and the company celebrated. But Union Mutual's approach to dealing with the issue may have had more long-term economic payoff than any modest differential in energy prices. The lowest common denominator always works better than the compromise.

Example #6: John and Mary Public

Conflicting demands or issues arise in most households. Some are more inflammatory than others, but all of them raise the household temperature to uncomfortable levels.

Suppose your teenage son complains that his $15-a-week allowance is insufficient for his needs and that by his calculations, $25 is the minimum he needs. You don't believe his allowance should be any higher than $15. Arguments ensue, and there are the usual "when I was your age" stories. Eventually a compromise of $20 is reached—$5 more than you want to give him, and $5 less than he says he needs.

A lowest common denominator would require removing the word *allowance* from the equation and seeing the real issues. On the one hand, you believe he should get no more than $15 for doing nothing but being a card-carrying junior member of the household. On the other hand, with movies costing up to $10, he doesn't see how less than $25 can get him through the week. Fine. You should give him only $15 but figure out a way for him to earn the other $10—either by doing a chore that pays $10 a week, or one that pays $40 a month, or a major task that might earn him $500 for the year. Both parties get what they really want or need, and both are satisfied.

Son:

$$\frac{\text{I want a \$25-a-week allowance. (numerator)}}{\text{I need \$25 a week to get by. (denominator)}}$$

Parent:

$$\frac{\text{I resent giving my son more than \$15 a week.}}{\textbf{(numerator)}}$$

I don't care how much money my son has, as long as he doesn't get more than $15 a week for doing nothing. **(denominator)**

Multiply the denominators ($25 a week × only $15 a week for doing nothing) and the result is "Find a way to earn the additional $10 a week."

A couple we know (she is Hispanic, and he is Israeli) just had a second baby. They had arguments before their first child was born because they wanted an unusual ethnic name, but everything he wanted in Hebrew sounded horrible to her Spanish ear, and everything she wanted in Spanish sounded equally bad to his Israeli ear. One of their favorite places in the world is Hawaii. So, in the end, they gave both their children Hawaiian names. And they are delighted with the results.

The Bottom Line

You can now see that failure is likely to result whenever a solution is based on compromise. Longer-term success is more likely to come from finding the lowest common denominator.

It's not always easy to find one or more common denominators in the real world. Math is much easier than life. For all of us, the pressures to arrive at consensus make compromise the quickest, easiest way out. The extra effort, and perhaps the extra time, needed to find the lowest common denominator instead of the compromise will, in the long run, serve you much better. The real problem is that our minds fall into the trap of easy solutions, and too few of us think about looking away from where the streetlight is shining. Try it. The other side of the street is not completely dark. It's just puzzling. Express it as a mathematical puzzle, and your mind will be freed to find solutions that work.

Part IV

IMAGINING THE WAY: USING METAPHORS TO FREE YOUR MIND

People translate information into images. To a computer, the numbers in its memory are reality; to a human, the words in his or her memory are only symbols that create images. The word "chair" is not the reality of a chair; it is a symbol for a chair, and the word enables us to picture the actual object.

That's why some of the most effective learning devices are metaphors or similes. When we say that a woman's hair is like silk, we create a mental image both striking and concrete. We can both see and remember strongly. The best teachers and the best writers enable us to see vivid images and therefore to learn. The enduring popularity of Shakespeare owes much to his extraordinary genius in creating memorable images.

Good teachers have always enlisted metaphors. They shift the frame of reference away from the expected and usual, and, in providing a good story or illustration, help you see a particular situation more astutely and vividly. That is why metaphors can be among the most useful thinking techniques for understanding in a time of rapid change. The five that we believe are most important to a professional strategist's needs are the *Three-Legged Stools of the Political Agenda, Right-of-Way, Football Meets Shopping, Managing by Harnessing Evolution,* and *Self-Defeating and Self-Fulfilling Prophecies.*

Focusing on narrow political issues and social debates can prevent you from seeing the more important bigger picture. Politicians and socially conscious business executives get mired in the controversies of the moment. Looking on a larger scale can give you a clearer understanding of public wants and needs. The simple three-legged stool metaphor can help you do that.

Right-of-way, using images ranging from railroads to the Internet, reinforces a fundamental business truth that is too often neglected—even by those who should know better, such as academics.

Our football game metaphor illustrates in a striking way what really matters in the business-customer relationship.

More and more astute observers of business are looking to biological models to help create understanding of organizations and their behavior. Darwin's Theory of Evolution may be best at enabling executives to not only understand but effectively manage.

Ideas have power only if they lead to effective action. Things predicted or imagined can be made to either happen or not happen. Knowing that there are self-defeating and self-fulfilling prophecies could be the most powerful thinking technique of all.

12

THE THREE-LEGGED STOOLS OF THE POLITICAL AGENDA

So often people get mired in the mental traps and clichés of political ideology that it's a good idea to step back, take in the whole political landscape, and say, "If I had to summarize it all in a few sentences, what would I say?" Because we are asked this question so often and because today's over-informationed people want something brief (preferably a sound bite), our response is to see political forces for change more clearly by using a simple metaphor: It's all about *three-legged stools*.

Example #1: The Foundation of the Republic

Obviously, different countries are based on different political ideologies. We'll confine our metaphor to the U.S. and similar democracies. Let's assume that we can summarize the U.S. political entity in one word: the Republic. That, then, becomes the seat of the stool on

171

which we all sit. And that stool is balanced on three legs that under-
pin our Republic: *individual responsibility, institutional accountability*, and *charity*. That's it. In the end, all our sociological and economic attitudes and values, all our public and private judgments and
decisions, boil down to how we feel about and balance these three.
You may come to these out of religious leanings or teachings, out of
community experience, out of successes and travails, or out of exposure to all the good and bad aspects of the world. However you shape
your opinions within the body politic, they all come down to how you
feel about each of these three legs: individual responsibility, institutional accountability, and charity.

Individual responsibility is the expectation we have of ourselves
and others that, person by person, we share the load of preserving
what was good in the past, maximizing the productivity of the present,
and stewarding all that will come to be in the future. We are expected to pull our own weight and meet our commitments to ourselves,
our loved ones, and the greater community. This means providing
and caring for those who depend on you, protesting what you believe
is wrong, voting in order to preserve democracy, serving the country
in war and peace in whatever way may be demanded, paying your fair
share of taxes, and being mindful and watchful of anyone or anything
that could threaten to undermine your way of life. It means serving
on juries, keeping your property clean, not abusing public resources
and amenities, obeying the laws of your community and your nation,
being in charge of your health and well-being, and not relying on others for that which you are able-bodied and able-minded enough to do
for yourself. It also means conducting yourself in a mature and reasonable manner in all aspects of public intercourse.

This all sounds like a tall order, but it is, after all, the ingredients
of one leg of the stool on which this country rests. Individual responsibility does not necessarily entail all of this in other societies and cultures, but it has always been all of this in the U.S.

The second leg is *institutional accountability*. This is the integrity you expect of the systems and structures put into place to guard our personal liberties, pave the way for executing our personal responsibility, and oversee the infrastructure needed to keep our society going. Whether the institutions are our legislative and regulatory bodies, our armed forces, our incorporated economic entities, our schools, the White House, or the Social Security Administration, you expect them all, along with all the other thousands of institutions out there designed to serve you, to do just that—serve you. The *social contract* on which that all rests, that binds them into one leg of the stool, is their accountability to us: we the citizens, the workers, the students, the investors, the retirees. We take that social contract seriously, and as a result of progress and abuse, accountability is written and rewritten into the system day by day, year by year, century by century. It means that all institutions—including business—must earn and retain the consent of the people by conforming with how they perceive the social contract. It is a hallmark of our Republic. Thus, it is one of the three legs on which that Republic rests.

The third leg of the stool, *charity*, would have escaped the notice of most observers, but not those who are most astute. One of Alexis de Tocqueville's most insightful observations about early America was that our fledgling society was characterized by people organizing themselves around causes. Good works, he noted, were carried out voluntarily by civic organizations created around these causes. To de Tocqueville, this was uniquely American and uniquely effective in establishing and maintaining a sense of community.

It is an essential foundation of our Republic that we take the business of charity seriously. We have always personally committed our dollars, time, attention, and energy to those who, for reasons of physical or mental disability, cannot pull their own weight or represent themselves through their own voice. This goes beyond people to include natural resources, artistic endeavors, animals, and posterity. We would not be American if this were not a fundamental part of our political fiber.

It is from this single three-legged stool metaphor that all else flows.

Example #2: The Political Parties

Everyone has a different view on how to interpret these three legs and how long to make each one. Here, too, we will simplify to more easily describe political life. The Republic has traditionally been based on a two-party system that, at present, means Republican and Democrat, and a third group—those who elect to be considered neither. Again, three legs.

Republicans, usually more conservative, have traditionally sought to lengthen the individual responsibility leg, shorten the institutional accountability leg, and weaken the charity leg by cleaving it in half and attempting to bind one of those halves to individual responsibility while imposing moral judgments on the other half.

The more liberal Democrats, on the other hand, have typically sought to shorten the individual responsibility leg, lengthen the institutional accountability leg, and greatly lengthen the charity leg while making no moral judgments about any of its components.

All of us who sit on the stool observe the obvious. Under neither Republican nor Democratic condition is the stool perfectly balanced. We constantly experience discomfort, dislocation, and, on occasion, fear of falling off. That's why, in December 2000, when a Gallup poll asked Americans about their political affiliation, 42 percent identified themselves as independent rather than as Republican or Democrat. In their book *The Radical Center: The Future of American Politics*, Ted Halstead and Michael Lind observe that, while analysts talk about electoral "realignments" in favor of one party or another, what is really occurring is a large-scale political "dealignment." There is a great deal of popular resentment of what is perceived as extremist holds on both parties. This gives the illusion of a sharply divided nation when, in truth, the alienated majority has a great deal in common with each other and is more interested in balancing the stool than in fighting culture wars. While the extremes inform the middle (see Chapter 4), and the middle does move, it is never happy being dictated to or governed by either extreme.

In a similar vein, George Lakoff writes, in *Moral Politics: How Liberals and Conservatives Think*, that this political division is a moral division, at the extremes, about what makes a "good" person and what is "right." He sees it as harking back to the family metaphor of child raising and the debate between strictness and nurturing. The more that children are brought up with "strict father" values, the more future conservatives we will have because this morality promotes self-discipline, individual responsibility, self-reliance, enterprise, competitiveness, and the free-market system. The "nurturing parent" model, on the other hand, leads to empathetic behavior, the promotion of fairness, and helping those who cannot help themselves.

Conservative Republicans versus liberal Democrats. Those are the two legs of the political system that represent the extremes. The rest of us are holding up the third leg, even while we all pile on top of the seat—an acrobatic feat to be sure. As leg *and* occupant, we hold on for dear life. But more and more, through hope or despair, we try to rise above it all. We keep the stool, the Republic, below us as a point of reference but don't completely trust those in charge of maintaining the integrity of those three legs—whether party or principle—upon which it is based. This is the dynamic of U.S. politics. It has always been so. And it will always be so. At least as long as we are the Republic we know ourselves to be.

When your employer took care of your health-care and retirement needs, it was not so important to you that the institutions delivering these were subject to strict accountability. Your individual responsibility was lessened, and therefore so was your concern for institutional accountability.

Now that you must take on more responsibility for your health expenditures and retirement income, however, it becomes more important to you that elected officials and regulators hold the health-care system and financial services industry more accountable. This is a clear example of how the more we lengthen one leg, the more we must lengthen the other. These three-legged stool metaphors, therefore, help you put political forces in balance with regard to both our Republic and the political parties that set the agenda.

Example #3: The Male/Female Perspective

Ever since the early part of the 20th century, and the granting of suffrage to women, the body politic has had to face a new reality. The female of the species was going into the American voting booth, and politics would never be the same. Roughly half the population, and an even larger segment over time of those who actually vote, women have advanced a different agenda and therefore have introduced more debate and confusion into the process. All to the good. And all to the chagrin of those who liked the days of private deals made during poker games in cigar-filled rooms, using old boys' networks, brute force, or competitive one-upmanship.

But can we simplify the difference between the male and female agenda in the political arena by using the three-legged stool? Yes.

The male perspective, stereotypically (always with ample exception), is that the seat of our modern world is the *economy*, and the three legs are *transportation systems, communication systems*, and *capital formation*—a noble agenda that has taken us quite far from the hunter-gatherer society, past the industrial era, and well through the post-industrial era. Money, wealth, and progress were all seen to derive from these three legs. Build them strong, and the seat—the economy—can hold more and more people piled on top of each other in a hierarchy.

Most women, on the other hand, see a world in which the seat of the stool is *society*, and the three legs are *health*, *education*, and *ecological integrity*. Tend to these legs, value them, and strengthen them, and the future is assured and more people have room to sit side by side.

This is not a question of who is right and who is wrong; both are right. Thus, we can safely predict a more complex set of political priorities in which all these factors combined will be expected to meld into a six-legged chaise lounge. Businesses will play a part in this by increasingly awakening to the blended opportunities that range from micro-lending to energy alternatives to educational software.

Many more large companies are reporting openly on their efforts to contain or reduce environmental damage. Other companies strive to be known as family-friendly by establishing such things as parental leave programs and part-time or odd-hour tracks for both mothers and fathers. As more women affect corporate legislation and regulation by gaining political office, as has happened in recent elections, and as more women arrive in executive suites, business can expect that there will be growing pressures to encourage both the male and female stools. In recent years, some of the leading law and accounting firms have come to understand the pressing need to accommodate women's different requirements and circumstances. They have made it possible for women to become partners even though they can't necessarily work full time all the time. And as these women gain more clout in legal and financial arenas, this too will further strengthen the three legs of the female/societal stool.

Astute politicians are also coming to understand the importance of combining the stools. They see that this is what people expect, and the political entities will have to respond to survive. They also understand that, in a time of great change, what the combined stools look like will change. That will require constant monitoring for leadership to be truly and constantly responsive. We are not so naïve as to think it will be easy. Along with the conflicts between the Left and the Right, the tension between the male and female views will fuel much political debate—from war to welfare, from criminal justice to civil rights, from the welfare of children to the welfare of the aged, from foreign aid to domestic abuse—over the next half-century and probably for as long as the Republic holds.

Using the three-legged stool image is a powerful way to see the pulls and tugs of the political arena clearly and accurately and to predict when controversy will arise. It will also help you to see how organizations can capture the enthusiasm of a broad array of stakeholders and constituents and to better understand how new and emerging issues will affect that.

13

RIGHT-OF-WAY

Some business school professors like to make the point that the railroads went into decline in the U.S. because they thought they were in the railroad business. Their error, the professors say, was not realizing that they were in the *transportation* business. This seemingly enlightened view is, in reality, another example of educated incapacity. The truth is that the railroads' really big mistake was not realizing that they were in the *right-of-way* business. When the telegraph and telephone companies and mail deliverers came along and sought to use the land alongside the tracks, the railroads, being in only the railroad business, said sure, why not? In doing so, they missed the opportunity to own and profit from the entire communications business. They gave away their right-of-way.

For the railroads to be built in the U.S., the federal government had to invest a great deal of resources in the effort. Indeed, the government did three things that could not have been done by the private sector: It revised immigration policy to attract cheap labor to lay the tracks, it used the military to protect the advancing enterprise, and, perhaps most important of all, it exercised the right of eminent domain to take private property from citizens to allow the railroad to pass through. Then, with the private sector thus protected and subsidized, vast investments were made in the leading-edge technologies of the day: steel, power, bridge-building, tunneling, blasting. All these enabled the railroads to pass over water, through mountains, over deserts, into forests, and past marauders.

From 1849 to 1882, thousands of young Chinese peasants were brought to the U.S. to provide cheap labor, primarily for the railroads. The Central Pacific Railroad Company alone employed some 15,000 Chinese laborers.

Challenges to using eminent domain to take private property for the benefit of commercial enterprises were defeated by the courts in the 19th century. Eminent domain was justified on the grounds that railroads were the equivalent of highways, and the government has a duty to provide public ways.

Many people got very rich from railroads (like Vanderbilt), and many others lost their shirts on railroad stocks. In the end, after all this sweat, toil, and good will, the telegraph companies came along and asked the railroads if, in exchange for free telegraph service, they could use the right-of-way alongside the track to erect their telegraph poles, and the railroads said, "Sure, go ahead." Then the telephone companies asked the same, and the railroads said, "Sure, go ahead." Then the post office asked the same for its postal drops, and the railroads said, "Sure, go ahead." Western Union's relatively low cost railroad contracts enabled that company to dominate communication in the mid-to-late 1800s. They did it because the railroads so thoughtlessly bartered away, for access to communications, the real key to their future—their right-of-way.

The railroads are the closest parallel we have to the recent development of the Internet. It was begun by the government as the DARPAnet to ensure uninterrupted communication between academia, the military, and the government. Then private investors moved in. The leading-edge technologies of the day were employed, and billions were spent to "lay down the tracks" to the general public. But this time around, the right-of-way is not being given away. It is central to any revenue model that might exist for the dot-coms that haven't blown up. Yahoo!, Amazon, eBay, and others are using the tracks they have put down to collect tolls from those who want to sell using those rights-of-way.

Every business and professional has spent years laying down commercial tracks. It is curious and, indeed, amazing that few have understood how to capitalize on their right-of-way—to their customers, suppliers, creditors, investors, employees, and so on. Valuing this metaphor and converting it to opportunity could leverage one of the most currently underutilized assets in the economy.

Right-of-way, the lesson the railroads didn't learn, will be a key to business success in the future. Having and controlling access to customers (and suppliers) is what will separate many winners from losers. In an increasingly competitive environment, the key to survival will be holding on to customers—something that is becoming difficult in these competitive times.

The Internet continues to offer more efficient distribution options. Distance is unimportant in an economy dominated by electronic activities, and industries such as financial services, software, and data processing are, in effect, "weightless." Thus, they all can explore strategic alliances in the rights-of-way of cyberspace. Online grocery delivery services expanded into video and dry cleaning delivery, shoe repairs, and firewood orders.

Example #1: Customer-Centered Versus Sale-Centered

Most businesses today, certainly those that deal directly with consumers, like to think they have a lock on their right-of-way because they think of themselves as being *customer-centered*. Are they really? Reflect on your own experiences when you had problems with companies you have done business with. Think of the impersonal automated telephone system. Think of the customer service department, perhaps operating out of another country, that doesn't know who you are and doesn't really care. Think of the overriding emphasis on the company's rules and procedures over the customer's well-being. Do you really believe those companies are customer-centered?

The truth is, most companies are *sale-centered* rather than customer-centered. That is, their focus and all their resources are directed to that first transaction in the acquiring of a customer—the initial sale. Service after the sale, particularly at a time when there are worker shortages and labor costs are rising, is seen as a controllable cost, an investment that should get maximum returns. In reality, this area often experiences cutbacks and quotas.

These developments in business, often guided by cost-benefit analyses, are generally seen as resulting in more efficient companies. We question that on several grounds. First, the focus on running a business should be *effectiveness* rather than *efficiency*. It would be nice if they were the same thing, but they are not. Efficiency is doing things right; effectiveness is doing the right things. When it comes to keeping customers, it's more in any company's long-term interest to be effective.

Focusing on right-of-way enables companies to see and benefit from the potential in all customers. Amazon.com looks not necessarily at the customer but at the customer's shelves. What other things, the company asks itself, does the customer need on those shelves? Why shouldn't we, already having access to the customer, be the one to supply those things? This is recognition that access to the customers—right-of-way—may well be the most valuable asset a business can have in a time of growing competition.

Years ago, you often heard people say such things as "I always buy Fords; my dad always bought Fords." How often do you hear that kind of thing today? Not very. Trends indicate this is likely to be heard even more rarely in the future. Ford will have to re-create its right-of-way to the next generation of consumers, as will other automakers.

Add to this what appears to be a growing hostility toward business, fueled by such developments as the Enron, Arthur Anderson, and Tyco scandals. In addition, surveys consistently show that people see big companies as insensitive to consumers. In recent years, we have seen significant increases in multimillion-dollar judgments against businesses in product liability and discrimination cases. According to an article in *Forbes* on May 13, 2002, the average jury award in product liability cases quadrupled between 1994 and 2002—to $6.8 million. *American Demographics*, in May 2002, reported on a 2001 Harris survey showing that trust in business and its leaders has fallen substantially since 1994. In 1994, more than half of those polled believed government regulation of business does more harm than good. Only about 40 percent believed that in 2001.

In such an environment, building a brand becomes as important for the company as it is for the product. For people faced with an abundance of choices and an overwhelming volume of information, trust in a brand can be enormously helpful in decision-making and actually becomes a right-of-way. In today's more skeptical environment, trust in the company brand is created by the perception that the customer receives fair, honest, just, and consistent treatment from the company.

Example #2: Tunnel Vision

In 1930 the book *The World in 2030 A.D.*, by the Earl of Birkenhead, forecast transatlantic air transport. The book also forecast that, since this was a development in intercontinental transport, it would be run by the steamship companies. Those companies, after all, were in the business of crossing oceans. However, they believed themselves to be in the steamship business. So they could not see what Lord Birkenhead saw, and now all they have is the cruise business.

Every state in the U.S. has a Department of Motor Vehicles. This agency, as motorists (often angrily) know, controls access to and granting of drivers' licenses and vehicle registrations. That's all it does. But what an enormous and unrealized opportunity this represents for state governments. The DMV owns an immensely valuable right-of-way. Everyone who wants to get a license and register or transfer a car or truck has to go through the DMV. The question state governments should, but don't, ask is what other products, programs, and messages can be sent along that right-of-way?

How about selling driver-education materials and programs? How about low-cost loans for low-income people? How about insurance pools for people insurance companies don't want to insure? How about securing insurance for new drivers? How about charging a fee for those who want an appointment so they won't have to stand in line?

This is not to say that state governments should usurp the prerogatives of—or compete with—business. But thinking about the DMV as possessing a right-of-way could help governments make that operation profitable and at the same time more useful and beneficial to the public. Indeed, many private enterprises might want to use the DMV as a right-of-way to reach millions of drivers.

Movie theater operators know, at least to some degree, that they have an opportunity to sell other things to their customers. Take popcorn, for example. That snack and others are sold at elevated prices to what amounts to a captive audience. According to one study, most movie theater profit—one-third of gross revenues—comes from selling food and beverages. Given this example of leveraging a right-of-way, and the obvious willingness of moviegoers to spend money at the theater as part of their pleasurable self-indulgence, what else can theater operators provide? What can they do further that would fatten their profits and enhance their customers' experiences? How can we all learn from their example?

Example #3: The Infrastructure Dilemma

There have been many changes in how we plan for, finance, and build infrastructure today. The telecommunications industry, in particular, is developing substantial infrastructure, whether it is Internet applications, optical technology, satellite radio, or third-generation (3G) mobile communication services.

In the past, infrastructure was largely built based on predictable future demands. Today, it is increasingly being built based on unknowable future demand. Previously, projects typically were financed in the public sector. Today, the money comes from a large pool of private capital.

The Internet began as a U.S. government program to make sure that our communications system would be able to function should the country come under attack. Only later did it become commercial as the technology became more widely available and affordable. Although dot-com mania has been curbed for now, diverse Internet infrastructure applications are constantly emerging.

European operators have spent more than $174 billion on licenses for a 3G wireless communications systems. They now face building the necessary infrastructure while their credit ratings suffer. Many skeptics are asking if sufficient demand exists to justify this investment. It is estimated that Britain will need to build at least 100,000 new towers for 3G to function.

In today's fast-moving economy and market, it is increasingly common to plan, develop, and build projects before we know for sure if they will even be needed. Just as companies produce smaller-scale goods and services that they *anticipate* the consuming public will want, the same thing is happening with large-scale infrastructure products and services. Planners anticipate the need for 3G to satisfy greater bandwidth and the continuing convergence of wireless and the Internet. They anticipate that consumers will want the service, and the infrastructure is built before that belief is tested.

Corporations and organizations that serve them need to be aware of the lead time, investment, and supply-chain ripple effect that can occur when major infrastructure is involved—not to mention the enormous risks. Investors are increasingly leery of investing in capital projects that are likely to lead to more backlogs. Consumers are warier about moving to new technologies, because the infrastructure won't be there. These same consumers are being pushed forward rapidly by technology, but back-office systems and willingness to invest are lagging behind. More technological advances—such as computer-controlled vehicles, smart cards, and smart materials—will all require massive infrastructure construction or overhaul. Business risks are heightened because leadership, knowledge, and the direction of technology are not in sync, and large-scale public funding is unlikely. Yet we continue to see proposed megaprojects not based on current demand.

The challenge for businesses and governments with enhanced distribution efficiencies is that the *competition* also benefits from these structural shifts. In many cases, the decreased distribution expense allows new companies to enter markets that were previously untapped. Therefore, it becomes increasingly important to know not only who your competitors are now but who they will be in the future. Netgrocer.com, an Internet grocery delivery service, was a classic example of companies totally unrelated to the grocery business— American Airlines, Microsoft, IBM, and FedEx—joining forces to distribute groceries. What this strategic alliance was *really* doing was gaining access to the customer using the companies' existing right-of-way. New business opportunities can proliferate because the rules about who is in what business are being rewritten. Access to the customer will become more important than one's initial business strategy or distribution channel, and the points of access will multiply manyfold. The massive investment in 3G may yet portend rights-of-way we can only now speculate about—for use by organizations from hospitals to stock markets, and for everything from automobiles to refrigerators.

There are new opportunities for doing business globally that were previously hindered by the lack of infrastructure in developing countries. These countries can now participate in global markets because they can, for example, forgo building massive power plants and instead build point-of-purchase fuel cell power plants. Eliminating this huge energy infrastructure expense is analogous to circumventing the traditional telephone land-line infrastructure and going straight to a cellular system. That has leveled the playing field in terms of global communication, so it has the potential to do the same for energy. And who will have the right-of-way in supplying fuel cells? Will current gas stations utilize it, or will they give it away, to, say, parking lots or Wal-Mart?

At a time of Wall Street-induced timidity, when businesses fear that massive investments in infrastructure will adversely affect analyses of their stock potential, a long-range perspective is essential. For tomorrow's relentlessly competitive environment, right-of-way may well be *the* key asset of business. It costs money—lots of it—to establish and control access. Failure to leverage it will be disastrous.

Example #4: The Amazon River

Why, after not making a profit year after year, was Amazon.com's stock valued so highly? Because, to astute observers, it represented the present value of Amazon's future business. Amazon is the model for the future. As discussed earlier, its true value lies in its ability to control access to a growing number of customers. That asset, unlike a specific product or products, becomes even more valuable in a world in which products are increasingly short-lived.

Like forts that dominated the banks of rivers of old, control of distribution channels means power. As authors have long known, writing a very good book may not profit you much if your publisher has no clout with bookstores.

What Are Your Potential Rights-of-Way?

Having invested months or years in building a business or a professional practice or an organization or a network, one or more of the following represent assets that you need to leverage adequately to provide additional returns:

- **Your customers or clients**—Who else wants access to them?

- **Your real estate**—To whom can you sublease, or comarket products or services with on-site—as supermarkets have done with pharmacies and banks? The flagship Macy's department store, located on Herald Square in Manhattan, is only now using its 7th Avenue building front as an automated billboard, leveraging a right-of-way to millions of eyeballs each year.

- **Your suppliers**—What can you do that is valuable to them in expanding their client base and that you can charge for? A major automobile company provides "stamps of approval" to all its suppliers, which enables them to do business with the company. These suppliers then use that approval to market themselves to other companies. The auto company never charged for that, in effect giving away a precious right-of-way.

- **Your advertising**—Whose logo or message can you profitably share your space with, as cobranding has allowed some companies to do?

- **Your contacts**—What might they need that you can procure for them for a fee, such as referring potential hires or running networking events? One entrepreneur, Susan Stautberg, has leveraged her rights-of-way over the course of her career. A veteran of White House journalism and a major public relations agency, she went on to leverage her people contacts by starting a publishing company and speaker's bureau. When the book publishing business became difficult in the mid-'90s—especially for independents—she was at an impasse. We advised her to once again leverage her right-of-way, which was clearly embedded in a network of diverse, highly-placed, talented, knowledgeable people. Stautberg developed PartnerCom, a company that sets up advisory boards for companies, governments, and nonprofits. Her ability to tap almost anyone is multiplied by each new person she connects with. Stautberg represents the growing number of individuals who, like larger organizations, are figuring out how to profit from the investments they have made in developing a right-of-way.

Remember, the right-of-way is grounded in what has already been a sizeable investment for purposes of providing a known product or service to a known user group. When you escape the mental trap of the business you think you're in, creative leveraging is not only possible, it is desirable. One caveat: You must establish trust that whatever you promise can and will be delivered. Therefore, it's critical that the integrity of your original entity is not only maintained but enhanced in leveraging your right-of-way.

14

FOOTBALL MEETS SHOPPING

Human activity has almost from the beginning been centered around both family and commerce, with commerce composed of trading, buying, and selling.

Anthropologists tell us that the primitive human, the hunter-gatherer, was programmed to seek out success in two important ways. The man sought rank and status, which enabled him to get the most desirable women and lead the hunt and territorial activities. The woman sought resources, whether to garner daily food for the family or to assure her children a healthier, longer-lived existence.

As we advance into the new millennium, we are still subconsciously guided by those same primitive programs. But with the economy radically changed many times over since those earlier societies, it seems that perhaps the most significant way we have evolved to match the biological imperatives of our past with the new economic environment is via shopping.

We Always Shopped

In past centuries, successful towns grew up around merchant trade. Whether the stops on the Silk Road of the Ancient East or the frontier towns of the American Wild West, both men and women were drawn to the resources and opportunities of commercial avenues, open-air markets, and busy ports. We have come a long way from those earlier bazaars and docks. Even in the underdeveloped world, goods are more in demand, and consumer activity is expanding into the most unlikely venues. For example, regional high-tech jails are replacing county jails, and the first thing to be built after communications and water and sewer systems are retailers such as Wal-Mart.

Stores of all kinds appear everywhere. There is no question that a glut of stores could be a problem if stores do not evolve in response to consumers' changing expectations. When that happens, retail shakeups occur, and traditional stores focus on cost-cutting and customer satisfaction. Discount stores and warehouse clubs boom at the expense of slow-to-change middle-brand retailers.

Discretionary shopping is now about lifestyle experiences, and these keep evolving over time, too, changing how people shop. One store in San Francisco and another in New York make you feel as if you're in someone's home, able to buy the furniture, clothing, and accessories in each, as well as eat gourmet meals. Mobile commerce and messages targeted to individual customers further alter shopping.

Even in an area such as health, Americans are changing how they shop, now spending almost $30 billion for alternative therapies. Despite heavy opposition from the medical establishment, there is great competition, even among hospitals, for patients (customers) and revenue. Pharmaceutical companies now spend over $2 billion on TV ads. In 1991, only one prescription medicine was advertised; now more than 50 are.

We have changed greatly since our hunter-gatherer roots. No longer is all shopping a practical task to be done quickly. With each succeeding century it becomes who we are and how we live. It now includes entertainment, adventure, and emotional rewards.

America and Americans are the forerunners of 21st century shopping society. One indicator of the future is how people exhibit status. For example, they no longer do it just by prominently attending cultural events. What makes towns and cities great are no longer just physical assets (ports, rivers, mineral resources). People want "livability" and technology. They want hip environments, with all that means, in terms of cafés, a diversity of culture, and shopping all becoming far more important in sustaining vibrant centers of population.

Men, who in the past were the merchants and guild members, are now on an equal shopping footing with women. In an economy that casts employee loyalty adrift, men now express their rank and status through their purchases, whether electronic or automotive or recreational, or through venture capital. These are the modern equivalents of bringing home the largest mammoth or the most booty from the enemy or buying the biggest house in the suburbs. Home improvements have become a major form of shopping, and even here, men and women are participating in equal numbers.

Even antimaterialists shop. They may not buy things, but they shop for experiences, and they buy into causes. Maybe you can't sell them SUVs, but you can sell them hybrid cars, meditation tapes, and even concert tickets.

This brings us to the institutions that must now market to all these people, wants, and needs. Modern commerce, a product of post-agricultural societies, takes its place in the passage of all modern history. In that timeline, some time has gone by, but much is left to go. What we think of as today's advanced marketplace may be the equivalent of being only 10 minutes into a 60-minute football game. To explain the hierarchy of strategies needed in this highly competitive environment, let's use a football metaphor in which it's 10 minutes into the game.

First Down

You are a marketer. You are on offense. It's only the first quarter, and it's first down. For you and all the other sellers of goods and services today, the first-down move is some combination of one or more of the following: *price, quality, convenience, assortment.* Today, it all starts there. If you can't compete on any of these fronts, you could lose the ball immediately to the opposition (competition). So you have to concentrate on having a product or service that is of excellent quality, or great price, or that offers a full range of options from which the buyer might choose, or is very convenient to shop for. One of these is good; two or more is better.

But the problem is that the defense is lining up against the offense.

Competing on Price

Linux, a *free* operating system, will soon become the number 1 version of UNIX (an open approach at the opposite end from Microsoft, which keeps its system proprietary). Increasingly, firms are giving away web-based services to fuel product sales on their sites or to gain revenue from advertisements. While drug companies widely advertise their prescription drugs, employers and health plans are pushing cheaper generics. Private-label makers have long been gaining shelf space against such powerful brand names as Kellogg and Nabisco. Supermarkets earn 25 percent more on store brands even though they are priced 10 to 24 percent below name brands. Day traders have accounted for 12 percent of NASDAQ volume, putting pressure on the big market makers to trim their spread, saving investors billions of dollars. Digital distribution of content, like music, makes pirating (free and unauthorized downloading of information) commonplace. Deregulation of the energy utilities is sending companies scrambling to keep old customers and find new ones as lowest cost begins to erode monopolistic pricing. Even low-income residential areas—where the few retailers that remained charged higher prices and could corner the $85 billion spent there—are now becoming attractive to lower-price chains.

Fast travel and the Internet make global comparison shopping a reality, forcing an entire country, the UK, to lower prices in all categories from cars to supermarkets. The Net allows consumers everywhere to find the lowest price anywhere through comparisons and auctions. Within 25 years, businesses and individuals will routinely use mobile intelligent agents to perform tasks such as shopping and negotiating online. In one simulation of the upcoming digital marketplace, the cybereconomy degenerated into vicious price wars and market crashes. For now, more and more consumers are getting a free ride from retailers because customers go into stores to see, feel, experience and learn about products, and then they go home and order them at the best price over the Internet.

Lowest cost has made companies, but it can break them because of an even lower cost and more convenient entrant. Except perhaps for Wal-Mart, whose size and ruthlessly efficient buying system enable it to profitably keep its prices lower, competing on the basis of least cost can become a dangerously short-lived game. For a while it looks as if, with sufficient volume, profits are guaranteed, so companies seek to cut costs everywhere through the value and production chains to get to the consumer as cheaply as possible. In doing so, competitors block each other's advantage, and few yards, if any, are gained.

New measures of a company's value emerge all the time. Two of the latest, EVA (economic value added) and MVA (market value added), are increasingly attracting CEOs, money managers, and analysts. Interestingly, none of the companies with the biggest market caps as well as highest MVA compete as lowest-cost sellers (GE, Coca-Cola, Procter & Gamble, Philip Morris, Bristol-Myers Squibb, Microsoft, Intel, Exxon, Pfizer).

According to J. Bradford DeLong, professor of economics at the University of California, Berkeley, the current economy is new because of its potential to create never-ending cost reductions driven by technological innovation. Money is being made by selling goods for *less* than they cost and relying on the learning curve to lower costs the next year.

Competing on Quality, Assortment, and Convenience

In the future, *caveat emptor* will matter less. The purchaser will increasingly expect quality from the seller and, if it isn't delivered, will demand redress. So quality has become a given if one is to succeed in the marketplace in the long run. Because of advances in quality control, most of the time it is harder to distinguish between deliverers on the basis of quality alone.

In the case of assortment, retailers, beginning with big-box formats like Toys 'R' Us and culminating in cyberspace with eBay, have raised the bar. Now, within categories, assortment is assured by many more players than ever. In office supplies, there are Office Depot, Staples, and Wal-Mart. In hardware, there are Home Depot, Lowe's, and Wal-Mart. Of course, an equal variety of choices is available in these same categories at Target, Ikea, Sears, local chains, from catalogs, and on the Internet.

In the case of convenience, product is everywhere—at the click of a mouse, in strip malls and regional malls, via catalogs and telephone, from TV, at flea markets, at airports—all via technology on our person or within the moment of wherever we may be. The real differentiator here is time until delivery, not accessibility of purchase. This all means that the defense has lined up against this price/quality/convenience/assortment first-down offense. The seller doesn't get as many yards as it used to, and now it's second down.

Second Down

The second-down move, in the majority of cases, is personalization or customization, whether of the product or the service itself, or the service attendant to it, or the environment in which it is delivered.

Sometimes, customization can be a first-down strategy. For example, there are times when you will travel 30 miles to a restaurant that has a limited menu, high prices, and mediocre food because it is the most romantic place within a 40-mile radius. But if there are many romantic places within a 40-mile radius, this restaurant couldn't get away with its below-par offerings, and it would have to satisfy the basics.

If done well, customization is a good offensive move. More often than not, it is executed rather poorly. In the early 1970s, we ran a futures-research program called the Trend Analysis Program for an insurance industry trade group. It was the dawn of computerized personalization of mass mailings, which aimed to make the recipient of the marketing message feel as though the seller was talking individually to him or her. At that time, one of us got a letter from *Newsweek* addressed to Mrs. Trend A. Program. It was an offer "that wasn't made to everyone, Mrs. Program. We believe you and the entire Program family will benefit from this highly targeted offer."

Three decades later, few people feel differently about the so-called personalization or customization in mass selling. When pet dogs receive preferred-customer credit card offers, and seniors receive select offers for parenting magazines, all pretending to be designed especially for their needs, you know why cynicism here remains high. On the other hand, clothing fitted to one's body using virtual reality or interactive shopping services, bicycles or cars that are manufactured based on each customer's choices of options, and paint that can be mixed based on one person's preference are all advances onto the customization front in a meaningful way. Still, in each category the competition moves in more quickly to execute equally well (or equally poorly, as the case may be). Furthermore, customization—individually tailoring products and easy do-it-yourself items, from home décor to health remedies to food to artwork—may work as a differentiator for a while, but eventually mass customization will drive down prices here too. Thus, the defense is more effectively lining up against this offense, and you get fewer yards on second down.

Third Down

Now it's third down. Most of the time the third-down move is *reputation*. This refers not to the quality of the particular good or service, but to the overall image of the delivering institution. It also refers to being aligned with the values of consumers. All other things being equal, what the organization stands for in the eyes of the greater community becomes an important consideration. It would be nice if, in an advanced and civilized society, this were the first-down move. But that's not the case most of the time. First the customer thinks about herself, and then she considers the seller's citizenship.

Reputation is like ice. It takes a long time for it to freeze and take shape. But a 1-degree increase in temperature can destroy it almost immediately. So a negative reputation (use of child labor, executive wrongdoing, merchandising misinformation) is far more likely to have an adverse impact on the seller than a positive reputation is to benefit it. That's because the defense has been lining up against this offense, too, with many more purveyors of goods and services going into cause-related marketing (saving the environment, funding research into breast cancer, supporting education) and image-enhancing programs (being family-friendly, promoting women and minorities, touting morality and ethics, loaning out executives). The paradox is that, although it is becoming necessary to execute this move, it is getting harder to make the customer sit up, take notice, and act selectively based on it. Thus, it's more difficult than ever to get enough yards on this third-down tactic to score a touchdown.

Fourth Down

This brings us to fourth down. The fourth-down move is generally prescribed by the seller's perceived field position. If the seller believes it is in lousy field position (say, on its own 25-yard line), the fourth-down move at this point in the game invariably is a punt. In the end, punting is giving the ball to the opposition and putting yourself on the defense.

In the world of competitive marketing, this is basically saying, "I give up. I've tried everything, it hasn't worked, and I don't feel good about where I stand, so let me do some damage to my competitors and see what they do. I'll spend all my energies for the next part of the game defending against them. If they do well, I'll learn from their moves and hopefully do better next time." The reason this sounds so familiar is that, in this hotly contested marketplace, we see a great deal of punting taking place. It seems the majority of sellers see themselves in poor field position.

Some marketers have more confidence and vision. They are surer of their potential, they see themselves on the competitors' 30-yard line, and as a fourth-down strategy they elect to attempt a field goal. If they make it, they put 3 points on the scoreboard, which may eventually win the game. This puts the ball in the air, away from the playing field (which would mean going head-to-head with the competitors for a touchdown with customers). As such, in the world of commerce this translates into a joint venture, strategic alliance, merger, or acquisition. Maybe it will win the day. But it is no guarantee of long-term success.

However, if the seller sees itself as being in a really good field position—say, 3 yards from the goal—the fourth-down move is clearly to go for the touchdown—to go all the way to win the customers and conceivably the game. This is the toughest option because getting the ball over from here is met with serious defense on the part of the competition. That's why this fourth-down move is the toughest of all to execute, although the rewards are greatest. What is the most difficult thing to execute well in the world of commerce? *Relationship*. Creating a true relationship with the customer.

Marketers and business executives everywhere bemoan what they see as a severe decline in customer loyalty. But loyalty is as impermanent as everything else today. It's not given; it has to be earned anew every day. In today's business environment and increasingly in tomorrow's, every business will be like Hemingway's old fisherman, desperately trying to keep the predators away from the big fish he caught. The question becomes, how do you attach your customers to you so they cannot easily be detached by the competition?

Many, if not most, businesses naïvely believe they do relationship marketing. That's because they use the word relationship cavalierly. If you penetrate beyond the world of marketing and ask people who they have *real* relationships with, you get answers like spouse, fellow employees, family, friends, neighbors, fellow churchgoers, doctors, bartenders, hairdressers. Go one further and ask what each of these relationships has in common. Many people will say "trust," but this is not true. There are people who do not trust their spouse or coworkers one bit.

All real relationships have only one thing in common—a *barrier to exit*. In other words, if it is a real relationship, it costs something to leave it. That is why some people, when they are transferred to another city, wait until they return to their previous location to have their hair done. The barrier to exit from the hairdresser they are used to is too great to contemplate. A divorce, a loss of neighbors or friends or family, for whatever reason does not come without a price.

Business schools spend a good deal of time teaching about barriers to entry. But barriers to entry are falling all the time. The real key to the touchdown is executing the successful *barrier to exit*. This is true relationship marketing. If it costs the customer nothing to leave—indeed, if the customer gains by going elsewhere—there was no relationship, despite what the marketer would like to believe.

Perhaps the best example of a relationship-based product is level-premium whole-life insurance. When you buy such a policy, you pay higher-than-necessary premiums for the earliest years of coverage, but the premium never goes up as you get older. A few years into the policy, a cash value begins to build that grows exponentially with each succeeding year you participate. If you've had the policy for a few years, it becomes costly to exit. Being older now, you would probably have to pay higher premiums with a new policy, you sacrifice at least part of the cash value you've been building, and you may have to undergo a new physical, with a risk of not passing. The whole-life policy is a forced savings, a risk reliever, a near-perfect barrier to exit. Term insurance, on the other hand, offers no such barrier to exit, and you are at the mercy (or advantage) of market forces with each term renewal.

More recent introductions that fit this description include auto leases and frequent-flyer miles, but these are "unfriendly" relationships. Sometimes the user feels trapped, or the competition offers the same incentives and the market gets crowded with offers to the point where the seller begins to lose the advantage.

Perhaps the best go-forward model of relationship marketing is still the King Gillette model. King Gillette made a high-quality, hefty, stainless steel manual razor and offered it way below value, knowing that it would be an irresistible buy. Then he made money on selling, for a reasonable price, the only blades that fit the razor. Buyer and seller both received equal advantage, and there was a barrier to exit that constituted a mutually reinforcing relationship.

If you do the hard work of creating such a win-win relationship, not only do you, as a marketer, get a touchdown (6 points), but you also have the opportunity to make the extra point conversion. In the case of our marketplace/football metaphor, you actually have the opportunity to get 2 extra points.

One is the chance to screw up with the customer. If you have a true barrier to exit, a real relationship, you can screw up once with the customer and still keep him or her. Most companies screw up at least once. In today's highly competitive marketplace, this is of great value because it costs so much more to get a customer than to keep one.

The second extra point is the opportunity to cross-sell. If you have a relationship, you can cross-sell because the customer is more likely to listen to what you have to say. If there is no relationship, cross-marketing is just so much junk mail or annoying telemarketing. Cross-selling is becoming a much more important proposition for all those companies with more than one product or service to offer the customer.

To recap, football is a useful metaphor for how sellers must approach the modern marketplace. There's first down, which is some combination of price, quality, convenience, and assortment. Second down is personalization or customization. Third down is company reputation. Fourth down is the punt (giving up and going on defense), the field goal (a business-to-business strategy), or the touchdown (the relationship).

That's it. It's an imperfect metaphor, to be sure, but it helps bring you into the modern world, puts all these strategies into perspective, highlights the way the game goes, and encourages companies to do the right thing.

15

MANAGING BY HARNESSING EVOLUTION

Biologist Stuart Kauffman is one of many leading scientists who say that an understanding of biology can tell us something profound about business and engineering. We explored one aspect of this in Chapter 5, "Efficiency Breeds Vulnerability." The Theory of Evolution is another biological principle on which 21st century management practice is increasingly relying. For that reason, it becomes a critical technique in freeing your mind to see the future of institutions and systems more clearly.

The Theory of Evolution is rather recent, a product of the scientific era. It is predated by other ideas about God, humanity, and the individual. Its validity, in whole or in part, in biology is not in question here. But its usefulness is clear in harnessing change and profiting from it.

Simply put, the Theory of Evolution is based on natural selection, more commonly but not necessarily accurately known as survival of the fittest. It has two major components:

- **Differential reproduction**—Organisms that breed the most offspring survive; those that do not breed die off.

- **Sexual selection**—That which is bigger or stronger or smarter or more colorful will tend to have the most offspring because it is seen as a more attractive mate. This can be managed artificially through genetic engineering and cross-breeding. Inbreeding tends to lead to weakness and vulnerability.

A newer, disputed addition to evolution theory is *punctuated equilibrium*, which is when a sudden event, such as a natural catastrophe (a crisis) or a mutation (a new development), creates an abrupt new path toward development. If this new development is adaptive, it might survive. If not, it will die. A case in point can be seen in the coral reefs. In many parts of the world where these reefs exist, some unadapted species of coral or whole reefs are killed off by dumping and pollution. In other areas, different species actually thrive on the debris.

The evolution paradigm now seems to be underpinning progressive management. It may always have for the most successful companies, but the process is greatly speeding up. Advances on all technological fronts are leading to the rapid breeding and cross-breeding of disciplines, products, services, and systems. The offspring of these are cross-breeding with each other to create even newer disciplines, products, services, and systems. Rather than wait for these to play themselves out, rapid change causes punctuated equilibrium, and once again there is a rush toward survival of the fittest.

On a global scale, the cross-breeding of disciplines is accelerating. Sociobiologist Edward O. Wilson calls this *consilience*—a lumping together of knowledge as a result of linkings, such as chemical physics, physical chemistry, molecular genetics, chemical ecology, and ecological genetics.

Cross-breeding of disciplines will aid in eco-efficiency (doing more with less). It could transform industry from a system that takes, makes, and wastes into one that integrates economic, environmental, and ethical concerns. This concept, being adopted globally, is one in which nature is not so much efficient as it is *effective*. In the next industrial evolution, the cross-breeding of technologies could allow waste to become food, not poison.

Evolution will continue to inspire industrial and technological systems applications as we move further into the 21st century. A group of Danish scientists announced in 2002 that they had used a genetic algorithm to develop super-strong metal alloys through an evolutionary process. Using a kind of genetic crossover and mutation, they "crossbred" the fittest permutation of materials for 45 generations until they produced the new metal.

The New Natural

To be seen as natural has been a positive image in the past, and companies have spent millions of dollars to create the illusion of natural. The image of what is natural today and what it will be in the future, however, is undergoing a makeover. The mating of *nature* and *technology*—formerly seen as concepts with conflicting objectives—is paving the way for the "new natural."

Example #1: Cross-Breeding to Manage the Biosphere

James Lovelock's Gaia hypothesis is based on the theory that Earth acts like a superorganism, with all its biological and physical systems cooperating to keep it healthy.

Even algae-produced DMS (dimethyl sulfide) is seen as an evolutionary adaptation to control Earth's temperature and climate, making weather not just a physical science but a biological one as well. Columbia University's recently established Earth Institute, seeing that Earth's problems are integrated, is linking earth sciences with biology and the social sciences. The burgeoning water crisis that threatens survivability of massive populations is seen as needing a cross-breeding approach, including technologies related to pollution, irrigation, composting, recycling, marketing, desalination, agriculture, and energy. Seawater agriculture, growing salt-tolerant crops on land with water pumped from the ocean, represents a possible solution to both the global water shortage and the food shortage.

A 1991 report of the Academy of Sciences called for research into *geoengineering*. This involves managing things like mosquito populations, water sanitation, trees, and energy—a kind of industrial ecology to offset the punctuated equilibrium of the greenhouse effect. Included in the environmental forecasts are *agrogenetics* (genetic engineering combined with plant manipulation) and *bioprocessing* (designing microorganisms and plants to "breed" environmentally friendly chemical and biological products, such as drugs, enzymes, and proteins). Food and fiber could be bred cheaply indoors as tissue cultures in giant bacteria baths at a fraction of the cost of today's agriculture and manufacturing. Within five years farmers may be planting naturally colored cotton to reduce the need for dyeing. Genetically modified plants will, at least in the minds of many scientists, yield healthier, more nutritious food. Children may be able to get vaccines through bananas, thereby avoiding the need to use a needle. The cloning of beef muscle cells allows the growth of beef without growing or slaughtering cattle.

Even with all these potential benefits, human intervention into natural processes meets with significant levels of resistance because many people fear unintended consequences. Since the extremes inform the middle on issues such as this (see Chapter 4), you can expect that there may well be speed bumps here occasionally. However, they are unlikely to prevent movement toward major forms of human intervention in biological evolution.

Example #2: Evolution and the Management of Health and Social Services

Computer languages are evolving to adapt, leading to the evolution of software languages to suit the Net. HTML (Hypertext Markup Language) was inadequate, so it was replaced by XML (Extensible Markup Language). XML is a metalanguage, something that provides rules for constructing other markup languages. It makes data searchable and malleable, allowing for more "offspring" data. Hospitals, for example, might pool their information and search for patterns of disease or successful treatments among the records of tens or hundreds of thousands of patients, ensuring the survival and procreation of the best treatments. In much the same way, health-care funders are looking for a metadiscipline to test the survivability of their investments. Hospitals are teaming up, and cross-disciplinary teams of professionals are being established in allied specialties.

Managers in the education sector are also cross-breeding toward survival of the fittest by mating the most successful aspects of programs demanding higher standards and tougher discipline to achieve the best outcomes.

Example #3: Managing Telecom

With technology driving down costs and barriers to entry, all sorts of new competitors are merging to transform the traditional telecommunications companies: cable TV operators, software manufacturers, banks, water companies, railways, and so on. Industries as different as hotels and advertising agencies now offer communications as an incidental part of a host of other services.

The cross-breeding of communication satellites, fiber optics, and the finite radio spectrum, along with advanced semiconductor technologies, such as silicon germanium (SiGe), combine with new breakthroughs in digital signal processors (DSPs) and software to develop ever more advanced telecom offspring. These joint technologies will, among other things, enable data to be transmitted over electric power lines into homes faster than 1 megabit per second. The Net is leading to mutations in commerce. Small companies now have the ability to challenge what were previously the "fittest" (the giants), and large companies can now adapt by pursuing micromarkets once served only by local companies. Japanese giants, such as Sony and Matsushita, are becoming vulnerable to a new species of predator (combinations of sophisticated chips and software) in much the same way that IBM lost ground in the 1990s to Intel and Microsoft. And in the future, all devices will evolve into specialized computer offspring through the addition of digital technology.

More companies and business schools are offering managers live, interactive classes delivered via satellite, and universities as well as businesses are becoming telecommunications institutions. Customers can buy stock from ATMs.

Videoconferencing kiosks, located in office buildings and bank branches, are staffed by experts who handle transactions from mortgage loans to mutual funds. In the mid-1990s, Chase built a $130 million satellite network global transaction center to connect New York, Hong Kong, Luxembourg, and Tokyo. IBOS (Interbank Online Systems) plans to link 500 banks and thousands of branches around the globe with one fiber-optic system.

New technologies promise even greater evolution in telecom service. The prefix *nano* means one billionth. A nanometer is a billionth of a meter. A nanosecond is a billionth of a second. Nanotechnology will provide the impetus for all forms of evolutionary developments. Nanomanufacturing strategies that enable machines and materials to virtually make themselves via molecular self-assembly are emerging. Chips that can activate each other and form electrical connections from telecom and computing are being developed. Quantum computing uses pulses of light as the new information carriers. Intelligent materials that can repair themselves and animate inert substances are leading to music emanating from doors, floors, and ceilings. Communications and computational networks are increasingly mated with biology to mimic brain and spinal cord functions. Optical fibers will be imbedded in materials that take on sensory capacity and provide signals. RFID (Radio Frequency Identity) tags on products such as clothing will communicate with manufacturers and retailers, providing useful information for marketing and security tracking, but causing concern among consumers about privacy intrusions.

We are rapidly approaching the time when you will no longer be able to point to any company as being typical of the telecom industry. Existing players are meeting increased competition from all manner of newly evolving connection and distribution technologies. What business(es) will current telecom companies eventually be in in the 21st century? What aspect of telecommunications will every other business or association be in? Since many refer to the next economy as the "communications" economy, it is critical to understand the role evolution is playing in managing the telecom future.

Example #4: Managing Biotech

Following the evolutionary path, you can also expect the convergence of companies as divergent as soaps, cosmetics, beverages, pig farming, food, energy, health care, and family counseling. The result may be a biotech industry that could rival or even surpass infotech as a dominating force in the market and in your life.

Microorganisms on the seafloor may become a source of energy, as might hydrogen-producing algae. As the search for natural energy-producing bioorganisms advances along with genetic engineering, you may see many more energy companies going the way of Monsanto and evolving into agriculture and cloning.

Biosensors will increasingly be imbedded in clothing or made wearable; so too will computers. Biosensors using nanotechnology bundles similar to those found in living cells may also be used to warn you of biological or chemical warfare. This could all lead to biocomputing environments that marry translation, monitoring (for things like temperature, health, and behavior), and caring for humans. Robotics now used in surgery may eventually evolve to surround you in all manner of caregiving.

With the aging of the U.S., along with much of the rest of the world, businesses related to aging, and especially the amelioration of it, will undergo extensive cross-breeding. Cloning and genetic mapping might well lead to unlocking the secrets of the genes that trigger aging. New collaborations based on genetic mapping will bring together researchers in behavior, aging, and drugs. A person's genotype will be known at birth, and much of the expert knowledge to manage that individual's health will be programmed into software.

Scientists are learning much more about the teen years, brain development, and hormones. For example, researchers are compiling a complete pediatric neuroanatomy map—the world's first database of normal brain development—and at the end of the 6-year study, there will be access to the map on the web. In the marriage of biotech and computing, progress is being made toward a simulation of the complete human body—a virtual human, for total analytic purposes (environmental, mental health, behavior, and so on).

Biotech is making major inroads in farming, from discoveries related to resistant strains of blights to genetic modifications—such as in rice—that can boost yields and cut global warming. How we see some crops will change as we make more discoveries about food and health, such as the positive influence of chocolate on the heart (hooray!). With depression emerging as a major global health issue, and with earlier links between certain depression-relieving foods (such as chocolate) and eating behaviors, agriculture will be increasingly tied directly to health management. The cloning and genetic modification of animals originally meant for food purposes is now extending to replacement organs for humans, production of pharmaceuticals, and even the re-creation of beloved pets.

Just as in the telecom/computing convergence, not only will a host of companies find themselves in crossover businesses, but companies not now in biotech will find that cross-breeding will put them, directly or peripherally, in the biotech business.

Examples of direct crossover include

- Food retailers in the health-care field

- Food manufacturers engaged in biosensors for everything from freshness of product to health of consumer to stocking the consumer's refrigerator based on the consumer's genotype to tracing movements of agrichemicals into the environment

- Jewelry containing pharmaceutical-dispensing schedules and processes

- Foodaceuticals (food and pharmaceuticals), cosmeceuticals (cosmetics and pharmaceuticals), cosmerobotics (cosmetics and self-organizing nanochips), pharmafoods (agricultural breeding of animals for everything from insulin to antibiotics), and genetifitness (health clubs, exercise equipment, and workout routines geared to genetic readouts)

Examples of peripheral engagement include

- The financial sector's investments in biotech

- New magazines springing up to cover the various areas of biotech explosion and application

- Insurers engaged in efficacy studies matching genotypes with lifestyles and treatments

- Educational software utilizing knowledge of brain function

- The drafting of legal precedents based on biodefenses in criminal and civil cases

- Niche marketing of religion based on natural dispositions

- TV shows on biothemes

Over the next few years, cosmetics companies will become more like biotech companies, and automation companies will be drawn more into the world of biosensors, cybernetics (the man/machine interface), and bioenergy. In the biotech age, GM may stand not just for genetically modified foods, but for cars that provide bioenvironments that ensure your safety and well-being, potentially geared to your circadian (daily) rhythms, hormonal balances, and brainwave patterns, whether you are a driver or a passenger. Business publications will find biotech-related companies rivaling infotech companies in column content and ad space, so advertising agencies will have to develop expertise and creativity in the biotech arena. Insurers will have to reassess risks in a biotech age, and newsletter publications may find unique genotypical niches to cater to with physical and mental and lifestyle advice. Consulting firms may find that bioethics is one of the most lucrative new areas of practice.

In short, just as was true in the infotech convergence, few companies will escape being drawn into the biotech evolution, and current companies may find themselves completely transformed by the oncoming cross-breeding of breakthroughs and their applications.

Example #5: The Business of Managing Human Evolution

Genetic engineering and mapping the human genome are racing onward like a speeding train. This is leading to all sorts of possibilities, including interference in the natural selection of human traits. Researchers are inducing stem cells to copy themselves without turning into anything else. Others are finding ways to turn stem cells into makers of needed body parts. This will spur genetic engineering and human cloning, and *Homo sapiens* may be supplanted by *homo geneticus*. Some researchers expect to create life in a test tube from inanimate chemicals within the next few years. The resulting primitive microbe will represent a huge technical advance in humans' ability to manipulate the natural world. The search for the smallest number of genes necessary to make a living organism promises a leap in our understanding of biology and evolution.

Living cells are beginning to yield their secrets about the aging process so that we may one day halt or even reverse it. The ability to map the human brain, synapse by synapse, is potentially leading to a capacity to download and grow our minds. Human identity may be based on evolving infinitely-sized "mind files" rather than based merely on our physical bodies.

We are at a point of evolution where the spectrum of species from animals to humans to machines is blurring. For example, the discussion of the similarities between humans and the great apes has led to assertions that great apes should be afforded some of the legal rights of humans. Philosopher Peter Singer takes this a step further, suggesting that if you deny rights to the great apes, you need to deny rights to intellectually disabled children as well.

At the other end of the spectrum are the development of new supercomputers and the mimicking of the human brain. Computers can now process up to 10 trillion operations per second, and even faster ones are on the way. Large-scale biocomputers in the form of supercomputers the size of grapefruits are being developed. Called "human brains," they are capable of real-time image processing, speech recognition, and logical inference. Researchers have also encoded strands of DNA with data that can perform computation inside a flask.

While mainstream computer science is comfortable with the concept of intelligent computers, an unanswered issue is whether computers are becoming more human-like or humans are becoming more computer-like. Jaron Lanier poses the possibility of computers becoming a successor species to humans. He observes that medical science, neuroscience, computer science, genetics, biology—separately and together—seem to be on the verge of abandoning the human plane altogether.

Raymond Kurzweil suggests several possibilities emerging from brain mapping. One is the design of neural nets that operate like the human brain. Another is scanning a brain that will be downloaded to a computer, resulting in re-creation of the human brain on a neural computer. Kurzweil speculates that human knowledge can be stored in an internal database and that death could disappear. In the future, he believes, identity will be based on our evolving mind file. Consequently, humans will become more like software than hardware. Some already call humans *wetware*.

In 2002, researchers placed three electrodes in a rat's brain and created what some are calling "Robo Rat." Using a keyboard, they could make the rat twist, turn, and jump on command. How many electrodes would be required to create Robo Human? These evolutionary developments are generating some profound questions: Will machines be compatible with each other and with humans? We already know what it is like when software is incompatible—or when people are incompatible. Imagine the iterations when there are "smart" human-machines and "dumb" humans, "dumb" human-machines and "smart" humans, "smart" human-machines interfacing with "dumb" human-machines, and so forth. How do you manage this?

One of the more intriguing applications of evolution theory is now occurring in software development. Software engineers are literally breeding and cross-breeding software programs to maximize the most desirable qualities and eliminate the less-desirable ones. This "unnatural" selection intends to have as a result the survival of the fittest software.

Researchers in Sweden recently developed software to enable a winged robot to learn how to fly by itself. The program randomly fed instructions to the robot about flapping its wings. Feedback from built-in motion detectors let the program figure out which sets of instructions did the best job of generating lift. The superior ones were mated to produce offspring that combined their best characteristics.

This was done for several iterations—or generations—until the robot knew the best way to create lift.

Hal, the human-like computer featured in the classic Stanley Kubrick film *2001: A Space Odyssey*, has been a popular-culture symbol of this cybernetic potential. Hal's destruction was a result of defending itself. If human-machines are programmed to defend themselves, they will protect themselves at whatever cost—including the cost of humans. At the end of the day, it may be that we need genetic engineering more than ever—as a way to stay ahead of machines. This suggests yet another argument in favor of biotechnology: Without its evolutionary advances, humans may become an endangered species.

Well before the end of this century, *Robo sapiens* may be as common as people with heart transplants are today. Already, approximately one in 10 Americans has some kind of synthetic body part—a pacemaker, a defibrillator, a heart valve, a knee joint. According to *Wired* magazine, before long we will be able to replace everything from legs to livers. As humans increasingly have some combination of corneal implants, artificial limbs, and brain chips, they are assuming robotic features. This will presumably work in tandem with chronological discoveries to alter the timing of our life paths. "Full-immersion virtual reality" mated with wireless Internet access will change your life in even the smallest ways, such as searching for misplaced items or dreaming in concert with others. This tactile virtual reality is a natural to combine with *chronobiology* (your body and its relationship to time and seasons) and to alter your perceptions, timing, and outcomes.

When the preliminary map of the human genome was announced in 2001, Francis S. Collins, the director of the National Human Genome Institute, said, "We have caught the first glimpses of our instruction book, previously known only to God." This statement's mixture of humility and arrogance reflects our ambivalence, confusion, fear, and hope as we face the possibilities now open to us.

Genomics, the new science of genetics, will shorten the process of biological evolution, according to physicist Stephen Hawking.

Survival of the Fittest

Cross-breeding is becoming the engine by which progress is occurring on all fronts. In this era of relentless competition, the truth is that every organization can no longer know for certain where its competition will come from. The banks were caught by surprise two decades ago when such unexpected competitors as GE Capital and Fidelity Investments grabbed large chunks of their business. Now they are being caught by surprise again as department stores and grocery stores invade their turf. Stepped-up cross-breeding will mean that traditional forms of competitive intelligence no longer suffice. Businesses will have to find more appropriate tools.

In prior eras, stability allowed *event pacing*—change didn't happen until events caused it to happen. Now intense competition and technology create constant punctuated equilibrium and require what Kathleen Eisenhardt and Shona Brown, in a 1998 article in *Harvard Business Review*, called *time pacing*. This means no longer waiting for things to happen, but actually creating a rhythm that managers can use to speed up the intensity of their efforts. Netscape introduces a new product every six months; Intel adds a new facility every nine months. Managing by creating punctuated equilibrium gives the organization considerable competitive momentum.

As competition becomes more intense, as the pace of everything continues to quicken, organizations increasingly find it necessary to do more than keep up: They must try to get ahead.

Managing by way of evolution requires a vision, a bold new way of seeing the future. All organizations—businesses, nonprofits, governments, schools, and even philanthropies—must make themselves into accelerators of evolution. No one can afford to remain passive.

Sephora, for example, was a new way to sell cosmetics. Its CEO, Myron Ullman III, believed that "retailing is about change," and he made Sephora a leader by mating art with vanity with the megastore concept. Mercato enabled online shoppers to pool their purchase requests and save money, which is an example of a growing trend on the Internet—*monopsony*: consumers banding together to exert market power. Adobe Systems has created an "incubator" for putting new conceptual offspring on a fast track to the marketplace. UPS has developed e-Ventures for cross-breeding and for developing new ideas in-house. Both Hewlett-Packard and Intel have set up venture funds to invest in outside companies that can follow up on good ideas, thereby avoiding the pitfalls of inbreeding.

In the area of customer service, organizations are increasingly using advanced technology to determine their best customers, and these customers become even fitter because they are rewarded and given the best service. Recent conventional wisdom says that technological literacy will polarize the haves and have-nots, but one's standing as the fittest customer may actually play a larger role in determining success. The 80-20 rule—that 80 percent of the profit comes from 20 percent of the customers—is now likely to create greater survival advantage for the 20 and even disadvantage for the 80.

Increasingly, outsourcing will take into account a global labor pool. Global moves will no longer be limited to professional staff or specialized labor. As labor moves to where work is being done, country-by-country employment statistics will become less relevant. As work migrates globally, new communities and affiliations will evolve based on this transience. Twenty-first century guilds may be the offspring of this community-building, and associations will have opportunities to cross-breed with these guilds to create new affinity programs.

The Next Big Management Tool

The idea of time pacing—of deliberate recombination, procreation, and mutation at predetermined intervals—is likely to become an increasingly important management tool for all organizations across divisions and functions. Creating cross-disciplinary teams, outsourcing strategic thinking, creating novel alliances, and mating good solutions with better ones to create the best possible outcomes may be the only ways to ensure more competitive offspring and therefore survival. From a human resources perspective, it may be the only way to manage good talent at two-year intervals. From a profitability perspective, it may be the only way to diversify risk.

Management these days is too often seen as controlling systems and processes. We will have to become more comfortable with a world that places us in a more evolutionary, if not revolutionary, context. Management will increasingly become the facilitation, acceleration, and evaluation of the evolution of the organization and its people.

There will be fewer models and precedents to light the way into the future. Things will be constantly new. Morphing, the ability to change shape and character almost effortlessly, will be an ideal and no longer an aberration.

Traditional market research will become increasingly difficult. As people combine their aspirations, and the conflicting messages they increasingly receive from all forms of media, they will change as rapidly and seemingly randomly as the weather. New techniques will evolve through similar cross-breeding that could make market research more effective. In some cases, survey research is slated to become extinct as brain mapping advances and we can tap directly into the human mind for answers to questions.

Human resources management also will require new processes. The creation of new forms of middle management based on cybernetic (human-machine interface) skills will be necessary in all organizations.

Compensation will need reinvention to keep up with the diversity of reinvented and cross-bred jobs and workers. For young workers, changing jobs is encouraged. Every job is conceived of as an evolutionary stepping-stone to the next job—and the more job offerings (offers and possibilities), the greater one's expectations of survival and success.

Organizations will have to adopt a culture whose central characteristic is flexibility. A critical issue will be how to combine that with some strands of organizational tradition to create a cohesive entity. Perhaps the only constant will be the organization's vision. Achieving that could mean a constantly evolving set of missions.

Managing by the evolutionary model ushers in a time characterized by knowing how to move comfortably with the flow. As a result, people, organizations, and societies will all have to become able to function effectively in a time when evolution moves so quickly that it becomes revolution. Understanding that this evolutionary tidal wave is sweeping over all aspects of society, the economy, and your life can open your mind to an infinite world of future possibilities and emerging opportunities. Using evolution as a metaphor provides the foundation for thinking and acting creatively and avoiding the trap of seeing tomorrow as a simple extension of today.

16

SELF-DEFEATING AND SELF-FULFILLING PROPHECIES

You are now fully aware that if we don't escape the mental baggage that traps us, the human tendency is to project the known present into the future. The result generally, as Mark Twain wrote, is that we get "wholesale returns of conjecture out of a trifling investment of fact." But some people can envision a different future. What often happens with them, depending on how effectively they communicate their visions, is that their prophecies become either *self-fulfilling* or *self-defeating*. They can actually change the future; they can make it happen, or they can prevent it from happening.

Example #1: Orwell and Gates

George Orwell gives us a perfect example of the self-defeating prophecy. In *1984*, written in 1948 and published in 1949, he showed us his stark and indeed terrifying vision of a future made unbearably bleak by a tyranny in control of all information and communication.

He could well have been right; that's how it could have turned out. But Orwell's vision of Big Brother was so disturbing that it helped prevent, through legislation and oversight agencies, what he feared 1984 would be. The awareness and concern created by one character in his book protected us to a considerable extent from the imposition of the controls and restraints on human independence he foresaw.

Bill Gates, on the other hand, gives us an example of the self-fulfilling prophecy. When he had his vision of a computer platform monopoly, everything at the time indicated he was wrong. The U.S. was embarking on an era of relentless competition. People had (and expected) multiple choices in everything, including multidirectional technologies, heightened customer expectations of choice, demands for ease and quality of interfaces, and work-life balance (begun by Silicon Valley inhabitants in their casual clothes and desire for "quality of life" alternatives to the IBMs of the world).

But Gates was a driven and determined man. He made his unlikely vision happen. He was able to triumph over higher-quality competitors and force onto the market products riddled with flaws. Leading his own people through a grueling 24/7 work environment, he muscled competitors out of his way through creative and preemptive initiatives. He's an example of how fierce intelligence, focus, determination, and—yes—ruthlessness can allow one person to make even an unlikely prophecy self-fulfilling.

But there are discontinuities, happenings whose impacts can radically alter the course of events. September 11, 2001, was such a discontinuity. One result is that there are renewed pressures to move to a surveillance society (Orwell may yet be proven partially right). And, in the wake of antitrust suits, Bill Gates may be proven partially wrong.

Orwell and Gates tell you that you needn't be trapped in destiny; you can create it. For better or worse, outstanding visionaries have done that for millennia. They have wiped out civilizations and, in the case of John F. Kennedy, sent men to the moon. Yet, in the less-daunting task of creating a successful business, those at the helm often just steer on the same course, believing that everything that brought them to this point is all there is or will be, and they unknowingly succumb to the weight of their mental baggage.

Gates also gives a good example of a self-defeating prophecy. In 1998, casting his company's lot with the Internet, he proclaimed that the Net would enable the achievement of "frictionless commerce"—no intermediaries between buyers and sellers. By his very words, he encouraged a forty-niner-like gold rush to get on the Internet and do commerce there. This, in turn, resulted in such a profusion and confusion of business that using new or existing intermediaries became essential for many if not most transactions. So much for frictionless commerce.

Example #2: Government and Nongovernmental Organizations

Bill Clinton presented himself and won the presidency in 1992, as an anti-big-government Democrat. He famously proclaimed that "the era of big government is over." Yet one of the first initiatives he took was to attempt the nationalization of health care. Because he was contradictory right off the bat, his proclamation became a self-defeating prophecy as he actually *strengthened* the opportunity for the entrenched powers, aroused to action by the challenges to their authority, to reassert that authority in new areas. One such new area is what has come to be called "nanny government"—getting citizens to eat right, drink less, stop smoking, and be sexually responsible. This time the resurgence of activist government is not just from the left. Whereas liberals seem to want government less involved in the bedroom and more in the boardroom, conservatives seem to want exactly the opposite. Even before 9/11 and Enron, the demise of big government was not to be. By calling for it, Clinton set the stage for it not to happen.

Perhaps the most striking example of self-defeating prophecy was in the ecological arena. When Rachel Carson published *Silent Spring* in 1962, her prediction of a world poisoned, perhaps fatally, by chemicals marked the real beginning of the environmental movement. Ten years later, with the publication of the Club of Rome's *Limits to Growth* in 1972, the believers in environmental doom were in full flower. There had been nothing like it since the Reverend Thomas Malthus' gloomy predictions of doom at the end of the 18th century.

Armies of concerned citizens mobilized themselves into Sierra Clubs and Greenpeaces to protect the environment from further degradation. Environmental advocacy groups began to succeed during the '70s and '80s in getting legislation and regulation to protect the environment and punish polluters. The U.S. Environmental Protection Agency was established, and with it the idea of demanding environmental impact assessments before projects and business undertakings could be approved. The Green Party rose to importance in Europe.

This culminated in the '90s with the emergence of the *precautionary principle*—the effort to determine ahead of time not only how much damage to the environment might occur, but how little is acceptable to the affected parties.

The old English common-law principle of *unavoidable ignorance* said that if it was not possible for you to know something, you could not be held liable for not knowing it. The precautionary principle increasingly makes that invalid. Consequently, decision-makers will want to be informed of all possible risks before they decide. With technologies, particularly new ones, this is impossible.

So what happened? Carson and the Club of Rome, by the very act of predicting environmental catastrophe, helped make sure it didn't happen. We haven't run out of resources; the air and water are now considerably cleaner and less polluted than they were 30 years ago. Population growth rates, according to the most recent UN statistics, have decreased considerably. Indeed, the latest projections from the UN show world population reaching no more than eight billion by 2050—and then declining. There is a greater supply of cleaner energy, and the possibility of even cleaner energy supplies in the future—hydrogen, wind, fuel cells—is far more promising than anyone would have guessed 20 or even 10 years ago. It has reached the point, as suggested by two eminent economists, Kenneth Arrow and Larry Guilder, that environmentalists and businesspeople are converging on mutual acceptance of the need to have both economic growth and protection of our natural capital, the environment.

None of it—not the improvement in air and water quality, not technological advances in clean energy, not the decline in population growth rates, not the awareness of the economic value of a healthy environment, and certainly not the growing convergence of viewpoints about environmentalism—none of it would have happened without the frightening forecasts that ultimately became self-defeating.

Example #3: Your Mind and Body

An example of a product in the U.S. whose promise became self-defeating is health insurance. It was believed that not only would health insurance help people pay for medical care (and, of course, make sure that doctors and hospitals got paid), it would also become a way to control the cost of health care. Impartial insurance companies and their disinterested claims managers would see to it that costs didn't escalate unreasonably. Insurance company profits, after all, were dependent on keeping costs down.

To some extent, that did happen. Mounting complaints from both doctors and patients testified to that. But what also happened, and what ultimately made the health insurance promise self-defeating, was what always happens when someone else pays the bill: People do things they otherwise would feel they could not afford to do. This is even more true when someone else is paying all or most of the premium, as employers did for many years. That tendency has, in the case of health care, been much stronger than the cost-reduction forces.

Psychics succeed to a considerable extent by creating self-fulfilling prophecies. Someone who is told by a psychic she has faith in that she will have two children is more likely to try to have two children in her life and not stop at one or go on to three. Someone who is told he will stay with his wife forever is less likely to be tempted to leave his marriage if he believes the prophecy.

Mothers use guilt every day to affect self-fulfilling prophecies, as do religions. If they say a particular form of behavior will result in your feeling remorseful or regretful, that's what you are more likely to feel. If they had never drummed that into you, your actions would have no such consequences.

Another striking example of self-fulfilling prophecy is the placebo effect. Every year, more than 200,000 Americans have arthroscopic knee surgery. According to a study reported in *The New England Journal of Medicine* in 2002, it's all in vain. In an experiment done at the Houston Veterans Affairs Medical Center, the operation was done on some patients, while a control group was sedated and had minor incisions made in their knees, leading them to believe they had had the surgery. Two years later, both groups had just about equal results, as measured by diminished pain and greater mobility. According to Nelda Wray, the head researcher on the study, "The entire driving force which bolsters this billion-dollar industry is the placebo effect." This is the self-fulfilling prophecy—tell them they'll get better, and they will.

Example #4: How to Make It Happen

When it comes to forecasting the future, not all people and not all organizations are equal. Most allow the future to happen to them. A few create the future. One of our most challenging tasks as consultants has been to help convert the former into the latter.

In 1996, we began discussing with a senior team at Rockwell Automation the future of energy use and alternatives, and our conviction that fuel cell (hydrogen conversion) technology was a promising possibility.

These senior staffers first asked who else in their industry was active in fuel cell work. They asked what the current numbers were regarding fuel cell research and application. They asked what the projection was for percentage of energy use that fuel cells would capture. None of their questions could be answered—some were even unknowable. They were willing to discuss this topic as interesting but not currently pressing.

When we asked this senior team, "Who at Rockwell is in charge of fuel cell initiatives?" we were met with head shaking and assumptions, but there was no definitive answer. We told these executives, from a cross section of line and staff functions, about an upcoming conference on fuel cell technology. They suggested perhaps they should send someone. We countered that they should send *everyone*. When one person attends a meeting and comes back energized, unless it's the CEO, nothing tends to happen because the energy dissipates without support (see Chapter 7, "Entropy"). But when a critical mass is energized, things do happen (see Chapter 9, "The Law of Large Numbers").

Rockwell sent 15 people, including engineers and financial executives, to the conference. As a result of their enthusiasm upon returning, they generated scenarios educating others in the company. Eventually a new fuel cell division was created, and a president was named to head it.

The company was now involved in a self-fulfilling prophecy as opposed to passive observation. They created the opportunity to shape the energy future and to be a profitable player in it. We were successful that time. But it's always a challenge to convince people that they can make something new happen, especially when their first questions are "Who else is doing this?" and "What are the numbers?"

More and more, as people, businesses, and societies seek to look ahead and anticipate change, you will increasingly see, hear, and read forecasts and predictions. What this book has been about is showing you how to escape the traps that cause you to believe only futures that mimic the present. Now that your mind is freer, and now that you have all these tools to see future possibilities more clearly, the final lesson is simple but awesome. Go ahead and see the future. See *a* future. If you don't like what you see, find fulfillment and profit in some way to head it off. If you like what you see, find fulfillment and profit in making it happen. You can do this as one person in a large organization, one person in a small business, one member of a family, or one member of society.

The future is now yours for the making and the taking. You no longer have to be overwhelmed or frightened by this time of constant change. You can be energized by it, and by using one or more of the thinking technologies in this book, you can profit greatly from it.

CONCLUSION

If you want to make God laugh, goes an old business adage, show Him your plan. In a time of rapid and massive change, such as we now live in, formal planning is too often an exercise in futility. It's not just change that makes this so. The narrowness of most business planning—or personal planning, for that matter—contributes as well.

Planners tend to make three really big mistakes:

- Faulty or inadequate analysis
- Not seeing the big picture—the *context*
- Failure to link information to action

The first of these cannot be corrected easily. It requires a wrenching change in ordinary or usual thinking. The techniques in this book can help you *think* better in order to *act* more effectively. It is very difficult to change how you think, but the times demand it. Among other things, you have to see and understand how important factors such as social trends are. You have to see these factors for what they really are, not for what you think or believe or hope they are. In its early years, for example, environmentalism remained a fringe movement, unconnected to the majority. Its pioneers were focused on aesthetics. Only when they realized that for most people it was really a health issue were they able to achieve a critical mass of believers.

The second flaw, not being aware of the big picture, comes from seeing things only discretely rather than holistically. This can be corrected by linking trends and events so that you see patterns and connections rather than single stand-alone events. For example, the burst of patriotism among young people following 9/11 makes sense when you know from tracking their beliefs and behavior that they had been almost desperately seeking meaning and significance in their lives.

As for the third problem, linking information to action, that also takes conscious effort. You must constantly ask yourself, if I know what this means for me, and I have some ideas of what to do about it, and I think I or we can profit from it, why isn't action being taken? Many employees, especially at the management and executive levels, say that stress is not about having more work, but about work that does not get done because inertia is blocking efforts to contribute in a meaningful way.

If your idea matters to you, and you are employed in a large organization, begin to enlist others in support of it and to identify the barriers to implementing it. If that fails, you can always try to take it elsewhere. If you manage people, remove the roadblocks—bureaucratic or other—to their ability to contribute to their fullest. If you are the boss, instruct your staff to continually identify the clogs in the organization that prevent creativity and innovation from flowing. If you are self-employed, be alert to your own personal inertia and how it can rob you of an exciting opportunity.

Anticipation Is Key

The first step is to get good information. That means clearly and consistently seeing what is happening in the world around you. The next step is to try to understand objectively what it could mean to you. Forget your knee-jerk reaction. Stop ignoring what could be significant just because it doesn't fit your current thinking. If you do this, you will find yourself less surprised by events. You will become better at *anticipating* change—which in today's rapidly changing world is the foundation of *managing* change. As a result, you and your organization will be quicker, smarter, more nimble, and more likely to prosper.

A case in point is the horrific events of 9/11. The magnitude and the audacity were surprising, but the fact that such an attack occurred was not. Over the past decade, many signals told us that things were coming to a head.

In the early 1990s, it was becoming increasingly clear that tensions were growing between the Islamic and non-Islamic worlds. Militancy in Islam was increasing, especially among the fundamentalists, and there was a noticeable escalation in terrorist groups driven by religious fanaticism. Contagious weapons, such as biologicals, were becoming easier to make and therefore more likely. Observation and analysis led even then to the conclusion that the world was moving into a much more fluid and uncertain military environment, where borders would be less clearly delineated, the nature of conflicts less easily defined, and the participants less likely to be in the military tradition we were all used to.

It was also apparent that massive migrations from South to North and from East to West were creating a potentially explosive situation. Displaced and alienated people, feeling increasingly victimized and angry, could well become recruits for terrorists.

By the mid-1990s, it was obvious that the U.S. could no longer consider itself reasonably well insulated from terrorism. The trends contributing to the "mainstreaming" of terrorism included the following:

- Growing urban concentrations of populations both susceptible and recruitable to terrorism

- An expanding gap between the haves and have-nots

- Increasing vulnerability of electronic-based societies and economies

- New weapons, such as biologicals, that could make terrorist acts both easier and more terrible

- Expanding religious and cultural conflicts

Importantly, you could see that as knowledge workers are increasingly recognized as businesses' most important assets, terrorists would be more likely to target people and not just things.

Well before the end of the decade, religion was increasingly important in determining the course of events in the world. Indeed, the spread of a very secular American culture around the world was contributing to a countertrend of impassioned adherence to indigenous religion-based cultures, as in Islam, which was often manifested as anti-Americanism. As religion became a more important force in people's lives, the divisive sentiments that emerged were certain to be more aggressive, hostile, and angry.

There was also the critical demographic component of the clash of cultures. In both the Islamic world and the West, young people were transforming religious institutions and practices. In the West, particularly in the developed countries, much of the new youthful energy was aimed at increasing tolerance. The opposite appeared to be true in Islam. And, it should be noted, the exuberant Christianity now blossoming in the Southern Hemisphere will also be accompanied by militancy.

A Congressional investigation concluded in September 2002 that there had been specific advance warnings that terrorists were planning to use airplanes as weapons. In 1998, for example, a CIA report asserted that Arab terrorists intended to crash planes into the World Trade Center. For at least three years prior to 9/11, U.S. intelligence agencies received reports that al Qaeda intended to launch attacks on New York and Washington. Apparently neither the CIA nor the FBI found these reports credible. It is the Cassandra myth (with which we opened this book) brought forward to modern times.

What Type of Business Will Succeed?

In the future, there are likely to be three types of businesses and businesspeople:

- **Type A**—Advanced/Anticipatory organizations and people, who begin with a vision and an actionable idea about how to position and present themselves

- **Type B**—Brains/Brawn organizations and people, who do not have new ideas but who have resources and staying power and can bring their assets to bear effectively under different circumstances

- **Type C**—Copycats, who can do no better than follow the lead of others and hope to survive

Frenzied merger and acquisition activity or desperately trying to coax or threaten employees into becoming more creative—the things B and C companies and people are likely to stress—are of little value unless they are driven by an understanding of change, a knowledge of how to respond to it, and a willingness to evolve.

Type A organizations and people are often characterized by *green shoots*. Like plants that get around obstacles by sending out green shoots to seek sunlight, water, or fertile soil, Type As face impediments by finding informal ways to get around, over, or under them. They are *nimble*. They or their leaders know that they must encourage initiative and innovation. To some extent, this requires a shift from the comforts of traditional thinking. Although this can be scary for some people, freeing the mind leads to the kind of unconventional thinking that is the essential element of nimbleness and that is increasingly necessary in today's fluid and unpredictable environment.

Question Consensus

Between us, we've spent more than 70 years looking at and analyzing trends. We have watched closely how people see and respond to information about change. We have learned, among other things, that a conclusion arrived at by a committee is more likely than not to be wrong. That is because the driving force, if we can call it that, in any committee is consensus. Consensus usually leads to seeing the future in today's terms. This kind of trap is a powerful enemy of thinking.

We have trained ourselves and our clients to look at things differently, to challenge conventional thinking (an oxymoron). This is not because we always disagree with the consensus; sometimes we agree. But we won't let that stop us, nor should it stop you, from saying "What if?" What if we're all wrong? What if there is another way of looking at it, another line of reasoning, another possible solution?

"Give a man a fish," say the Chinese, "and you feed him for a day. Teach him how to fish, and he feeds himself for life." This book is about learning how to fish. It is about freeing your mind to think in ways that will sustain and nourish your organization—and you—in the sure-to-be-tumultuous years ahead.

REFERENCES

Chapter 1, "Looking Through Alien Eyes"

Armoun, Stephanie. "More Gen Xers Juggle Jobs, Parents' Care." *USA Today*, 26 April 2002.

Barack, Lauren. "Kids Take the Corner Office." *The Industry Standard*, 4 September 2000, p. 156+.

Daly, Emma. "U.N. Says Elderly Will Soon Outnumber Young for First Time." *The New York Times*, 9 April 2002.

DeCordoba, Jose. "As Violence Worsens, Business Leaders Flee Colombia, Venezuela." *The Wall Street Journal*, 30 August 2000.

England, Robert Stone. "The Fiscal Challenge of an Aging Industrial World." *Future Survey*, March 2002, p. 22+.

Hewitt, Paul and Robert England. "Meeting the Challenge of Global Aging: A Report to World Leaders." *Future Survey*, March 2002, p. 23.

Jeffrey, Nancy Ann. "The New-Economy Family." *The Wall Street Journal* (Weekend), 8 September 2000.

Lyall, Sarah. "For Europeans, Love, Yes; Marriage, Maybe." *The New York Times*, 24 March 2002.

Ono, Yumiko. "In Japan, to Nail a Job as a Manicurist, Take a Trip to Long Island." *The Wall Street Journal*, 10 October 2000.

Parker-Pope, Tara. "Rise in Early Puberty Causes Parents to Ask 'When Is It Too Soon?'" *The Wall Street Journal*, 21 July 2000.

Shapiro, Joseph P. "Enjoying Life After Death." *U.S. News & World Report*, 11 September 2000, p. 76+.

Suro, Roberto. "Movement at Warp Speed." *American Demographics*, August 2000, p. 61+.

Vinzant, Carol. "They Want You Back." *Fortune*, 2 October 2000, p. 271+.

Wellner, Alison Stein. "A New Flavor in the Melting Pot." *American Demographics Forecast*, May 2002, p. 1+.

Yee, Chen May. "High Tech Life for India's Women." *The Wall Street Journal*, 1 November 2000.

Zachary, G. Pascal. "People Who Need People." *The Wall Street Journal*, 25 September 2000.

_____. "Battle for Brains." *The Financial Times*, 12–13 August 2000.

_____. "Making the Most of Midlife." *U.S. News & World Report*, 18 September 2000, p. 20.

_____. "10 TIMES 10^{10}—What Is in a Number?" *Geneva Association Information Newsletter*, May 2000, p. 2+.

_____. "A Wizened World." *American Demographics Forecast*, January 2002, p. 11.

Chapter 2, "Trend/Countertrend"

Alba, Richard D. "Assimilation's Quiet Tide." *The Public Interest*, Spring 1995, p. 3+.

Allen, Charlotte. "A Conservative's Lament." *UTNE Reader*, March/April 1995, p. 91+.

Anderson, Alun. "Are You a Machine of Many Parts?" *The World of 1999*, supplement of *The Economist*, p. 109+.

Bernstein, Nell. "Goin' Gangsta, Choosin' Cholita." *UTNE Reader*, March/April 1995, p. 87+.

Bernstein, Peter L. "The New Religion of Risk Management." *Harvard Business Review*, March/April 1996, p. 47+.

Bertman, Stephen. "Hyperculture—Stress." *Vital Speeches of the Day*, 15 January 1999, p. 204+.

Boynton, Robert S. "The New Intellectuals." *The Atlantic Monthly*, March 1995, p. 53+.

Burns, Greg. "The New Economics of Food." *Business Week*, 20 May 1996, p. 78+.

Carlson, Tucker. "God Is My Campaign Manager." *The Weekly Standard*, 21 June 1999, p. 15+.

Cleland, Kim. "Ad, Promo Strategies Make New Converts." *Advertising Age*, 10 April 1995, p. 1+.

Comarow, Avery. "Not Too Young for Heart Disease." *U.S. News & World Report*, 8 March 1999, p. 74.

Concar, David. "Get Your Head Round This..." *New Scientist*, 10 April 1999, p. 20+.

Crowley, Elizabeth. "More Young People Turn Away from Politics and Concentrate Instead on Community Service." *The Wall Street Journal*, 16 June 1999.

Cushman, John H. Jr. "E.P.A. Plans Radical Change in Calculation of Cancer Risk." *The New York Times*, 16 April 1996.

Diller, Lawrence H., M.D. "Running on Ritalin: A Physician Reflects on Children, Society, and Performance in a Pill." *Future Survey*, March 1999, p. 7.

Donovan, Doug. "Angst on the Cybersofa." *Forbes*, 5 April 1999, p. 47.

Flynn, Julia. "Gap Exists Between Entrepreneurship in Europe, North America, Study Shows." *The Wall Street Journal*, 2 July 1999.

Furedi, Frank. "The Blame Game." *New Scientist*, 25 August 2001, p. 48.

Gedmin, Jeffrey. "The New Europe-Menace." *The Weekly Standard*, 29 March 1999, p. 19+.

Gitlin, Todd. "We're All Authorities." *The New York Times Book Review*, 23 May 1999.

Gladwell, Malcolm. "Dept. of Disputation: Blowup." *The New Yorker*, 22 January 1996, p. 32+.

Godschalk, David R., T. Beatly, P. Berke, and E.J. Kaiser. "Natural Hazard Mitigation: Recasting Disaster Policy and Planning." *Future Survey*, July 1999, p. 17.

Gunther, Marc. "God & Business." *Fortune*, 9 July 2001, p. 58+.

Hecht, Jeff. "Wavelength Division Multiplexing." *Technology Review*, March/April 1999, p. 72+.

Henneberger, Melinda. "Provocateur Is Back to 'Spit' on Detractors of U.S." *The New York Times*, 30 October 2001.

Heuberger, Frank and Laura Nash, "A Fatal Embrace? Assessing Holistic Trends in Resources Programs." *Future Survey*, February 1995, p. 9+.

Jones, Malcolm. "Touched by the Angels." *Newsweek*, 3 May 1999, p. 71+.

Kakutani, Michiko. "When Fluidity Replaces Maturity." *The New York Times*, 20 March 1995.

Kirwan-Taylor, Helen. "How to Spend It." *The Financial Times* magazine supplement, March 1999, p. 69+.

Koretz, Gene. "Do Large Stakes Inhibit CEO?" *Business Week*, 6 May 1996, p. 24.

Labash, Matt. "What's Wrong with Dodgeball?" *The Weekly Standard*, 25 June 2001, p. 17+.

Lardner, James. "The Urge to Splurge." *U.S. News & World Report*, 24 May 1999, p. 48+.

Leary, Warren E. "Gene Inserted in Crop Plant Is Shown to Spread to Wild." *The New York Times*, 7 March 1996.

Léger, Dimitry Elias and Felecia A. Williams. "Soul on the Edge." *The Source*, December 1998, p. 162+.

Leo, John. "Learning to Love Terrorists." *U.S. News & World Report*, 8 October 2001, p. 48.

Lippin, Richard A. "Responsible Pleasures: A Doctor's Prescription for What Ails You." *The Futurist*, June/July 1999, p. 34+.

Mayo, John S. "Information Technology for Development." *The New York Times Magazine*, 9 April 1995, p. 38.

Morris, David B. "Illness and Culture in the Postmodern Age." *Future Survey*, March 1999, p. 2.

Nash, Laura L. "How the Church Has Failed Business." *Across the Board*, July/August 2001, p. 26+.

Niebuhr, Gustav. "Protestantism Shifts Toward a New Model of How 'Church' Is Done." *The New York Times*, 29 April 1995.

Niebuhr, Gustav. "Where Religion Gets a Big Dose of Shopping-Mall Culture." *The New York Times*, 16 April 1995.

Ogden, Michael. "Politics in a Parallel Universe: Is There a Future in Cyberdemocracy?" *Future Survey*, February 1995, p. 4.

Orr, Deborah. "Damn Yankees." *Forbes*, 17 May 1999, p. 206+.

Peterson, Ivers. "Big-League Computing." *Science News*, 12 December 1998, p. 383.

Raeburn, Paul. "From Silent Spring to Barren Spring?" *Business Week*, 18 March 1996, p. 42.

Raloff, Janet. "Does Light Have a Dark Side? Nighttime Illumination Might Elevate Cancer Risk." *Science News*, 17 October 1999, p. 248+.

Raloff, Janet. "Languishing Languages: Cultures at Risk." *Science News*, 25 February 1995, p. 117.

Richtel, Matt. "Consumers Warm to 'Free' PCs." *The New York Times*, 15 April 1999.

Roszak, Theodore. "Shakespeare Never Lost a Manuscript to a Computer Crash." *The New York Times*, 11 March 1999.

Rybczynski, Witold. "This Old House." *The New Republic*, 8 May 1995, p. 14+.

Schifrin, Matthew and Om Malik. "Amateur Hour on Wall Street." *Forbes*, 25 January 1999, p. 82+.

Schonfeld, Erick. "Betting on the Boomers." *Fortune*, 25 December 1995, p. 78+.

Schrof, Joannie and Stacey Schultz. "Melancholy Nation." *U.S. News & World Report*, 8 March 1999, p. 56+.

Sletcher, Michael A. "Fewer of Us Are Saying 'I Do.'" *The Washington Post National Weekly Edition*, 12 July 1999.

Sunstein, Cass R. "Vanity Fair." *The New Republic*, 29 March 1999, p. 42+.

Tabor, Mary B. W. "Schools Profit from Offering Pupils for Market Research." *The New York Times*, 5 April 1999, p. A1+.

Tierney, John. "Suitable Men: Rare Species Under Study." *The New York Times*, 7 June 1999.

Uchitelle, Louis. "A Top Economist Switches His View on Productivity." *The New York Times*, 8 May 1996.

Vogelstein, Fred. "A Virtual Stock Market." *U.S. News & World Report*, 26 April 1999, p. 47+.

Walljasper, Jay. "Sustainable Extravagance." *UTNE Reader*, March/April 1999, p. 63.

Weir, Margaret. "In the Shadows." *The Brookings Review*, Spring 1995, p. 16.

Zill, Nicholas and John Robinson. "The Generation X Difference." *American Demographics*, April 1995, p. 24+.

_____. "The Christian Capitalists." *U.S. News & World Report*. 13 March 1995, p. 52+.

_____. "A Civil Self-Service." *The Economist*, 1 May 1999, p. 49+.

_____. "Dead Workers Society." *Across the Board*, May 1999, p. 1.

_____. "Detroit Discovers the Consumer." *The Economist*, 17 February 1996, p. 61.

_____. "Econo-Mix: Job Listings On-Line, *Futurific*, March 1999, p. 6+.

_____. "Fire and Forget?" *The Economist*, 20 April 1996, p. 51.

_____. "The Grand Illusion." *The Economist*, 5 June 1999, p. 52+.

_____. "Healthy Pit Stop." *Science*, 14 May 1999, p. 1115.

_____. "Hormonal Sabotage." *Natural History*, March 1996, p. 42+.

_____. "How Safe Is Your Bank?" *The Economist*, 27 April 1996, p. 15+.

_____. "Is Working Out Uncool?" *The Numbers News*, March 1996, p. 1+.

_____. "Making Cities Safer: Good Fences..." *The Economist*, 25 March 1995, p. 30+.

_____. "News from the War Against Death: 3D Crunch to Impact Drug Discovery." *Futurific*, March 1999, p. 25.

_____. "Non-Profits Cash in on Names." *Happenings*, March 1995, p. 4.

_____. "North America: Sales of Religious Books..." *National & International Religion Report*, 6 March 1995, p. 4.

_____. "Pay Dirt." *The Economist*, 5 June 1999, p. 28.

_____. "Pension Funds: Dutch Coverage." *The Economist*, 6 April 1996, p. 81.

_____. "Scientists, Copying Cells, Produce Identical Sheep." *The New York Times*, 17 March 1996.

_____. "Space Inc: Breakthroughs in Aerospace." *Futurific*, March 1999, p. 10.

_____. "Transport Nation: Cars." *Futurific*, March 1999, p. 14+.

_____. "Who's Wearing the Trousers?" *The Economist*, 8 September 2001, p. 26+.

Chapter 3, "Substituting the Spiral for the Pendulum"

Beckett, Paul. "SEC Order Forces Executives to Swear by Their Names." *The Wall Street Journal*, 5 July 2002.

Belkin, Lisa. "For Women, the Price of Success." *The New York Times*, 17 March 2002.

Fisher, Daniel. *The Kondratieff Wave*. Angelfire.com, 1998.

Friedman, Elyse M., ed. "The New-Economy Almanac." *INC.—The State of Small Business in 1997*, July 1997, p. 108+.

Gardyn, Rebecca. "Animal Magnetism." *American Demographics*, May 2002, p. 30+.

Hopkins, Michael. "The State of Small Business 1997." *INC.—The State of Small Business in 1997*, July 1997, p. 11+.

Liesman, Steve. "Consumer Spending: A Sentimental Journey?" *The Wall Street Journal*, 8 April 2002.

Lyall, Sarah. "For Europeans, Love, Yes; Marriage, Maybe." *The New York Times*, 24 March 2002.

Pertman, Adam. "Adoption Nation: How the Adoption Revolution is Transforming America." *Future Survey*, January 2002, p. 7.

Raspberry, William. "The Nonparent Trap?" *The Washington Post National Weekly Edition*, 6 May 2002.

Sheler, Jeffrey L. "Faith in America." *U.S. News & World Report*, 6 May 2002, p. 40+.

Tyre, Peg. "Bringing Up Adultolescents." *Newsweek*, 25 March 2002, p. 38+.

_____. *The Kondratieff Wave*. Commodity Research Bureau, 2002.

_____. "Lighting's Dark Side." *Science*, 15 February 2002, p. 1227.

Chapter 4, "The Extremes Inform the Middle"

Allen, Michael. "As Dot-Coms Go Bust in U.S., Bermuda Hosts an Odd Little Boomlet." *The New York Times*, 6 January 2001, p. A1+.

Ashdown, Paul. "From Wild West to Wild Web." *Vital Speeches of the Day*, 1 September 2000, p. 699+.

Band, Jonathan. "The Copyright Paradox." *Brookings Review*, Winter 2001, p. 32+.

Barlow, John Perry. "The Next Economy of Ideas." *Wired*, October 2000, p. 240+.

Bellenson, John Lloyd. "Sensory Download." *Business 2.0*, 26 September 2000, p. 122.

Binswanger, C. K. "Gimme 20 Push-Ups—Now!" *Newsweek*, 27 October 1997, p. 54.

Brown, Arnold. "Listening to the Luddites." *USA Today*, September 2002, p. 25+.

Carnahan, Ira. "Insurance by the Minute." *Forbes*, 11 December 2000, p. 86+.

Clemetson, Lynette. "Trying to Right Mr. Wong." *Newsweek*, 31 July 2000, p. 55.

Cohen, Roger. "Germany's Shift East." *The New York Times*, 29 September 1998, p. A1+.

Coleman, Brian and Thomas Kamm. "Germany's Schroder Backs Controls." *The Wall Street Journal*, 1 October 1998, p. A16.

Dery, Mark. "Alien Nation." *Red Herring*, October 2000, p. 350+.

Dionne, E. J. Jr. "Is There Really a 'Third Way'?" *The Washington Post National Weekly Edition*, 17 August 1998, p. 28.

Drucker, Peter F. "The Next Information Revolution." *Forbes ASAP*, 24 August 1998, p. 46+.

Fox, Barry. "Patents: Where Am I?" *New Scientist*, 18 December 1997, p. 11.

Friedman, Robert I. "Red Mafiya: How the Russian Mob Has Invaded America." *Future Survey*, January 2001, p. 17.

Gates, Jeff. "Twenty-first Century Capitalism: To Humanize, Ownerize." *The Humanist*, July/August 1998, p. 9+.

Goodstein, Laurie and Sam Dillon. "Scandal Is Stirring Catholics to Push for More Power." *The New York Times*, 10 November 2002, p. 1+.

Grande, Carlos. "Dawn of the Cyberbabes." *Financial Times*, 17 August 2000, p. 10.

Harney, Alexandra. "Japanese Men Warm to Virtual Girlfriends." *Financial Times*, 24 November 2000, p. 6.

Hatlestad, Luc. "Privacy Matters." *Red Herring*, 16 January 2001, p. 48+.

Kate, Nancy Ten. "What If...There Was One Car for Every Adult?" *American Demographics*, December 1997, p. 43+.

Katz, Michael. "Who (Gonna) Dunnit." *Forbes*, 11 December 2000, p. 216.

Kristof, Nicholas D. "Experts Question Roving Flow of Global Capital." *The New York Times*, 20 September 1998, p. 18.

Kurtz, Paul. "Beyond Humanist Manifesto II." *The Humanist*, September/October 1998, p. 25+.

Kurzweil, Ray. "Dear PC: RIP." *Business 2.0*, 26 September 2000, p. 162+.

The New York Times, 1 February 2001, p. A16.

Lake, Anthony. "6 Nightmares: Real Threats in a Dangerous World and How America Can Meet Them." *Future Survey*, January 2001, p. 5.

Lanier, Jaron. "Taking Stock: So, What's Changed in the Last Five Years?" *Wired*, January 1998, p. 60.

Le Beau, Christina. "The E-Training Evolution." *Grok*, October 2000, page 128+.

Lemmey, Tara. "Your Next Identity Crisis." *Business 2.0*, 26 September 2000, p. 180+.

Lewis, Peter H. "Spy Software Puts Home PCs Under Surveillance." *The New York Times*, 22 June 2000, p. G1+.

Lilla, Mark and Christopher Caldwell. "America's Two Revolutions." *Wilson Quarterly*, Summer 1998, p. 119+.

Manuel, Gren and Leslie Chang. "Will Language Wars Balkanize the Web?" *The Wall Street Journal*, 30 November 2000, p. A17+.

Markoff, John. "The Soul of the Ultimate Machine." *The New York Times*, 10 December 2000, p. BU1+.

Matthews, Robert. "The Ideas Machine." *New Scientist*, 20 January 2001, p. 26+.

McAfee, Andrew. "The Napsterization of B2B." *Harvard Business Review*, November/December 2000, p. 18+.

McDonough, William and Michael Braungart. "The NEXT Industrial Revolution." *The Atlantic Monthly*, October 1998, p. 82+.

Miller, Daniel. "The Internet: An Ethnographic Approach." *Future Survey*, December 2000, p. 6.

Miller, Riel. "The Internet in 20 Years: Cyberspace, the Next Frontier?" *Future Survey*, December 2000, p. 3.

Monastersky, R. "Sizzling June Fires Up Greenhouse Debate." *Science News*, 25 July 1998, p. 52+.

Mullins, Justin. "Next-Generation Fashion." *New Scientist*, 6 January 2001, p. 12.

Munk, Nina. "Girl Power!" *Fortune*, 8 December 1997, p. 312+.

Neal, Douglas and Nicholas Morgan. "Our Data, Our Selves." *The Wilson Quarterly*, Autumn 2000, p. 51+.

Northington, Suzanne. "Tater Tots Again?" *Upside*, November 2000, p. 58.

Olson, Walter. "Unified Kvetch Theory." *Reason*, August/September 1998, p. 64+.

Parloff, Roger. "Can We Talk?" *Fortune*, 2 September 2002, p. 102+.

Perine, Keith. "The Trouble with Regulating Hate." *The Industry Standard*, 31 July 2000, p. 94+.

Perkin, Julian. "Switched-on PCs Will Mind Your Manners." *Financial Times*, 4 October 2000, p. 1+.

Powell, Bill and Kim Palchikoff. "Sober, Rested and Ready." *Newsweek*, 8 December 1997, p. 50+.

Purton, Peter. "Good Prognosis for Mobile Health Services." *The Financial Times*, 20 September 2000, p. xxiv.

Raloff, J. "Estrogen's Emerging Manly Alter Ego." *Science News*, 6 December 1997, p. 356.

Rodrik, Dani. "The Global Fix. *The New Republic*, 2 November 1998, p. 17+.

Rose, Frederick. "Work Week: Is Canada Emerging?" *The Wall Street Journal*, 25 November 1997, p. 1.

Rosen, Jeffrey. "The Fall of Private Man." *The New Republic*, 12 June 2000, p. 22+.

Rosen, Jeffrey. "Here's Looking at You: Does the Supreme Court Value Privacy?" *The New Republic*, 16 October 2000, p. 24+.

Rosen, Jeffrey. "Why Privacy Matters." *The Wilson Quarterly*, Autumn 2000, p. 32+.

Russell, Glenn and Bernard Holkner. "Virtual Schools." *Future Survey*, December 2000, p. 7.

Schiro, Anne-Marie. "Power Suits Fade, and Romance Comes into Focus." *The New York Times*, 18 November 1997, p. B15.

Schuman, Michael. "Asian Governments Bid Adieu to Invisible Hand." *The Wall Street Journal*, 24 August 1998, p. A1.

Sheehy, Gail. "Beyond Virility, a New Vision." *Newsweek*, 17 November 1997, p. 69.

Shosak, Arthur B. "Organized Labor Reawakens Online." *Business 2.0*, 26 September 2000, p. 162+.

Southwick, Karen. "Physician, Wire Thyself." *Forbes ASAP*, 27 November 2000, p. 249+.

Stelzer, Irwin M. "There's No Way Like the Third Way." *The Weekly Standard*, 21 September 1998, p. 26+.

Tibbs, Hardin. "Humane Ecostructure: Can Industry Become Gaia's Friend?" *Whole Earth*, Summer 1998, p. 61+.

Turkle, Sherry. "When Toys Are Us." *Forbes ASAP*, 2 October 2000, p. 213+.

Verton, Dan. "The Threat from Within." *Business 2.0*, April 2000, p. 329+.

Wallraff, Barbara. "WHAT Global Language?" *The Atlantic Monthly*, November 2000, p. 52+.

Webb, Jeremy and Duncan Graham-Rowe. "Everything, Anywhere." *New Scientist*, 21 October 2000, p. 33+.

Weiss, Daniel Evan. "You, Robot." *The Industry Standard*, 7 August 2000, p. 168+.

_____. "Bangladesh: Acid Horrors." *The Economist*, 17 January 1998, p. 35+.

_____. "Complaint Department." *Y&R's Brand Futures Group*, 26 May 2000, p. 1+.

_____. "Decline in Doing Home Repairs Suggests Shift in DIY Market." *The Public Pulse*, September 1997, p. 5.

_____. "Digital Family." *Technology Review*, January/February 2001, p. 25.

_____. "Look, Ma, No Hands!" *Science News*, 13 September 1997, p. 168+.

_____. "Monkeying Around with the Brain." *Newsweek*, 27 November 2000, p. 76.

_____. "Mother Nature Is Striking Back." *Business Week*, 26 October 1998, p. 143.

_____. "Office Supplies and E-Learning." *Futurific*, November 2000, p. 14.

_____. "Police System Analyzed Every Face at Super Bowl."

_____. "The Technology Review Ten." *Technology Review*, January/February 2001, p. 97+.

_____. "Top Ten Trends 2001." *Red Herring*, 4 December 2000, p. 99+.

Chapter 5, "Efficiency Breeds Vulnerability"

Amato, Ivan. "Crossed Signals." *U.S. News & World Report*, 16 December 2002, p. 54+.

Crystal, Ben. "NASA's New Shuttle Designs Stolen by Hacker." *New Scientist*, 17 August 2002, p. 13.

Flicker, Barry. "Working at Warp Speed: The New Rules for Project Success in a Sped-Up World." *Future Survey*, August 2002, p. 11.

Fraser, Nicholas. "Le Divorce." *Harper's Magazine*, September 2002, p. 58+.

Grabosky, Peter, Russell Smith, and Gillian Dempsey. "Electronic Theft: Unlawful Acquisition in Cyberspace." *Future Survey*, November 2002, p. 22+.

Lee, Jennifer. "Dirty Laundry, Online for All to See." *The New York Times*, 5 September 2002, G1+.

Malone, Michael S. "Welcome to Feedback Universe." *Forbes ASAP*, 7 October 2002, p. 20+.

Pontin, Mark. "Power Trouble Ahead for the Grid." *Red Herring*, September 2002, p. 27.

_____. "Plumbing Revolution." *The Economist*, 16–22 November 2002, p. 71.

_____. "Top of the Hacks." *New Scientist*, 24 August 2002, p. 7.

Chapter 6, "The Multiplier Effect of New Distribution Channels"

Comerford, Richard. "Computing." *IEEE Spectrum*, January 2000, p. 45+.

Drucker, Peter. "The Next Society." *The Economist*, 3–9 November 2001, p. after 54.

Fetto, John. "Will It Do Laundry, Too?" *Forecast*, February 2000, p. 4+.

Fukuyama, Francis. "How to Regulate Science." *The Public Interest*, Winter 2002, p. 3+.

Fulford, Benjamin. "Highly Mobile." *Forbes*, 7 February 1999, p. 113.

Hiu, Alice S. Y. et al. "An Investigation of Decision-Making Styles of Consumers in China." *The Journal of Consumer Affairs*, Winter 2001, p. 326+.

Kaufman, Jonathan. "Marketing in the Future Will Be Everywhere—Including Your Head." *The Wall Street Journal*, 1 January 2000.

Kurzweil, Ray. "The Web Within Us." *Business 2.0*, December 1999, p. 173+.

Martinez, Barbara. "Health Plan That Puts Employees in Charge of Spending Catches On." *The Wall Street Journal*, 8 January 2002.

McCartney, Neil. "Challenges Ahead as Networks Start Building the Future." *The Financial Times*, 17 January 2001.

Pinker, Steven. *How the Mind Works*. W. W. Norton & Company, Inc., New York, NY, 1997, pp. 89–90.

Platt, Charles. "You've Got Smell!" *Wired*, November 1999, p. 256+.

Poe, Robert. "Optical Illusion." *Business 2.0*, 14 November 2000, p. 116+.

Ransdell, Eric. "Network Effects." *Fast Company*, September 1999, p. 208+.

Rosenzweig, Mark R. *Biological Psychology*. SinaverAssociates, Inc., Sunderland, MA, 1996, pp. 624–625.

Ryan, James. "Innerspace Invaders." *Business 2.0*, October 1999, p. 225.

Walker, Leslie. "Big Business Wants a Piece of the Auction." *The Washington Post National Weekly Edition*, 30 July–12 August 2001, p. 18+.

Weber, Joseph. "The New Power Play in Health Care." *Business Week*, 28 January 2002, p. 90+.

Wolfson, Adam. "Biodemocracy in America." *The Public Interest*, Winter 2002, p. 23+.

_____. "Battelle: New Millennium Strategic Technologies for the Next 20 Years." *Technology Forecasts*, December 1999, p. 1+.

_____. "Busier Signals?" *Science*, 14 January 2000, p. 189.

_____. "Communication Is the Name of the Game." *Futurific*, September 1999, 21+.

_____. "A Dozen Millennium Forecasts from *The Futurist*." *Future Times*, Fall 1999, p. A6+.

_____. "The Great Telecoms Crash." *The Economist*, 20 July 2002, p. 9.

_____. "Industry's Switch to Digital Television." *Futurific*, September 1999, p. 24.

_____. "The World in Your Pocket." *The Economist*, 9 October 1999, p. 5+ (special section).

Chapter 7, "Entropy"

Adler, Jerry and Tara Weingarten. "Mansions Off the Rack." *Newsweek*, 14 February 2000, p. 60+.

Andrews, Edmund L. "Europe Plans to Collect Tax on Some Internet Transactions." *The New York Times*, 2 March 2000.

Baum, Geoff et al. "Introducing the New Value Creation Index." *Forbes ASAP*, 3 April 2000, p. 140.

Bodenstab, Jeffrey. "An Automaker Tries the Dell Way." *The Wall Street Journal*, 30 August 1999.

Borrus, Amy and Richard S. Dunham. "Tech: The Virtual Third Party." *Business Week*, 24 April 2000, p. 74+.

Brooke, James. "Rising Tax Bills Fuel Anger in Canada." *The New York Times*, 27 February 2000.

Brooks, David. "The New Upper Class." *The Weekly Standard*, 8 May 2000, p. 21+.

Cohen, Norma. "Retailers Count the Cost of Shopping Spree." *The Financial Times*, 5 May 2000.

Corcoran, Elizabeth. "The E Gang." *Forbes*, 24 July 2000, p. 145+.

Croal, N'Gai. "The Art of Darkness." *Newsweek*, 12 June 2000, p. 48+.

Daley, Suzanne. "The Pedestal Is Cracking Under an Elite in France." *The New York Times*, 9 July 2000.

Dolan, Kerry A. "The Age of the $100 Million CEO." *Forbes*, 3 April 2000, p. 122+.

Ehrenfeld, Tom. "Intellectual Capital: Small Is Beautiful." *The Industry Standard*, 29 May 2000, p. 206+.

Eisenhardt, Kathleen M. "Survival of the Swiftest." *Red Herring*, April 2000, p. 374+.

Ewing, Jack. "Surprise, The German Greens Are Marching with Business." *Business Week*, 28 February 2000, p. 59+.

Findlay, Mark. "The Globalization of Crime: Understanding Transitional Relationships in Context." *Future Survey*, February 2000, p. 9+.

French, Howard W. "Internet Recharges Reformers in Korea." *The New York Times*, 29 February 2000.

George, Nicholas and Clare MacCarthy. "Ageing Population Brings Jobs Crisis to Scandinavia." *The Financial Times*, 11 April 2000.

Gerstner, Louis V. Jr. "Guest Commentary: Blinded by Dot-Com Alchemy." *Business Week*, 27 March 2000, p. 40.

Hayden, Thomas. "Safaris and Sensitivity." *Newsweek*, 5 June 2000, p. 56.

Jovin, Ellen and Jennifer Lach. "Online with the Operator." *American Demographics*, February 1999, p. 36+.

Kaiser, Jocelyn, ed. "NetWatch: Free Online University?" *Science*, 24 March 2000, p. 2111+.

Kantrowitz, Barbara. "Busy Around the Clock." *Newsweek*, 17 July 2000, p. 49.

Karmin, Craig. "The Global Shareholder." *The Wall Street Journal*, 8 May 2000.

Kirsner, Scott. "Are You Experienced?" *Wired*, July 2000, p. 188+.

Koerner, Brendan I. "The Bugs in the Machine." *Wired*, August 2002, p. 27+.

Koretz, Gene. "Economic Trends: A Better Life for Our Kids." *Business Week*, 10 April 2000, p. 32.

Kruger, Pamela. "Why Johnny Can't Play." *Fast Company*, August 2000, p. 271.

Leach, William. "Country of Exiles: The Destruction of Place in American Life." *Future Survey*, February 2000, p. 8.

Levering, Robert and Milton Moskowitz. "The 100 Best Companies to Work For." *Fortune*, 10 January 2000, p. 82+.

Losco, Joseph and Brian L. Fife. "Higher Education in Transition: The Challenges of the New Millennium." *Future Survey*, February 2000, p. 18.

Montagnon, Peter and Khozem Merchant. "Virtual Banking Planned for Rural India." *The Financial Times*, 17 March 2000.

Rohwer, Jim. "Japan Goes Web Crazy." *Fortune*, 7 February 2000, p. 115+.

Sawhney, Mohanbir and Steven Kaplan. "Let's Get Vertical." *Business 2.0*, September 1999, p. 84+.

Schlegel, Jean. "Lifting the Lid Off Some Mysteries." *The Financial Times*, 17 May 2000.

Schrage, Michael. "Disruptive Teens Totally Rule." *Fortune*, 12 June 2000, p. 338.

Seybold, Patricia B. "Wrap Up Your E-Wallets for the Holidays." *Business 2.0*, September 1999, p. 58.

Sittenfeld, Curtis. "What Do Young People Want?" *Fast Company*, August 2000, p. 182.

Spindle, Bill. "Japan Becomes a Mecca for Venture Capitalists." *The Wall Street Journal*, 24 February 2000.

Spindle, Bill. "Japanese Economy Faces a Potential Bonanza as Nearly $1 Trillion in Savings Plans Mature." *The Wall Street Journal*, 24 March 2000.

Strom, Stephanie. "In Japan, Start-Up and Risk Are New Business Watchwords." *The New York Times*, 24 April 2000.

Swardson, Anne. "A Pension Crisis Looms in Europe." *The Washington Post National Weekly Edition*, 1 May 2000.

Tomkins, Richard. "Stretching a Selling Point." *The Financial Times*, 26 May 2000.

Useem, Jerry. "New Ethics...or No Ethics?" *Fortune*, 20 March 2000, p. 82+.

Wellner, Alison Stein. "The Perils of Hiring Stars." *Inc.*, August 2004, p. 31.

Winter, Greg. "Taking at the Office Reaches New Heights." *The New York Times*, 12 July 2000.

Woolley, Scott. "On-line or the Breadline." *Forbes*, 9 August 1999, p. 80.

Wysocki, Bernard Jr. "In U.S. Trade Arsenal, Brains Outgun Brawn." *The Wall Street Journal*, 10 April 2000.

_____. "A Continent on the Move." *The Economist*, 6 May 2000, p. 25+.

_____. "Drucker on Financial Services." *The Economist*, 25 September 1999, p. 25+.

_____. "Europe in Cyberspace." *The Economist*, 1 April 2000, p. 21+.

_____. "Global Economy Makes Taxing Harder." *The Futurist*, March/April 2000, p. 11.

_____. "The Heyday of the Auction." *The Economist*, 24 July 1999.

_____. "India's Economy: Many Obstacles Still Ahead." *The Economist*, 4 March 2000, p. 70+.

_____. "Into the Whirlwind." *The Economist*, 22 January 2000, p. 23+.

_____. "The New Spain." *Y&R's Brand Futures Group* (Internet report), 17 April 2000, p. 1+.

_____. "Nouveau Riche Numbers Jump." *American Demographics Forecast*, April 2000, p. 1+.

_____. "Online Finance: The Virtual Threat." *The Economist*, 20 May 2000, p. 5 Survey+.

_____. "Talking Trends: What's New with the World's Oldest Tradition?" *FGI Bulletin*, May 2000, p. 3.

_____. "The Taming of the Shrewd." *The Economist*, 6 May 2000, p. 75+.

_____. "Tax-Cut Fever." *Business Week*, 6 March 2000, p. 56+.

_____. "Under Pressure, China Blesses Private Sector." *The Wall Street Journal*, 13 March 2000.

_____. "US-India Business: On the Upswing." *The Economist Intelligence Unit Country Monitor*, 29 March 2000, p. 1.

_____. "The World of ResidenSea." *Avenue* (Advertisement), March 2000.

Chapter 8, "Integrity Begets Quality"

Allen, Michael. "As Dot-Coms Go Bust in U.S., Bermuda Hosts an Odd Little Boomlet." *The New York Times*, 6 January 2001.

Alsop, Ronald. "Perils of Corporate Philanthropy." *The Wall Street Journal*, 16 January 2002.

Alsop, Ronald. "Reputations Rest on Good Service." *The Wall Street Journal*, 16 January 2002.

Brady, Diane. "Why Service Stinks." *Business Week*, 23 October 2000, p. 118+.

Carnahan, Ira. "Insurance by the Middle." *Forbes*, 11 December 2000, p. 86+.

Drucker, Peter F. "They're Not Employees, They're People." *Harvard Business Review*, February 2002, p. 70+.

Dworkin, Ronald. "Sovereign Virtue: The Theory and Practice of Equality." *Future Survey*, July 2000, p. 20.

Grande, Carlos. "Dawn of the Cyberbabes." *The Financial Times*, 17 August 2000.

Hamilton, David P. "Going Places." *The Wall Street Journal*, 11 December 2000.

Hatlestad, Luc. "Privacy Matters." *Red Herring*, 16 January 2001, p. 48+.

Katz, Michael. "Who (Gonna) Dunnit." *Forbes*, 11 December 2000, p. 216.

Kolk, Ans. "Green Reporting." *Harvard Business Review*, January/February 2000, p. 15+.

Kuchinskas, Susan. "One-To-(N)one?" *Business 2.0*, 12 September 2000, p. 141+.

Le Beau, Christina. "The E-Training Evolution." *Grok*, October 2000, p. 128+.

Miller, Riel. "The Internet in 20 Years: Cyberspace, the Next Frontier?" *Future Survey*, December 2000, p. 3.

Neal, Douglas and Nicholas Morgan. "Our Data, Our Selves." *The Wilson Quarterly*, Autumn 2000, p. 51+.

Orey, Michael and Milo Geyelin. "Lawyers Find Jury Pools Polluted by Antibusiness Biases." *The Wall Street Journal*, 12 August 2002.

Rosen, Jeffrey. "Why Privacy Matters." *The Wilson Quarterly*, Autumn 2000, p. 32+.

Simons, Tony. "The High Cost of Lost Trust." *Harvard Business Review*, September 2002, p. 18+.

Whelan, David. "Wrapped in the Flag." *American Demographics*, December 2001, p. 37+.

_____. "Curse of the Ethical Executive." *The Economist*, 17 November 2001, p. 70.

Chapter 9, "The Law of Large Numbers"

Balu, Rekka. "Poor People." *Fast Company*, June 2001.

Stark, P. B. *Statistics Tools for Internet and Classroom Instruction with a Graphical User Interface*. 1997–2002.

Chapter 10, "Demography"

Cohen, Joel E. "Human Population: The Next Half Century." *Science*, 14 November 2003.

Longman, Phillip. "The Global Baby Bust." *Foreign Affairs*, May/June 2004.

Schoenfeld, Almut. "Germany Returns Generous Perks for Civil Servants." *The Wall Street Journal*, 5 April 2004.

Weiner, Edith and Arnold Brown. *Office Biology*. Master Media Ltd., 1993.

Wiseman, Paul. "No Sex, Please—We're Japanese." *USA Today*. 3 June 2004.

http://www.census.gov.

_____. "Forever Young." *The Economist*, 27 March 2004.

_____. "Replacement Migration: Is It a Solution to Declining and Aging Populations?" *United Nations Population Division of the Department of Economic and Social Affairs (DESA)*, 17 March 2000.

Chapter 11, "Compromise Versus Lowest Common Denominators"

Mortimer, John. "Blood Sport as Politics," *The New York Times*, 24 September 2002, p. A27.

Chapter 12, "The Three-Legged Stools of the Political Agenda"

Halstead, Ted and Michael Lind. *The Radical Center: The Future of American Politics*. Doubleday, New York, NY, 2001.

Chapter 13, "Right-of-Way"

Freedman, Michael. "The Tort Mess." *Forbes*, 13 May 2002, p. 90+.

McCartney, Neil. "Challenges Ahead as Networks Start Building the Future." *The Financial Times*, 17 January 2001, p. 1.

Paul, Pamela. "Corporate Responsibility." *American Demographics*, May 2002, p. 24+.

Ray, Jean S. *Railroads and Telecommunications*. Baton Rouge, LA, July 1995. (This article was adapted from a legal research memorandum.)

Wingfield, Nick. "In Latest Strategy Shift, Amazon Is Offering a Home to Retailers." *The Wall Street Journal*, 24 September 2003.

_____. "These Grocery-Delivery Services Might Even Do Windows." *The Wall Street Journal*, 12 February 1998, p. A1.

http://www.csmonitor.com/durable/2001/07/23/p11sl.htm. Copyright 2001 *The Christian Science Monitor*.

http://www.ggrpc.com/pulicus.htm.

http://www.needham.mec.edu/high school/cur/kane98/kane p.3 immig/China/china.html.

http://www.santacruzsentinel.com/archive/2002/May/26biz/ stories/01biz.htm. Copyright 1999–2002 *Santa Cruz Sentinel*.

Chapter 14, "Football Meets Shopping"

Balu, Rekha. "How a Pasta Maker Used Its Noodle to Whip the Giants." *The Wall Street Journal*, 9 December 1998, p. A1+.

Barnett, Megan. "Surviving the Shakeout." *The Industry Standard*, 5 March 2001, p. 43+.

Barron, Kelly. "Suburban Flight." *Forbes*, 30 November 1998, p. 146+.

Belkin, Lisa. "Primetime Pushers." *Mother Jones*, March/April 2001, p. 30+.

Boitano, Margaret. "Wired in West Virginia Jails (of All Places)." *Fortune*, 18 December 2000, p. 68.

Croal, N'Gai. "The Little Rio Is Causing a Grand Fuss." *Newsweek*, 14 December 1998, p. 58.

Dreyfuss, Joel. "Software That Comes Cheap." *Fortune*, 9 November 1998, p. 228J.

Flynn, Julia. "Sorry, But They're Not Gonna Take It Anymore." *Business Week*, 25 January 1999, p. 64.

Fricker, Janet. "This Pill Washes Whiter." *New Scientist*, 31 October 1998, p. 22+.

Graham, Nick. "Selling the Tale." *FGI Bulletin*, December/January 1998, p. 1+.

Hamel, Gary and Jeff Sampler. "The E-Corporation." *Fortune*, 7 December 1998, p. 80+.

Joel, Kotkin, Sarah E. Moran, Matthew Jaffe, and Kevin Roderick. "Best New Places to Do Business." *The Industry Standard*, 19 February 2001, p. 74+.

Lach, Jennifer. "Focusing the Lens on Energy Users." *American Demographics*, December 1998, p. 42+.

Liebmann, Wendy. "How America Shops 2000." *Vital Speeches of the Day*, 1 October 2000, p. 753+.

Meadows, Susannah. "Kinder, Gentler Clinics." *Newsweek*, 26 February 2001, p. 52+.

Meyer, Michael. "Fast, Yes. Easy? No." *Newsweek*, 11 September 1998, p. 42+.

Mills, Mike. "Playing Fair with Retailers." *The Washington Post National Weekly Edition*, 30 November 1998, p. 23.

Naughton, Keith. "Cheap Thrills for Shoppers." *Newsweek*, 16 April 2001, p. 45.

Ody, Penelope. "New Ways to Connect with Customers on the Move." *Financial Times*, 7 March 2001, p. xvi.

Peteson, Ivars. "Agents of Cooperation." *Science News*, 2 January 1999, p. 12+.

Tanouye, Elyse. "U.S. Has Developed an Expensive Habit; Now, How to Pay for It?" *The Wall Street Journal*, 6 November 1998, p. A1+.

Tully, Shawn. "America's Greatest Wealth Creators." *Fortune*, 9 November 1998, p. 192+.

Wellner, Alison Stein. "Make Love, Not Art?" *Forecast*, March 2001, p. 1+.

Winters, Wendi. "In Focus: Smells Like Teen Spirit." *FGI Bulletin*, January 2001, p. 4.

_____. "Brown Eyed Girl: Cross-Merchandising in a Unique Setting" and "The Apartment: The Feel of Home." *State of Retail, Tobé Report*, 4 January 2001, pp. 30–33.

_____. "Predictions for 1999." *Y&R's Brand Futures Group, Brain Snacks #59*, 25–29 January 1999, p. 1+.

_____. "10 Trends for the Post-PC World." *Red Herring*, December 1998, p. 52+.

http://www.YRBFG@aol.com. "Unique Recipes." *Y&R's Brand Futures Group*, 2 February 1999.

Chapter 15, "Managing by Harnessing Evolution"

Arnst, Catherine and John Carey. "Biotech Bodies." *Business Week*, 27 July 1998, p. 56+.

Auster, Bruce B. "The Fountain of Youth." *U.S. News & World Report*, 24 April 2000, p. 12.

Begley, Sharon. "A Gene for Genius?" *Newsweek*, 25 May 1998, p. 72.

Begley, Sharon with Thomas Hayden. "How Long Can You Go?" *Newsweek*, 22 February 1999, p. 50.

Bellenson, John Lloyd. "Sensory Download." *Business 2.0*, 26 September 2000, p. 122.

Benady, Susannah. "Mapping the Brain in Four Dimensions." *The Financial Times*, 10 April 2000.

Berman, Phyllis and Katherine Bruce. "Makeover at the Makeup Counter." *Forbes*, 19 April 1999, p. 82+.

Brown, Lester. "China's Water Shortage Could Shake World Food Security." *Future Survey*, July 1998, p. 17+.

Carey, John. "Playing God in the Lab." *Business Week*, 26 April 1999, p. 83+.

Chase, Bob. "Restoring the Impulse to Dream." *Vital Speeches of the Day*, 15 October 1997, p. 20+.

Dery, Mark. "Alien Nation." *Red Herring*, October 2000, p. 350+.

Dyson, Freeman. "Out of Sequence." *Red Herring*, June 1998, p. 158+.

Easterbrook, Gregg. "Hot and Not Bothered." *The New Republic*, 4 May 1998, p. 20+.

Easterbrook, Gregg. "Medical Evolution." *The New Republic*, 1 March 1999, p. 20+.

Eisenhardt, Kathleen and Shona Brown. "Time Pacing: Competing in Markets That Won't Stand Still." *Harvard Business Review*, March/April 1998, p. 177.

Eng, Sherri. "Hatching Schemes." *The Industry Standard*, 27 November–4 December 2000, p. 174+.

Enriquez, Juan and Ray Goldberg. "Transforming Life, Transforming Business: The Life-Science Revolution." *Harvard Business Review*, March/April 2000, p. 96+.

Gardyn, Rebecca. "What's on Your Mind?" *American Demographics*, April 2000, p. 31+.

Gilder, George. "Piping Hot." *Forbes ASAP*, 23 February 1998, p. 110+.

Glenn, Edward P. et al. "Irrigating Crops with Seawater." *Scientific American*, August 1998, p. 76+.

Graham-Rowe, Duncan. "Darwin Forges Fittest Metals." *New Scientist*, 6 July 2002, p. 18.

Graham-Rowe, Duncan. "Opinion Interview: God of the Norns." *New Scientist*, 1 April 2000, p. 42+.

Graham-Rowe, Duncan. "Say Hello to the RoboRat." *New Scientist*, 4 May 2002, p. 6+.

Hillis, Danny. "Massive, Parallel Supercomputers: Where They're Going." *Forbes ASAP*, 22 February 1999, p. 60+.

Hopkins, Patrick D. "Bad Copies: How Popular Media Represent Cloning as an Ethical Problem." *The Hastings Center Report*, March/April 1998, p. 6+.

Hunt, Lynn. "Send in the Clouds." *New Scientist*, 30 May 1998, p. 28+.

Kahn, Joseph. "Banking on the Unbanks." *The New York Times*, 4 February 1999.

Kornberg, Thomas B. and Mark Krasnow. "The Drosophila Genome Sequence: Implications for Biology and Medicine." *Science*, 24 March 2000, p. 2218+.

Krimsky, Sheldon. "Hormonal Chaos: The Scientific and Social Origins of the Environmental Endocrine Hypothesis." *Future Survey*, February 2000, p. 15+.

Kurzweil, Raymond. "Dear PC: RIP." *Business 2.0*, 26 September 2000, p. 162+.

Kurzweil, Raymond. "Piece of Mind: Downloading Brains in the 21st Century." *Forbes ASAP*, 22 February 1999, p. 79+.

Lanier, Jaron. "The Eternal Now." *Forbes ASAP*, 22 February 1999, p. 72+.

Lehmann-Haupt, Rachel. "Plug In, Start Up, Drop In." *Business 2.0*, 14 November 2000, p. 204+.

Lemmey, Tara. "Your Next Identity Crisis." *Business 2.0*, 26 September 2000, p. 180+.

Matthews, Robert. "The Ideas Machine." *New Scientist*, 20 January 2001, p. 26+.

Mayer, Caroline. "On the 800 Line: Why All Customers Aren't Treated the Same." *The Washington Post National Weekly Edition*, 3 August 1998.

McDonough, William and Michael Braungart. "The NEXT Industrial Revolution." *The Atlantic Monthly*, October 1998, p. 82+

Mitchell, William J. "e-topia: Urban Life, Jim—But Not as We Know It." *Future Survey*, February 2000, p. 7.

Moody, Glyn. "A New Dawn." *New Scientist*, 30 May 1998, p. 34+.

Motluk, Alison. "Grow Your Own." *New Scientist*, 12 February 2000, p. 25+.

Moukheiber, Zina. "Back to Nature." *Forbes*, 19 October 1998, p. 146+.

Moukheiber, Zina. "Dr. Robot." *Forbes*, 6 March 2000, p. 159+.

Mullins, Justin. "Next-Generation Fashion." *New Scientist*, 6 January 2001, p. 12+.

Munk, Nina. "The New Organization Man." *Fortune*, 16 March 1998, p. 62+.

Murray, Matt. "Retailers Use Legal Wrinkle to Link Sales, Bank Services." *The Wall Street Journal*, 8 February 1999.

Neff, Jeff. "It's Not Trendy Being Green." *Advertising Age*, 1 April 2000, p. 16+.

Nelson, Emily. "Wal-Mart's Garth-Quake May Spur Sales." *The Wall Street Journal*, 2 November 1998.

Nowak, Rachel. "Almost Human." *New Scientist*, 13 February 1999, p. 20+.

Norman, Donald A. "The Invisible Computer: Why Good Products Can Fail, the Personal Computer Is So Complex, and Information Appliances Are the Solution." *Future Survey*, January 1999, p. 6.

Palmaffy, Tyce. "The Gold Star State: How Texas Jumped to the Head of the Class in Elementary School Achievement." *Policy Review*, March/April 1998, p. 30+.

Paras, Wilhelmina and Santha Oorjitham. "Living Without Water." *World Press Review*, August 1998, p. 39.

Pelton, Joseph N. "Telecommunications for the 21st Century." *Scientific American*, April 1998, p. 80+.

Peterson, Ivers. "Big-League Computing." *Science News*, 12 December 1998, p. 383.

Raloff, Janet. "Chocolate Hearts." *Science News*, 18 March 2000, p. 188+.

Raloff, Janet. "More Waters Test Positive for Drugs." *Science News*, 1 April 2000, p. 212.

Regalado, Antonio. "Intellectual Capital: Universities Jump into the Venture Game." *Technology Review*, January/February 1999, p. 25.

Roane, Kit R. "Replacement Parts." *U.S. News & World Report*, 29 July 2002, p. 54+.

Rotman, David. "The Next Biotech Harvest." *Technology Review*, September/October 1998, p. 34+.

Rushkoff, Douglas. "Electronic Passalongs: The New Social Currency." *Business 2.0*, 26 September 2000, p. 121+.

Sample, Ian. "Robot Learns to Fly." *New Scientist*, 17 August 2002, p. 24.

Sander, Chris. "Genomic Medicine and the Future of Health Care." *Science*, 17 March 2000, p. 1977+.

Thurm, Scott. "On the Comeback Trail." *The Wall Street Journal*, 15 June 1998.

Tibbs, Hardin. "Humane Ecostructure: Can Industry Become Gaia's Friend?" *Whole Earth*, Summer 1998, p. 61+.

Travis, J. "Cloning Extends Life of Cells—and Cows?" *Science News*, 29 April 2000, p. 279.

Veit, Howard R. "Health Care Consumerism." *Vital Speeches of the Day*, 1 July 1998, p. 562+.

Vinzant, Carol. "Electronic Books Are Coming at Last!" *Fortune*, 6 July 1998, p. 119+.

Vogel, Gretchen. "An Institute for Planet Earth." *Science*, 22 May 1998, p. 1182+.

Weiss, Daniel Evan. "You, Robot." *The Industry Standard*, 7 August 2000, p. 168+.

Weiss, Peter. "Smart Outfit." *Science News*, 20 November 1999, p. 330+.

Wilson, Edward O. "Back from Chaos." *The Atlantic Monthly*, March 1998, p. 41+.

Wishard, William Van Dusen. "What the Future Holds." *Vital Speeches of the Day*, 1 March 1999, p. 313+.

Wrong, Michela. "Monsanto Opts to Work with the Grain." *The Financial Times*, 11 April 2000.

Wu, C. "Power Plants: Algae Churn Out Hydrogen." *Science News*, 26 February 2000, p. 134.

_____. "The African Connection." *The Wilson Quarterly*, Autumn 2000, p. 122+.

_____. "Breakthroughs Affecting Many Disciplines Foreseen from National Nanotechnology Initiative." *Technology Forecasts*, February 2000, p. 1+.

_____. "Cacao Trees Under Fungal Siege." *Science*, 14 April 2000, p. 259.

_____. "Environmental Technology Forecast." *Technology Forecasts*, May 1998, p. 1+.

_____. "Extrusion Processing Yields Cereals with Colon Cancer Fighting Properties." *Technology Forecasts*, October 1998, p. 11+.

_____. "Filling the Bowl." *New Scientist*, 1 April 2000, p. 19.

_____. "Getting Inside a Teen Brain." *Newsweek*, 28 February 2000, p. 58+.

_____. "Hospitals Within Hospitals." *Futurific*, December 1997, p. 8.

_____. "Hubris and the Human Genome." *Science*, 15 May 1998, p. 994+.

_____. "Melancholy Money." *New Scientist*, 12 February 2000, p. 21.

_____. "News from the War Against Death: Downloading and Eventually Duplicating Brains." *Futurific*, March 1999, p. 26.

_____. "NewsWire: Reconstructing Rover." *New Scientist*, 26 February 2000, p. 5.

_____. "Resistance Is Useless." *New Scientist*, 19 February 2000, p. 21.

_____. "Retail Bytes: June 1999." *Y&R's Brand Futures Group* (Internet: yrbfg@aol.com), 28 June 1999, p. 1+.

_____. "Switch On." *New Scientist*, 5 February 2000, p. 10.

_____. "Virulent Blight." *New Scientist*, 1 April 2000, p. 5.

_____. "Wearable Net Devices See Changing Human Interaction." *Future Trends*, January/February 2000, p. 1+

Chapter 16, "Self-Defeating and Self-Fulfilling Prophecies"

Meadow, Donella H., Dennis L. Meadows, and Jorgen Randers. "Beyond the Limits to Growth." In *Context Journal*. Context Institute, 1996.

_____. "Knee Jerk." *U.S. News & World Report*, 22 July 2002, p. 17.

_____. "A Survey of the Global Environment." *The Economist*, 6 July 2002, p. 4.

INDEX

A

able/challenged example (figure-ground experiments), 13-15

Adoption Nation, 47

adrenaline addiction, entropy, 99-101

Advanced/Anticipatory organizations (Type A businesses), 233

advertisements, as potential right-of-way, 188

aftermarketing, 108

aging population
demography, 137-142
taxation as entropic system, 97-98

aging/youth example (figure-ground experiments), 11-13

agrogenetics, 206

Amazon, 35
rights-of-way metaphor, 187-188

American Demographics, report on 2001 Harris survey, 183

antimodernity countertrend versus modernity trend, 24

Arab countries, demography, 130-133

Arrow, Kenneth, 225

Asia, demography, 134-135

assortment (competitive assortment), 196

assumptions, questioning personal biases, 4

attention, multiplier effect of distribution channels, 91

auto leases, 201
autonomy trend, 25

B
baby busts, 131
balance of power (U.S. government), 75
Banavar, Jayanth, 122
bandwagon effect, 122
barrier to exit (customer relations), 200
beautification, traditional versus nontraditional gender roles, 64
Belkin, Lisa, "The Odds of That" article, 119
bell-shaped curves, Law of Large Numbers, 123-125
benchmarking, entropy, 93
bias
  organizational traps, 69
    distribution channels, 81-91
    efficiency breeds vulnerability, 71-80
    entropy, 93-104
    integrity leads to quality, 105-116
  personal traps, educated incapacity, 1-68
    extremes informing the middle, 53-68
    figure-ground experiments, 8-18
    lessons from alternative perspectives, 18-21
    substituting the spiral for the pendulum analogy, 43-52
    trends/countertrends, 23-41

bioprocessing, 206
biosensors, 209
biotech management, 209-212
blocks
  organizational traps, 69
    distribution channels, 81-91
    efficiency breeds vulnerability, 71-80
    entropy, 93-104
    integrity leads to quality, 105-116
  personal traps, educated incapacity
    extremes informing the middle, 53-68
    figure-ground experiments, 8-18
    lessons from alternative perspectives, 18-21
    substituting the spiral for the pendulum analogy, 43-52
    trends/countertrends, 23-41
blogs, 62
brain mapping, 214
Brains/Brawn organizations (Type B businesses), 233
branding trend, 30
brawn (traditional versus nontraditional gender roles), 64
brazenness (traditional versus nontraditional gender roles), 64
breadwinning (traditional versus nontraditional gender roles), 64
breeding (traditional versus nontraditional gender roles), 64

"Bridge on the River Kwai
      Syndrome," 102
broncobusting (traditional
      versus nontraditional
      gender roles), 64
Brooks, David, 101
Brown, Shona, 216
business oversight cycles, 48-51
business planning, 229
   anticipation, 231-233
   dangers of efficiency, 79-80
   faulty analysis, 229
   lack of awareness of
      context, 230
   linking information to
      action, 230
   successful businesses types,
      233-234
Byron, Ada, 66

C
capital formation
      (economy), 176
Carson, Rachel, *Silent
      Spring*, 224
CDC (Centers for Disease
      Control), 31
censorship versus free speech,
      61-64
Centers for Disease Control
      (CDC), 31
challenged/able example
      (figure-ground
      experiments), 13-15
channels of distribution,
      disintermediation, 81
   choices/options, 88
   gaining client attention, 91
   health care, 87

institutional education versus
      distance learning, 85-86
   media, 82-83
   multiplication of identities,
      88-91
   print versus the Internet, 83-85
   retailing, 86-87
charity (the Republic), 172-173
children, demography, 146
China, demography, 134-135
chronobiology, 215
clients, as potential
      right-of-way, 188
Clinton, Bill, self-defeating
      prophecy sample, 223
cloning, 210-216
CLS (Continuous Linked
      Settlement) bank, 76
coastal living, demography, 147
COBOL, 66
Collins, Francis S., 215
colocation, 84
commerce (modern), as product
      of post-agricultural
      societies, 192-193
   competitive pricing, 194-196
   competitive quality, assortment
      and convenience, 196
   field position, 199-202
   personalization/customization,
      197-198
   reputation, 198-199
commercialization of
      community countertrend,
      38-41
communication systems
      (economy), 176
competitive pricing, 194-196

compromise, 151-154
  conflicting demands
    *compromise versus Lowest
    Common Denominator,
    165-166*
    definitions, 162-165
    employee diversity, 154-157
    *international conflict,
    158-159*
    majority rules, 157-158
    *when denominators are
    4 and 8, 160-162*
Comte, Auguste, 129
concentration of conformity
  (as danger of business
  efficiency), 80
concentration of power
  (as danger of business
  efficiency), 80
concentration of space
  (as danger of business
  efficiency), 79
concentration of systems
  (as danger of business
  efficiency), 79
concentration of time
  (as danger of business
  efficiency), 79
conflicting demands
  compromise versus Lowest
    Common Denominator,
    165-166
  definitions, 162-165
  employee diversity, 154-157
  international conflict, 158-159
  majority rules, 157-158
  when denominators are
    4 and 8, 160-162
conformity, concentration of
  (as danger of business
  efficiency), 80

consensus, 234
Consumer Project on
  Technology (Nader), 62
consuming safety trend, 36-38
contacts, as potential
  right-of-way, 188
context, lack of awareness, 230
Continuous Linked Settlement
  bank (CLS bank), 76
convenience (competitive
  convenience), 196
Copycats (Type C
  businesses), 233
corporate citizenship, 114
corporate social responsibility
  integrity leads to quality,
    112-114
  versus free-market capitalism,
    56-58
cosmeceuticals, 211
cosmerobotics, 211
Council of Europe cyberspace
  treaty, 59
countertrends/trends, 23
  consuming versus saving
    safety, 36-38
  decline of community/
    commercialization of
    community, 38-41
  emerging diseases of affluence,
    31-34
  Newton's Third Law, 41
  opting out/self reliance, 25-28
  sociology of apology, 28-31
  technology/poetry, 34-36
critical mass, Law of Large
  Numbers, 120-121
cross-breeding of disciplines,
  204-206
cross-sell opportunities, 202
crossover businesses, 211

customer relations, 200
 auto leases, 201
 barriers to exit, 200
 cross-sell opportunities, 202
 frequent-flyer miles, 201
 King Gillette model, 201
 level-premium whole-life
  insurance, 201
customer-centered businesses,
 181-183
customers
 as potential right-of-way, 188
 getting and keeping, 107-110
customization, football meets
 shopping metaphor,
 197-198
cyberspace transactions, 73
cycles in business oversight,
 48-51

D
decline of community trend,
 38-41
Dell Computer recycling
 program, 58
DeLong, J. Bradford, 196
Democrats (political party),
 three-legged stools of
 the political agenda
 metaphor, 174
demography, 117, 129
 aging population, 137-142
 Asia, 134-135
 caution regarding
  extrapolation, 148-149
 children, 146
 global middle class, 143-145
 immigration, 135
  environmental problems, 136
  food distribution, 136
  urbanization, 136

 Islam, 130-133
 Latino influence, 143
 long-range population
  projections, 147-148
 migration to urban areas and
  seacoasts, 147
 women, 145
 Ymigration, 142-143
 youths, 133-134
Departments of Motor Vehicles,
 rights-of-way
 opportunities, 184
dialectic (societal change), 54
differential reproduction,
 Theory of Evolution, 204
diffusion drift, 122
digital signal processors
 (DSPs), 208
direct crossover samples, 211
discretionary shopping, 192
disintermediation, 24, 81-82
 distribution choices/options, 88
 gaining client attention, 91
 health care, 87
 institutional education versus
  distance learning, 85-86
 media, 82-83
 multiplication of identities,
  88-91
 print versus the Internet, 83-85
 retailing, 86-87
distance learning, 85-86
distribution channels,
 disintermediation, 81
 choices/options, 88
 gaining client attention, 91
 health care, 87
 institutional education versus
  distance learning, 85-86
 media, 82-83

multiplication of identities, 88-91

print versus the Internet, 83-85

retailing, 86-87

drift (diffusion equation), 122

Drucker, Peter, 57

DSPs (digital signal processors), 208

Dworkin, Ronald, 107

E

Earl of Birkenhead, *The World in 2030 A.D.*, 183

Earth Institute, 205

eco-efficiency, 204

ecological arena, self-defeating prophecy sample, 224-225

ecological integrity (society), 177

economic value added (EVA), 195

economy, 176

educated incapacity, 1-68

extremes informing the middle, 53-56

corporate social responsibility versus free-market capitalism, 56-58

free speech versus censorship, 61-64

studying and applying extremes, 68

techies versus luddites, 58-61

traditional versus nontraditional gender roles, 64-68

figure-ground experiments, 8

able/challenged example, 13-15

male/female example, 9-10

stability/transition example, 15-18

youth/aging example, 11-13

lessons from alternative perspectives, 18-21

substituting the spiral for the pendulum analogy, 43-44

cycles in business oversight, 48-51

market cycles, 51-52

social fabric cycles, 45-48

trends/countertrends, 23

consuming versus saving safety, 36-38

decline of community/ commercialization of community, 38-41

emerging diseases of affluence, 31-34

Newton's Third Law, 41

no responsibility self reliance examples, 25-28

sociology of apology, 28-31

technology/poetry, 34-36

education

institutional education versus distance learning, 85-86

society, 177

efficiency, 72

dangers for businesses, 79-80

increased vulnerability, 71-73

acceleration through electronics, 73-74

governmental efficiency, 74-75

importance of redundancy, 78-80

working at warp speed, 75-78

Eisenhardt, Kathleen, 216

electromagnetic interference (EMI), 74

electronics, advances in efficiency, 73-74

emerging diseases of affluence (trends/countertrends), 31-34

EMI (electromagnetic interference), 74

employee diversity, 154-157

entropy, 93
  adrenaline addiction, 99-101
  benchmarking, 93
  countering mental trap of entropy, 101-104
  Internet, 98-99
  know-how gap, 102
  star performers, 94
  taxation, 94
    encouraging investment, 97
    global aging, 97-98
    intelliwealth, 95
    Internet, 96
    massive personal wealth, 95-96

Environmental Protection Agency (EPA), 224

Equator Principles, 57

EVA (economic value added), 195

Excite, 35

expertise, limits of (educated incapacity), 1-68
  extremes informing the middle, 53-56
    corporate social responsibility versus free-market capitalism, 56-58
    free speech versus censorship, 61-64
    studying and applying extremes, 68
    techies versus luddites, 58-61
    traditional versus nontraditional gender roles, 64-68
  figure-ground experiments, 8
    able/challenged example, 13-15
    male/female example, 9-10
    stability/transition example, 15-18
    youth/aging example, 11-13
  lessons from alternative perspectives, 18-21
  substituting the spiral for the pendulum analogy, 43-44
    cycles in business oversight, 48-51
    market cycles, 51-52
    social fabric cycles, 45-48
  trends/countertrends, 23
    consuming versus saving safety, 36-38
    decline of community/ commercialization of community, 38-41
    emerging diseases of affluence, 31-34
    Newton's Third Law, 41
    no responsibility self reliance examples, 25-28
    sociology of apology, 28-31
    technology/poetry, 34-36

Extensible Markup Language (XML), 207

extremes informing the middle, 53-56

corporate social responsibility versus free-market capitalism, 56-58

free speech versus censorship, 61-64

studying and applying extremes, 68

techies versus luddites, 58-61

traditional versus nontraditional gender roles, 64-68

F

failure to link information to action, 230

family, renewed focus on, 46

farming, biotechnology, 210

fat-tailed distribution pattern, 122

faulty analysis, 229

female/male example (figure-ground experiments), 9-10

female/male perspective, three-legged stools of the political agenda metaphor, 176-178

field position, football meets shopping metaphor, 199-202

figure-ground experiments, 8

able/challenged example, 13-15

male/female example, 9-10

stability/transition example, 15-18

youth/aging example, 11-13

fixed images, 83

Flicker, Barry, *Working at Warp Speed: The New Rules for Project Success in a Sped-Up World,* **75**

flood of information trend, 24

food distribution, immigration, 136

foodaceuticals, 211

football meets shopping metaphor, modern commerce as product of post-agricultural societies, 191-193

competitive pricing, 194-196

competitive quality, assortment and convenience, 196

field position, 199-202

personalization/customization, 197-198

reputation, 198-199

formal planning, 229

anticipation, 231-233

faulty analysis, 229

lack of awareness of context, 230

linking information to action, 230

successful businesses types, 233-234

foundation of the Republic, 171-174

Fox, Robin, 130

Fraser, Nicholas, *The Voice of Modern Hatred,* **78**

free speech versus censorship, 61-64

free-market capitalism, 56-58

Freedom of Information Act, 63

frequent-flyer miles, customer relations, 201

fuel cell technology, 227

fuel cell technology (Rockwell Automation), 226-228

future trends, Law of Large Numbers, 126-127

G

Gaia hypothesis (Lovelock), 205
garbage in, garbage out
    principle, 66
Gates, Bill
    self-defeating prophecy
        sample, 223
    self-fulfilling prophecy
        sample, 222
gender roles, 64-68
genetic engineering, 54, 212-216
genetic mapping, 210-216
genetifitness, 211
Genomics, 216
geoengineering, 206
Gladwell, Malcolm, *The Tipping
    Point: How Little Things
    Can Make a Big
    Difference*, 122
global aging
    demography, 137-142
    taxation as entropic system,
        97-98
global labor pool, 217
global middle class,
    demography, 143-145
Golden Rule, 107, 111-112
governmental efficiency, 74-75
Green Party, 224
Greenpeace, 224
Guilder, Larry, 225
Guinere, Lani, 157

H

Hague Convention, 60
Hal (human-like computer), 215
halo effect, 122
Halstead, Ted, *The Radical
    Center: The Future of
    American Politics*, 174
Hawking, Stephen, 216

health (society), female agenda
    in political arena, 177
health care
    distribution channels, 87
    management of, 207
    self reliance trend, 27
    self-defeating prophecy
        sample, 225
Hegel, George, 54
Heisenberg Uncertainty
    Principle, 44
Henderson, David, 113
Hopper, Admiral Grace
    Murray, 66
HTML (Hypertext Markup
    Language), 207
human cloning, 212-216
human evolution management,
    212-216
human resources
    management, 218
Hypertext Markup Language
    (HTML), 207

I

IBOS (Interbank Online
    Systems), 208
*Illness and Culture in the
    Postmodern Age*, 31
immigration, demography,
    135-136
The Imperial Animal, 130
in-your-face phenomenon
    (extremes), 55
inadequate analysis, 229
individual biases (educated
    incapacity), 1-68
    extremes informing the middle,
        53-56

corporate social
responsibility versus
free-market capitalism,
56-58
free speech versus
censorship, 61-64
studying and applying
extremes, 68
techies versus luddites,
58-61
traditional versus
nontraditional gender
roles, 64-68
figure-ground experiments, 8
able/challenged example,
13-15
male/female example, 9-10
stability/transition example,
15-18
youth/aging example, 11-13
lessons from alternative
perspectives, 18-21
substituting the spiral for the
pendulum analogy, 43-44
cycles in business oversight,
48-51
market cycles, 51-52
social fabric cycles, 45-48
trends/countertrends, 23
consuming versus saving
safety, 36-38
decline of community/
commercialization of
community, 38-41
emerging diseases of
affluence, 31-34
Newton's Third Law, 41
no responsibility self reliance
examples, 25-28

sociology of apology, 28-31
technology/poetry, 34-36
individual responsibility (the
Republic), three-legged
stools of the political
agenda metaphor, 172
information cascade, 123
infrastructure dilemma (rights-
of-way metaphor),
185-187
Institute for Community Design
Analysis, 40
institutional accountability
(the Republic), 172-173
institutional biases, 69
distribution channels, 81-82
choices/options, 88
gaining client attention, 91
health care, 87
institutional education
versus distance learning,
85-86
media, 82-83
multiplication of identities,
88-91
print versus the Internet,
83-85
retailing, 86-87
efficiency breeds vulnerability,
71-73
acceleration through
electronics, 73-74
efficiency in government,
74-75
importance of redundancy,
78-80
working at warp speed,
75-78
entropy, 93
adrenaline addiction, 99-101

benchmarking, 93
countering mental trap of
entropy, 101-104
Internet, 98-99
star performers, 94
taxation, 94-98
integrity leads to quality,
105-107
corporate social
responsibility, 112-114
getting and keeping
customers, 107-110
Golden Rule, 111-112
stewardship, 115-116
trust, 110-111
institutional education, 85-86
integrity, contribution to quality,
105-107
corporate social responsibility,
112-114
getting and keeping customers,
107-110
Golden Rule, 111-112
stewardship, 115-116
trust, 110-111
intelliwealth, taxation as
entropic system, 95
intentional families, 47
Interbank Online Systems
(IBOS), 208
international conflict, 158-159
Internet
as entropic system, 98-99
citizens (netizens), 40
distribution channels, 83-85
taxation as entropic system, 96
Internet-based education,
distribution channels,
85-86
investments, taxation as
entropic system, 97

Islam, demography, 130-133
iVillage, 35

J-K
Japan, demography, 134-135

Kauffman, Stuart, 203
King Gillette model (model
of relationship
marketing), 201
know-how gap, entropy, 102
Kondratieff Wave theory, 43
Kubrick, Stanley, *2001: A Space*
***Odyssey*, 215**
Kurzweil, Raymond, brain
mapping, 214

L
lack of awareness of
context, 230
Lakoff, George, *Moral Politics:*
How Liberals and
***Conservatives Think*, 175**
Latino influence,
demography, 143
Law of Large Numbers, 117-120
bell-shaped curves, 123-125
critical mass, 120-121
future trends/events, 126-127
peer pressure, 122-123
learned intermediaries, 99
Lego-Bio organization, 50
level-premium whole-life
insurance, customer
relations, 201
Levitt, Ted, 106
LiCari, Jerome, 106
limits of expertise (educated
incapacity), 1-68
extremes informing the middle,
53-56

corporate social
    responsibility versus
    free-market capitalism,
    56-58
free speech versus
    censorship, 61-64
studying and applying
    extremes, 68
techies versus luddites,
    58-61
traditional versus
    nontraditional gender
    roles, 64-68
figure-ground experiments, 8
    able/challenged example,
    13-15
    male/female example, 9-10
    stability/transition example,
    15-18
    youth/aging example, 11-13
lessons from alternative
    perspectives, 18-21
substituting the spiral for the
    pendulum analogy, 43-44
    cycles in business oversight,
    48-51
    market cycles, 51-52
    social fabric cycles, 45-48
trends/countertrends, 23
    consuming versus saving
    safety, 36-38
    decline of community/
    commercialization of
    community, 38-41
    emerging diseases of
    affluence, 31-34
    Newton's Third Law, 41
    no responsibility self reliance
    examples, 25-28

    sociology of apology, 28-31
    technology/poetry, 34-36
Limits to Growth, 224
Lind, Michael, The Radical
    Center: The Future of
    American Politics, 174
linking information to
    action, 230
long-range population
    projections, 147-148
long-term memory, 84
Lovelock, James, Gaia
    hypothesis, 205
Lowest Common
    Denominator, 118
    conflicting demands, 165-166
    definitions, 162-165
    versus compromise, 151-159
    employee diversity, 154-157
    international conflict,
    158-159
    majority rules, 157-158
    when denominators are
    4 and 8, 160-162
Lud, Ned, 58
luddites versus techies, 58-61

M
mainstreaming of terrorism, 232
majority rules, compromise
    versus Lowest Common
    Denominator, 157-158
Malcolm Baldrige Award, 105
male/female example
    (figure-ground
    experiments), 9-10
male/female perspective,
    three-legged stools of the
    political agenda
    metaphor, 176-178

management
  health and social services, 207
  telecom management, 207-209
  Theory of Evolution
    metaphor, 203
    *cross-breeding of
      disciplines, 204*
    "new natural," 205-216
**market cycles, spiral versus
  pendulum analogy of
  historical cycles, 51-52**
market value added (MVA), 195
marketing
  aftermarketing, 108
  children, demography, 146
**maternal use of guilt,
  self-fulfilling prophecy
  sample, 226**
**media, as distribution channel,
  82-83**
memory storage, 84
metaphors, 169
  football meets shopping
    metaphor, modern
    commerce as product of
    post-agricultural societies,
    191-202
  management by harnessing
    evolution, 203
    *cross-breeding of
      disciplines, 204*
    "new natural," 205-216
    *survival of the fittest,
      216-217*
    time pacing, 218
  rights-of-way, 179
    Amazon, 187-188
    *customer-centered
      businesses versus*

    *sale-centered businesses,
      181-183*
    *infrastructure dilemma,
      185-187*
    *potential rights-of-way,
      188-189*
    tunnel vision, 183-185
  three-legged stools of the
    political agenda, 171
    *foundation of the Republic,
      171-174*
    *male/female perspective,
      176-178*
    political parties, 174-176
Metcalf, Bob, Metcalf's Law, 121
**middle class, demography,
  143-145**
**migration to urban areas
  and seacoasts,
  demography, 147**
**modern commerce as product of
  post-agricultural
  societies, 192-193**
  competitive pricing, 194-196
  competitive quality, assortment
    and convenience, 196
  field position, 199-202
  personalization/customization,
    197-198
  reputation, 198-199
**modernity trend versus
  antimodernity
  countertrend, 24**
monopsony, 217
**monotheism countertrend
  versus paganism
  trend, 23**
***Moral Politics: How Liberals
  and Conservatives Think
  (Lakoff), 175***

multiplier effect of distribution channels, 81
distribution choices/options, 88
gaining client attention, 91
health care, 87
institutional education versus distance learning, 85-86
media, 82-83
multiplication of identities, 88-91
print versus the Internet, 83-85
retailing, 86-87
Muslim countries, demography, 130-133
MVA (market value added), 195

N
Nader, Ralph, Consumer Project on Technology, 62
nanny government, 223
nanotechnology, 208
National Human Genome Institute, 215
National Museum of Women's History, 66
navigators, 99
negative information countertrend versus flood of information trend, 24
netizens (Internet citizens), 40
Netscape, 35
neural computer (brain mapping), 214
neural nets (brain mapping), 214
"new natural" (management by harnessing evolution metaphor), 205
biotech management, 209-212
cross-breeding of disciplines, 205-206

human evolution management, 212-216
management of health and social services, 207
telecom management, 207-209
Newton's Third Law, trend/countertrend, 41
nontraditional gender roles, 64-68

O
"The Odds of That" article (Belkin), 119
OECD (Organization for Economic Cooperation and Development), 113
Office Biology, **137**
operational structure, 49
opting out countertrend versus self reliance trend, 25-28
Organization for Economic Cooperation and Development (OECD), 113
organizational traps, 69
distribution channels, 81
choices/options, 88
gaining client attention, 91
health care, 87
institutional education versus distance learning, 85-86
media, 82-83
multiplication of identities, 88-91
print versus the Internet, 83-85
retailing, 86-87

efficiency breeds vulnerability,
71-73
*acceleration through
electronics, 73-74*
*efficiency in government,
74-75*
*importance of redundancy,
78-80*
*working at warp speed,
75-78*
entropy, 93
adrenaline addiction, 99-101
benchmarking, 93
*countering mental trap of
entropy, 101-104*
Internet, 98-99
star performers, 94
taxation, 94-98
integrity leads to quality, 105
*corporate social
responsibility, 112-114*
*getting and keeping
customers, 107-110*
Golden Rule, 111-112
stewardship, 115-116
trust, 110-111
Orwell, George, self-defeating
prophecy sample, 221

P
paganism trend versus
monotheism
countertrend, 23
Panel on Audit Effectiveness
(Public Oversight
Board), 48
Pax World, 57
PDPs (personal development
programs), 41
peer pressure, Law of Large
Numbers, 122-123

pendulum analogy of historical
cycles, substituting with
spiral analogy, 43-44
cycles in business oversight,
48-51
market cycles, 51-52
social fabric cycles, 45-48
peripheral engagement
samples, 211
personal development programs
(PDPs), 41
personal planning
anticipation, 231-233
faulty analysis, 229
lack of awareness of
context, 230
linking information to
action, 230
personal traps, educated
incapacity, 1-68
extremes informing the middle,
53-56
*corporate social
responsibility versus
free-market capitalism,
56-58*
*free speech versus
censorship, 61-64*
*studying and applying
extremes, 68*
*techies versus luddites,
58-61*
*traditional versus
nontraditional gender
roles, 64-68*
figure-ground experiments, 8
*able/challenged example,
13-15*
male/female example, 9-10
*stability/transition example,
15-18*

youth/aging example, 11-13
lessons from alternative
    perspectives, 18-21
substituting the spiral for the
    pendulum analogy, 43-44
cycles in business oversight,
    48-51
market cycles, 51-52
social fabric cycles, 45-48
trends/countertrends, 23
consuming versus saving
    safety, 36-38
decline of
    community/commercializa-
    tion of community, 38-41
emerging diseases of
    affluence, 31-34
Newton's Third Law, 41
no responsibility self reliance
    examples, 25-28
sociology of apology, 28-31
technology/poetry, 34-36
personal wealth, taxation as
    entropic system, 95-96
personalization, football meets
    shopping metaphor,
    197-198
placebo effect, self-fulfilling
    prophecy sample, 226
poetry countertrend versus
    technology trend, 34-36
political forces, three-legged
    stools of the political
    agenda metaphor
foundation of the Republic,
    171-174
male/female perspective,
    176-178
political parties, 174-176

population projections, 147-148
potential rights-of-way, 188-189
Potential Support Ratio
    (PSR), 137
power, concentration of (as
    danger of business
    efficiency), 80
pricing (competitive pricing),
    football meets shopping
    metaphor, 194-196
print, distribution channels,
    83-85
pro-life/pro-choice debate, 54
PSR (Potential Support
    Ratio), 137
psychics, self-fulfilling prophecy
    sample, 226
Public Oversight Board, 48
pulsed images, 83
punctuated equilibrium, Theory
    of Evolution, 204

Q
quality
    competitive quality, football
        meets shopping
        metaphor, 196
    as result of integrity, 105
    corporate social
        responsibility, 112-114
    getting and keeping
        customers, 107-110
    Golden Rule, 111-112
    stewardship, 115-116
    trust, 110-111
"Quality Circles" (quality
    program), 106
quantum computing, 208
questioning assumptions, 4

R

The Radical Center: The Future of American Politics (Halstead and Lind), 174

Radio Frequency Identity (RFID), 209

railroad business, rights-of-way metaphor, 179-181

real estate, as potential right-of-way, 188

redundancy, 71, 78-80

reintermediation countertrend versus disintermediation trend, 24

relationships (customer relations)
auto leases, 201
barriesr to exit, 200
cross-sell opportunities, 202
frequent-flyer miles, 201
King Gillette model, 201
level-premium whole-life insurance, 201

relevance of aging population, demography, 139-142

religion revival, 46

renewed focus on family, 46

Republic, foundation of, 171-174

Republicans (political party), 174

reputation, football meets shopping metaphor, 198-199

retail, distribution channels, 86-87

RFID (Radio Frequency Identity), 209

Rheingold, Howard, 121

rights-of-way metaphor, 179
Amazon, 187-188
customer-centered businesses versus sale-centered businesses, 181-183
infrastructure dilemma, 185-187
potential rights-of-way, 188-189
tunnel vision, 183-185

risk-balancing effect (trend/countertrend), 36-38

Robo Rat, 214

Robo sapiens, 215

Rockwell Automation, 226-228

S

sale-centered businesses (rights-of-way metaphor), 181-183

Sarbanes-Oxley Act, 50

saving safety countertrend versus consuming safety trend, 36-38

secularism, 23

self reliance trend versus opting out countertrend, 25-28

self-defeating prophecies
Clinton, Bill, 223
ecological arena, 224-225
Gates, Bill, 223
George Orwell example, 221
health care sample, 225

self-fulfilling prophecies, 221
Gates, Bill, 222
maternal use of guilt, 226
placebo effect, 226
psychics, 226
Rockwell Automation fuel cell technology sample, 226-228

sexual selection, Theory of
    Evolution, 204
shopping, modern commerce
    as product of post-
    agricultural societies,
    191-202
    competitive pricing, 194-196
    competitive quality, assortment
        and convenience, 196
    field position, 199-202
    personalization/customization,
        197-198
    reputation, 198-199
short-term memory, 84
Sierra Clubs, 224
SiGe (silicon germanium), 207
Silent Spring (Carson), 224
silicon germanium (SiGe), 207
Simons, Tony, 106
Six Degrees: The Science
    of a Connected Age
    (Watts), 123
Six Sigma, 105
Slash and Burn value set
    (organizational), 111
smart mobs, 121
social fabric cycles, 45-48
social responsibility, 112-114
social services, management
    of, 207
socially responsible investment
    vehicle (SRI vehicle), 57
societal change, dialectic
    form, 54
sociology of apology
    (trends/countertrends),
    28-31
software development,
    evolution theory, 214
space, concentration of (as
    danger of business
    efficiency), 79

spiral analogy of historical
    cycles, 43-44
    cycles in business oversight,
        48-51
    market cycles, 51-52
    social fabric cycles, 45-48
SRI vehicle (socially responsible
    investment), 57
stability/transition example
    (figure-ground
    experiments), 15-18
Stanley, Eugene, 123
star performers, entropy, 94
stewards, 99
stewardship
    as organizational value set, 111
    integrity leads to quality,
        115-116
storage of memory, 84
substituting the spiral for the
    pendulum analogy, 43-44
    cycles in business oversight,
        48-51
    market cycles, 51-52
    social fabric cycles, 45-48
successful business types,
    233-234
suppliers, as potential right-of-
    way, 188
survival of the fittest, 216-217
swarming, 123
systems, concentration of (as
    danger of business
    efficiency), 79

T
taxation, as entropic system, 94
    encouraging investment, 97
    global aging, 97-98
    intelliwealth, 95
    Internet, 96
    massive personal wealth, 95-96

techies versus luddites, 58-61

technology trend versus poetry
    countertrend, 34-36

telecom management, 207-209

terrorism, mainstreaming, 232

Theory of Evolution
    differential reproduction, 204
    management metaphor, 203
        cross-breeding of
            disciplines, 204
        "new natural," 205-216
    punctuated equilibrium, 204
    sexual selection, 204
    survival of the fittest
        management, 216-217
    time pacing, 218

"Third Way" politics, 57

three-legged stools of the
    political agenda
    metaphor, 171
    foundation of the Republic,
        171-174
    male/female perspective,
        176-178
    political parties, 174-176

Tiger, Lionel, 130

time, concentration of (as
    danger of business
    efficiency), 79

time pacing, 216-218

The Tipping Point: How Little
    Things Can Make a Big
    Difference, 122

Tober, Barbara, 161

Total Quality Management
    (TQM), 105

TQM (Total Quality
    Management), 105

traditional gender roles versus
    nontraditional gender
    roles, 64-68

transactions in cyberspace, 73

transition/stability example
    (figure-ground
    experiments), 15-18

transportation systems
    (economy), 176

Trend Analysis Program, 197

trends/countertrends, 23
    consuming versus saving
        safety, 36-38
    decline of community/
        commercialization of
        community, 38-41
    emerging diseases of affluence,
        31-34
    Newton's Third Law, 41
    self reliance/opting out, 25-28
    sociology of apology, 28-31
    technology/poetry, 34-36

tunnel vision (rights-of-way
    metaphor), 183-185

2001 Harris survey, *American*
    Demographics
    report, 183

2001: A Space Odyssey, 215

Type A businesses
    (Advanced/Anticipatory
    organizations), 233

Type B businesses
    (Brains/Brawn
    organizations), 233

Type C businesses
    (Copycats), 233

U

U.S. Environmental Protection
    Agency, 224

Ullman, Myron, III, 217

unavoidable ignorance, 224

United Nations Development
    Program, 132